RACE, RACISM, AND REPARATIONS

ALSO BY J. ANGELO CORLETT

Terrorism: A Philosophical Analysis

Responsibility and Punishment

Analyzing Social Knowledge

RACE

racism

&REPARATIONS

J. ANGELO CORLETT

Cornell University Press

Ithaca and London

First published 2003 by Cornell University Press
First printing, Cornell Paperbacks, 2003

Printed in the United States of America

Library of Congress Cataloging-in-Publication Data
Corlett, J. Angelo
    Race, racism, and reparations / J. Angelo Corlett.
        p. cm.
Includes bibliographical references (p.   ) and index.
    ISBN 0-8014-4160-9 (cloth) ISBN 0-8014-8889-3 (paperback)
    1. Race.   2. Ethnic groups.   3. Racism.   4. Indians of North
America—Social conditions.   5. African Americans—Social conditions.
6. Minorities—Government policy—United States.   7. Reparation—
United States.   I. Title.
    HT1523.C67 2003
    305.8—dc21   2003005660

Cornell University Press strives to use environmentally responsible
suppliers and materials to the fullest extent possible in the publishing
of its books. Such materials include vegetable-based, low-VOC inks
and acid-free papers that are recycled, totally chlorine-free, or partly
composed of nonwood fibers. For further information, visit our
website at www.cornellpress.cornell.edu.

Cloth printing   10 9 8 7 6 5 4 3 2 1

Paperback printing   10 9 8 7 6 5 4 3 2 1

For Keith Lehrer,
whose brilliance of mind is matched by his greatness
of heart, whose relentless pursuit of truth has
rewarded him with plentiful wisdom, and bountiful
love and respect for others.

Contents

Acknowledgments ix

Introduction 1

1 Race and Ethnicity 6

2 What Is Latino Identity? 17

3 Defending the Genealogical Concept of Latino Identity 44

4 What Is Racism? 62

5 Surviving Evil in the United States: African and Native Americans 94

6 Affirmative Action for Latinos? 115

7 Ethnic Identity and Public Policy 124

8 Reparations to Native Americans? 147

9 Reparations to African Americans? 191

Conclusion 221

Selected Bibliography 227

Index 249

Acknowledgments

I wish to express my gratitude to Naomi Zack for her helpful comments on the topics of race, sex, ethnicity, and gender, especially pertaining to the content of chapter 1, which is a revised version of "Parallels of Ethnicity and Gender," in *Race/Sex*, edited by Naomi Zack (London: Routledge, 1997), pp. 83–94. I am grateful to Routledge for use of this material. An earlier version of chapter 2 was presented at a session of the American Philosophical Association (Eastern Division), December 29, 1996, as part of a session titled "Culture, Identity, and Intellectual Heritage," sponsored by the APA Committee on Hispanics in Philosophy. It was subsequently published as "Latino Identity" in *Public Affairs Quarterly* 13 (1999): 273–95, and I am grateful to North American Philosophical Publications for its use in revised form here and to Gustavo Segade for translating it into Spanish for reprinting in *Revista de Philosofia* (Mexico). I wish to thank Linda Martín Alcoff, Raymond Belliotti, Jane Duran, Jorge García, Jorge Gracia, Jan Narveson, Gregory Pappas, Ofelia Schutte, and Burleigh Wilkins, respectively, for their incisive comments on earlier drafts of the content of chapter 2. I am greatly indebted to Bernard Boxill, Garcia, and Howard McGary for their critical comments on earlier drafts of the content of chapter 4 on racism. Chapter 4 is a revised version of "Analyzing Racism," *Public Affairs Quarterly* 12 (1998): 23–50, and gratitude is expressed to North American Philosophical Publications for use of the material here. Chapter 5 is a revised version of "Surviving Evil: Jewish, African and Native Americans," *Journal of Social Philosophy* 32 (2001): 207–23, and gratitude is expressed to Blackwell Publishers for use of the material here. Chapter 6 is a revised version of "Latino Identity and Affirmative Action," in *Hispanics/Latinos in the United States,* edited by Jorge Gracia and Pablo DeGreiff (London: Routledge, 2000), pp. 223–34, and I am grateful to Routledge for the use of this material. A version of this paper was presented at the Conference on Ethnic Identity, Culture, and Group Rights, State University of New York at Buffalo, 3 October 1998, organized by Jorge J. E. Gracia and Pablo DeGreiff. I am grateful to those at the conference for incisive discussion of these issues. The content of chapter 7 consists of a revised version of a paper by the same title presented to the Department of Philosophy at the University of Hawai'i at Manoa, April 27, 2001. I appreciate the critical comments of Rodney C. Roberts and others, which led to improvement of it. Chapter 8 is a revised version of chapter 9 of *Responsibility and Punishment* (Dordrecht: Kluwer Academic Publishers, 2001) and is used herein in gratitude to Kluwer Academic Publishers. It is reprinted in Rodney C. Roberts, editor, *Injustice and Rectification* (New York: Peter Lang, 2003), pp. 147–64. A shorter version of this chapter is published as "Reparations to Native Americans?" in *War Crimes and Collective Wrongdoing,* edited by Aleksandar Jokic (London: Blackwell Publishers, 2001), pp. 236–69. I am grateful to Robert Audi, Boxill, Anthony Ellis, Margaret Gilbert, Richard W. Miller, Narveson, James Nickel, Michael Slote, and Wilkins for incisive comments on earlier drafts of this chapter. Parts of this chapter in earlier draft forms were presented at the Canadian Society for the Study of Practical Ethics, Canadian Learneds Society, 1997, and at the Conference on War Crimes: Legal and Moral Issues, University of California, Santa Barbara, 1997. A version of chapter 9 was presented at a special session on group rights and reparations at the American Philosophical Association (Pacific Division), Seattle, Washington, March 29, 2002. I am thankful for incisive comments by my fellow panelists, Boxill and McGary.

I am even more grateful to the following philosophers who read the penultimate version of the book manuscript and provided helpful critical comments: Alcoff, Boxill, McGary, Charles Mills, Roberts, and Zack.

I wish to thank an anonymous referee of Cornell University Press for having the courage to publish this book, along with Catherine Rice, Jack Rummel, and Teresa Jesionowski for their helpful suggestions on improving the overall quality of the book.

The contents of this book are intended to encourage readers to begin to think more deeply about issues of race, racism, and reparations. I hope that this book represents reasoned passion (as opposed to mere passion), and that the arguments and analyses contained herein genuinely advance our understanding of these intractable issues. I have attempted to clarify my assumptions along the way toward arguing for various claims and against others. Should certain of those assumptions prove implausible, then we owe it to ourselves to rethink the matters of race, racism, and reparations in light of alternative ways in which we might begin to better understand these vital concerns. In any event, we ought to, as Socrates would have it, follow earnestly the arguments wherever they may lead us, and bravely. Perhaps just as important, we ought to revise our lives in accordance with the best light of reason regarding such life-transforming problems.

J. ANGELO CORLETT

San Diego, California

RACE, RACISM, AND REPARATIONS

Introduction

The concepts of race, racism, and reparations play increasingly important roles in our daily lives. Racist harms such as those experienced at the hands of the United States government by Native and African Americans, for instance, raise questions of reparations to these groups. If it turns out that such means of compensatory justice are morally required, then what is the best way to determine who qualifies for reparations?

Although most social scientists today denounce the traditional notion of race in favor of a more nuanced idea of ethnicity,[1] the folk conception of what we are as humans nonetheless still includes that of race. Indeed, the ideas of race and ethnicity are often confused in everyday discourse, as evidenced by the fact that Mexicans are often referred to as a "race,"[2] even though the traditional notion of race includes no such category. So it is important to understand philosophically the idea of race and to evaluate it on rational grounds. This is the topic of chapter 1.

Should the notion of race not stand up to critical scrutiny, then perhaps it ought to be replaced. But with what? If the concept of race is so problematic and yet ought not to be replaced, what then would become of the justification for programs of affirmative action? Moreover, would appeals for reparations to groups that have been significantly harmed make sense? An assumption here is that the moral plausibility of policies of affirmitive

---

1. Cf. Ashley Montague, *Man's Most Dangerous Myth* (Cleveland: World, 1964); Orlando Patterson, *The Ordeal of Integration* (Washington, D.C.: Civitas/Counterpoint, 1997).

2. Evidenced perhaps by the Mexican and Chicano use of *La Raza* to refer to the collective that is *Mexicanos*.

action are contingent on a defensible classification of persons into ethnic groups.

Perhaps the concept of ethnicity, however imperfect, is a significant conceptual improvement over that of race. If so, then we ought to refer to ourselves as belonging to one single race: the human race. But we might also recognize that we as individual humans belong to a plurality of ethnic groups, implying the emptiness of the notion of a "pure race." The contents of chapters 2 and 3 explore philosophically the nature of Latino identity (or identification) with an aim toward positive public policy administration. (That I usually refer to Latinos in the male gender form does not mean that I am excluding Latinas from my analysis; I have chosen to do so to avoid the awkward amalgam "Latino/a.") It is the first philosophical analysis of the nature of Latino identity, or the conditions of membership in the stipulated umbrella term for a cluster of distinct but related ethnic groups that I shall call "Latinos." I refer to it as the "genealogical conception of Latino identity." Nothing in my analysis or argumentation is contingent on my employment of the controversial category: "Latino." Should we Latinos devise a more suitable replacement category for us, I will be happy to use it. But my arguments in this book would remain unaffected by such a change in terminology. And I have attempted to clarify my analysis so that recent concerns with it are addressed adequately. I should, however, point out that my use of "Latino" is an attempt to use it as an umbrella term to *unify* us as members of one or more of various and distinct ethnic groups, for instance, a "pan-Latino" identity.[3]

Even if the notion of race is conceptually empty, the reality of racism is, unfortunately, alive. Hence it is important to understand that the concept of race, being empty, not only serves as the foundation of racism, but that its emptiness demonstrates the depth of the wrongness of racism. This is not meant to imply that mere racial or group classification is itself racist. For as Anthony Appiah has argued, racialism (the belief that racial groups exist as categories) is not in itself a form of racism.[4] And it is one of the main tenets of this book that some form of human (ethnic) categorization or identification is important, both for purposes of public policy administration and the interpretation of medical research, but also for self- and group-esteem.

Not only is a philosophical exploration of race and ethnicity important

3. For an account of how precisely such an identity is forming in one New York City neighborhood, see Milagros Ricourt and Ruby Danta, *Hispanas de Queens* (Ithaca: Cornell University Press, 2002).

4. Anthony Appiah, "But Would That Still Be Me? Notes on Gender, Race, Ethnicity, as Sources of Ethnicity," *Journal of Philosophy* 77 (1990): 493–99.

in order to better understand the wrongness of racism and service public policy administration and self- and group-esteem, but it helps illuminate the foundations of racism. Chapter 4 is devoted to a philosophical exploration into the following questions: what *is* racism? What kinds of racism are there, and what are its motivations and origins? How universal is racism? Is everyone a racist? Is racism an all-or-nothing matter? Or, is racism such that it is a matter of degree? Whatever the case, how complicated is racism, and how might it be dealt with in a reasonably successful manner? I defend a cognitive-behavioral theory of racism that, because of its more comprehensive explanation of this concept, supplants doxastic theories. The reader is urged to not draw from my argument for the universality of racism the incorrect inference that racism is unimportant or that all instances of racism are on moral par with each other.

Two of the most profound examples of racist evil anywhere in human history are found in the history of the United States of America. One is the violent theft of the territory now known as the United States, and how this pertains to the genocide of Native Americans within U.S. territory. The other is the enslavement of Africans in the United States, along with the enforcement of Jim Crow laws that assisted in the oppression of African Americans subsequent to U.S. slavery. No other ethnic groups in the United States have suffered the kinds and durations of evils experienced by these two groups. It is for this reason that their experiences form the focus of my attention, especially regarding reparative justice. I make no apologies for this focus of attention. In fact, I find negligent philosophers who use the term "*the* Holocaust" to refer exclusively to the oppression of Jews by the Nazi regime. To do so is to ignore the "American Holocaust" of Native Americans, which was far worse in terms of duration of evil and amount of property taken violently and fraudulently by the U.S. government. Moreover, some might even argue that the enslavement of Africans in the United States and all that it entailed surpasses what happened to Jews under the Nazi regime. The point here is that if the Nazi oppression of Jews warrants reparations from Germany (which, of course, it does), then the racist oppression of Natives and African Americans warrants reparations from the U.S. government. But that issue awaits treatment in later chapters. Chapter 5 examines why some ethnic groups that were victims of U.S. racist oppression have fared better than others. For in the spirit of George Santayana, it is important to understand various dimensions of racist evils in order to guard against their recurrence.

Chapter 6 provides a philosophical discussion of whether Latinos in the United States are deserving, on moral grounds, of affirmative action benefits. No arguments are provided for or against affirmative action programs. The discussion assumes that such programs are justified—perhaps even required—on moral grounds.

Chapter 7 extends the basic conditions of analysis from my genealogical conception of Latino identity to the genealogical conception of ethnic identity. In terms of public policy administration, it seems that the basic conditions of ethnic group membership are similar throughout all ethnic groups. Furthermore, a new theory of affirmative action in hiring is set forth, one that is differential in its awarding of affirmative action benefits to certain targeted groups. Unlike current programs of affirmative action, some of which have been in place for almost four decades in the United States, my plan would award affirmative action benefits in proportion to the severity and duration of the harms experienced by various groups in the United States. In order to caution against an incorrect reading of my words as being antifeminist or misogynist, I would kindly request that readers pay due attention to the fact that I affirm that discrimination has existed and exists against European American women in U.S. society. (Again, I'd like to briefly explain my terminology. I've chosen the term *European American* to differentiate persons from European ethnic groups such as the English, French, Polish, German, and other like groups from African Americans and Latinos. Of course, many Latinos might consider themselves in part or wholly European. I acknowledge this complexity, but for the sake of concise terminology will stick to this usage nonetheless.) However, their role as oppressors of various folk of color does not make them equal beneficiaries of affirmative action benefits. Justice must be lexically prior to the whims of political power. And it is the power of politics and ideological dogmatism that blinds many to the fact that proportionality (both kind and duration) of racist/sexist harms must play the fundamental role in determining which groups ought to receive what degrees of affirmative action benefits. That I have explained clearly why European American women ought not to qualify except for only the least amount of such benefits in no way implies that I am somehow insensitive to their plight.

The demand for reparations to Native and African Americans is not a recent phenomenon, yet until recently, such demands were all but ignored by both the U.S. government and its citizenry. Indeed, the 2001 United Nations Conference on Racism in Durham, South Africa, included a condemnation (by implication) of U.S. slavery as barbaric and in need of compensation. Perhaps because the U.S. government fears the legal repercussions that might arise from such officially sanctioned condemnations, U.S. president George W. Bush sent an African American delegate to the conference to challenge this position.

Given the history and harshness of U.S.-perpetrated racism against Native and African Americans, what are reparations and are they owed to these groups? Subsequent to providing a philosophical analysis of ethnic group membership as a replacement of the concept of race, and following a philosophical analysis of the nature of racism that can be used by lawmakers and judges, in chapter 8 I clarify the idea of reparations and defend a basic reparations argument in terms of the Native American experience in the United States. The reparations argument is founded on the principle of morally just acquisitions and transfers, which posits that there is no moral statute of limitations on injustice and that those who would support such a statue of limitations clearly have the burden of moral argument. After considering and refuting several objections to the enactment of U.S. policies of reparations to Native Americans, I set forth and note the limitations of a range of possible reparations policies given the horrendous nature of Native American oppression in the United States and by the U.S. government. Finally, in chapter 9, I revise the reparations argument in terms of the African American experience, noting the differences between the respective cases of reparations to Native and African Americans. After considering and refuting several objections to such an argument as it pertains to African Americans, I conclude that race-based evils such as those experienced by Native and African Americans warrant reparations by the U.S. government. Mine is a moral argument that, if plausible, warrants serious political, economic, and legal attention.

1

Race and Ethnicity

The language of race is, in some respects, not unlike the parable of the emperor's new clothes. Words such as *Caucasian* (or *white,* or *Anglo*), *European American, Asian, Latino,* and *Hispanic* are used habitually and without much thought given to their meaning. "Primitive race theories," as I shall call them, purport to classify human individuals into distinct groups: for example, "Negroid," "Mongoloid," "Caucasoid."[1] Immanuel Kant, while admitting that his "opinions" on race are offered as "preliminary" and investigatory,[2] nonetheless gives a basic fourfold account of race consisting of "the white race," "the Negro race," "the Hun race (Mongol or Kalmuck)," and "the Hindu or Hindustani race." It is possible, Kant argues, "to derive all of the other hereditary characteristics of peoples from these four races either as mixed races or as races that originate from them."[3] So persuasive have been these primitive analyses of race that they have become part of the common language about how people are to be classified. Furthermore, as Charles Mills has argued, "'race' is the common conceptual denominator that gradually came to signify the respective global statuses of superiority and inferiority, privilege and subordination" as a matter of the "racial contract."[4] What is needed is a more holistic understanding

1. For a critique of primitive race theories in their distinctly biological forms, see Daniel Blackburn, "Why Race Is Not a Biological Concept," in *Race and Racism in Theory and Practice,* ed. Berel Lang, pp. 3–26 (Lanham: Rowman and Littlefield, 2000); James King, *The Biology of Race* (New York: Harcourt Brace Jovanovich, 1971).

2. Immanuel Kant, "Of the Different Human Races," in *The Idea of Race,* ed. Robert Bernasconi and Tommy Lott, p. 19 (Indianapolis: Hackett, 2000).

3. Ibid., p. 11.

4. Charles Mills, *The Racial Contract* (Ithaca: Cornell University Press, 1997), p. 21. This point is echoed in David Goldberg, *The Racial State* (London: Blackwell Publishers, 2002).

and clarification of the nature of humans. To accomplish this, the primitive conceptions of race must be abandoned in favor of a more precise categorization of humans into *ethnic* groups. Do ethnic groups share common properties? If so, then what are they?

In this chapter, I reject primitive race theories that categorize peoples into different "races" based solely on certain genetic traits possessed by members of each putative racial group.[5] A plausible analysis of ethnic group membership categorizes persons into groups of *ethnicity* (rather than the primitive race categories). This categorization in no way supposes, however, any distinctions between ethnic groups on the basis of genetic or any other kind of innate ordering so that one group is classified as "superior" to another. If any such distinctions of quality do exist, it is because, on average, one group or another has outperformed others in certain ways, perhaps because it has had greater social advantages or opportunities than other groups, or it exists in an environment more congenial to its own flourishing than other groups in the same or different environments.

Primitive "Race" Theories

Prior to understanding the plausibility of primitive race theories, it is helpful to come to terms with the ways in which such views attempt to ground themselves. First, primitive race theories may take a biological form wherein humans are categorized by genetic features shared by members of each group which also serve to demarcate that group from others. Morphological traits such as skin color and hair texture are passed genetically from one generation to the next within each group or race. Often, though not necessarily, this view of race assumes or argues that race as a human marker is a defensible, "natural" category. I shall refer to this version of primitive race theory as "race biologism."

Another variant of primitive race theory is what I shall call "race essentialism." Proponents of race essentialism define human races by a set of genetic or cultural traits shared by all members of a "racial" group. To be sure, there may be other ways to ground primitive race theories, but race biologism and race essentialism represent two of the more popular methods. Often times, these two primitive race theories are run together. Race biologism assumes a kind of race essentialism when certain genetic criteria are said to define human racial groups. Race essentialism may assume a kind

---

5. What I argue in criticism of primitive race theories is not inconsistent with objections to conceptions of race found in Anthony Appiah and Amy Gutmannn, *Color Conscious* (Princeton: Princeton University Press, 1996).

of race biologism when certain features are defined as essential to membership in a human racial group. For this reason, I shall use "primitive race theories" to refer to both race biologism and race essentialism.

Prior to offering a new philosophical analysis of ethnicity, it is helpful to clear the way by explaining why primitive "race" theories are inadequate.[6] There are numerous difficulties with such theories. Among the more obvious ones are their arbitrariness in the selection of which traits define racial groups, their fundamental incompleteness in accounting for the notions of race, and their apparent lack of significance. I shall refer to these as "the genetic arbitrariness objection," "the incompleteness objection," and "the insignificance objection," respectively. First, there seems to be an arbitrariness in the ways in which primitive race theorists have selected which genetic traits become decisive in distinguishing "racial" groups. Let us imagine that there are n traits that geneticists have identified as those which distinguish "Negroids" from "Caucasoids." There are various difficulties here. One is whether or not each member of, say, the "Negroid" group possesses each of the n features that distinguishes "Negroids" from "Caucasoids." Even if this is true, a deeper analysis of genetic traits might very well reveal that there are $n+1$ or more traits that would distinguish several—even hundreds—more such human groups. Surely it is plausible that the evolution of peoples results in the development of additional distinguishing traits between groups. If so, then there is a degree of arbitrariness concerning the selection of genetic traits that are said to categorize peoples into a mere few "racial" groups. If regress in the evolution of various and additional distinguishing genetic traits is found for these groups, then primitive race theories are in need of rethinking. How does the primitive race theorist know which and how many genetic properties distinguish one group from another, thus supporting the claim of racial difference?"[7]

One can imagine a somewhat less primitive race theorist revising her position in light of this concern, but arguing that the genetic arbitrariness objection is evaded by accepting the evolution of additional distinguishing genetic traits and, in turn, additional "racial" groups. But if this line is

6. For a discussion of some problems related to a species of primitive race theory (called the "ordinary concept of race"), see Naomi Zack, *Race and Mixed Race* (Philadelphia: Temple University Press, 1993), chapter 2.

7. As Appiah argues, "This is not, of course, to deny that there are differences in morphology among humans: people's skins do differ in color. But these sorts of distinctions are not—as those who believe in races apparently suppose—markers of deeper biologically-based racial essences, correlating closely with most (or even many) important biological (let alone non-biological) properties" (Anthony Appiah, "But Would That Still Be Me? Notes on Gender, 'Race,' Ethnicity, as Sources of 'Identity,'" *Journal of Philosophy* 87 [1990]: 496).

taken by the less primitive race theorist, she admits that primitive race theories are in need of revision in a rather crucial way.

Moreover, the less primitive race theorist faces the obstacle of the incompleteness objection. Even if the genetic categorization of "races" is nonarbitrary, it is implausible to suppose that a mere genetic analysis of human differences suffices as the conceptual means by which humans are differentiated. Is there not more to a "race" that mere genetic characteristics? Is there not a history, a culture, a certain life-form or experience? If so, then primitive race theory needs to provide an account of what *else*, besides genetics, suffices to categorize peoples into "races." However, once it accomplishes this in any important measure, it ceases to be *primitive* race theory, conceding that the very feature that makes itself "primitive" is theoretically inadequate.

Finally, primitive race theories face the insignificance objection. Even if it can be shown that the distinguishing of peoples into races is not arbitrary, and even if primitive race theory admits that it is incomplete and seeks only to provide a purely genetic analysis of commonalties and differences amongst humans, it is not obvious what significance the theory has beyond its giving an account of genetic similarities and differences among humans. It would still not warrant the categorization of humans into distinct races, unless by "races" it is meant merely that there are some genetic differences between "breeds" of humans as members of certain groups. But then it remains unclear as to whether such differences are significantly more interesting than the differences in biological traits between persons *within* "races." If genes are what give some people, say, kinky hair and dark colored skin and others neither of these traits, what makes such a genetic difference of sufficient importance to categorize persons into racial types? Here the genetic arbitrariness objection comes back to haunt primitive race theory. Moreover, anyone sorting persons into groups must acknowledge that a person's belonging to this or that group is a *matter of degree.*

Given the plausibility of the genetic arbitrariness objection, the incompleteness objection, and/or the insignificance objection, an adequate analysis of ethnicity ought to adopt the categories of ethnicity rather than of race. For ethnic categories do not presuppose that there are distinct groups of people based on purely genetic traits. Nor do they assume that specific traits of ethnic or gender groups are fixed in that they may evolve over time. They are not, moreover, natural kinds.[8]

---

8. Zack, *Race and Mixed Race*, p. 17. For discussions of natural kinds and natural kind terms, see Saul Kripke, *Naming and Necessity* (Cambridge: Harvard University Press, 1972), pp. 116–144; W. V. Quine, "Natural Kinds," in *Naming, Necessity, and Natural Kinds*, ed. Stephen P. Schwartz, pp. 155–75 (Ithaca: Cornell University Press, 1977).

The Genealogical-Experiential Analysis of Ethnicity

Is it plausible to argue that the terms of ethnicity are conditional? Are there ethnic essences? Naomi Zack argues that no such conditions and essences exist for race.[9] But consider the following analysis of the nature of ethnicity: A person, S, belongs to an ethnic group, G, to the extent that S is:

(1) a genealogical descendant of G.

This analysis, which I shall refer to as the "naive conception of ethnicity," seems to capture what is both necessary and sufficient for inclusion in an ethnic group. However, it is unclear whether or not (1) suffices for ethnic group membership. The reason for this is because (1) is ambiguous as stated. For the question arises as to which ethnic group one belongs if one is of mixed ethnicity. This poses particular problems for primitive conceptions of race, ones that insist on clear genetic markers between Caucasoid, Mongoloid and Negroid persons. Instances of mixed race where the mix is equal, genealogically speaking, seem not to admit of answers to the question, "Of which race is X?" Less primitive conceptions of ethnicity might argue that such cases of mixed race demonstrate that ethnicity is a matter of degree. Even so, the less primitive conceptions of ethnicity still do not provide a complete picture of ethnicity. There seems to be more to ethnicity than mere genealogical history. In an effort to bolster the naive conception of ethnicity, biological views of ethnicity might add:

(2) distinguished by (visible or apparent) features of her ethnic group members (e.g., hair texture, facial features, etc.)

to complete the analysis. But (2) poses certain troubles if it is construed as a necessary condition of ethnicity. For it raises questions of ethnic identity not unlike some problems of personal identity.[10] Consider the African American who, at t_1, possesses what are considered to be full African American features, biologically speaking, but who, for whatever reason, has those features surgically removed at t_2 such that he is no longer distin-

---

9. Zack, *Race and Mixed Race*, chapter 2; "Race and Philosophical Meaning," *APA Newsletter on Philosophy and the Black Experience* 94 (1994): 14.

10. Important discussions of personal identity include those found in A. J. Ayer, *The Problem of Knowledge* (New York: Penguin, 1956), chapter 5; G. F. Macdonald, ed., *Perception and Identity: Essays Presented to A. J. Ayer, with His Replies* (Ithaca: Cornell University Press, 1979); Robert Nozick, *Philosophical Investigations* (Cambridge: Harvard University Press, 1981), chapter 1; Derek Parfit, *Reasons and Persons* (Oxford: Oxford University Press, 1984); and Sidney Shoemaker, *Self-Knowledge and Self-Identity* (Ithaca: Cornell University Press, 1963).

guishable from, say, one of "pure" European descent. For example, this person has his skin color changed from a dark black to a pale color, has his nose and lips reworked such that they resemble the typical European features. The question is whether or not the surgical alterations have actually changed this person's ethnicity. If so, then (2) is a necessary condition of ones being an African American. But there is reason to think that the person in question has not, in having the deemed African American biological features altered, effected a change in his own ethnic identity. The reason for this is that there may be more to ethnicity than mere biology. It might be the case that this person shares a significant sense of self-pride in being an African American, including having a pride of a certain culture that he still deems as his own. Perhaps he even participates in cultural activities that are identified as African American, including the use of a recognizable African American dialect. Indeed, for these and other reasons, he considers himself to be an African American despite what some other African Americans might think of his having certain of his biological features altered. Here we assume that the reasons for the changes in physical appearance did not include self-deception or an attempt to opt out of the group African Americans. Now to say that this person is no longer an African American seems to beg the question concerning the nature of African American as an ethnic category. Yet there seems to be no non-question-begging way for one to insist that this person has lost his ethnicity as an African American due to the change in biology. It follows that (2) is *not* a necessary condition of ones ethnicity, and it follows that (1)-(2) is not an unproblematic analysis of the nature of ethnicity. It is of interest to note that similar difficulties arise for attempts to complete the analysis in terms of psychological, political, or linguistic factors of persons. There are no psychological, political, or linguistic features shared by all members of an ethnic group. For instance, the psychological trait of, say, being conscious of ones own ethnicity is shared by some African Americans, but not by all. The political standpoints of African Americans also differ widely. While many are of a Democratic bent, a growing number are aligning themselves with the Republican agendas. Furthermore, while many African Americans speak some dialect of "black English," others refrain from speaking in that way. In any case, such factors do not seem to figure into the analysis of ethnicity. Rather, they appear to be present as properties which, if possessed, identify a person as being more or less of a certain ethnic group.

Now it might be argued that the analysis be modified in order to properly define "ethnicity." To (1) might be added:

(3) has an *intentionally shared experience* with the members of G.

(1) and (3) evade the above mentioned ambiguity with (1). In addition to its stipulating degrees of ethnic group membership based on shared genealogical traits among members of *G*, (1) and (3) also admit degrees of ethnicity as shared experience among ethnic group members. For one might share the experience of being an African American with most but not all African Americans. Or, one might share such an experience with relatively few such persons. In the former case, we might say that the person in question is an African American in a stronger sense (but not less qualitatively significant a sense, morally speaking) than is the person in the latter instance. Anthony Appiah argues that ethnicity involves a shared culture among a group of people,[11] one which they can call their own. I would argue that a shared culture is part of what is meant by "shared experience" in (3). I would add that it is not just a matter of genealogical ties between persons in a group that makes them part of the same ethnic group, but also a matter of one's having a sense of shared values, language, and a life-form with others of a certain group. Moreover, one might argue that binding in-group members of the ethnic group is a common myth or culture established by convention and sustained from one generation of group members to the next. One might refer to this as an *ethnic heritage.*

Note that the experience shared in (3) must be intentional. This means that whatever ethnic experience there is cannot be shared by accident or coercion. It must result from the intentional and free action of humans. The language shared by members of *G*, the shared culture among *G's* members, the manners in which members of *G* experience the world and are perceived by out-group members are not the result of moral good or bad luck, but are the consequence of intentional choices by members of *G*.

It is this set of factors that primitive race theorists ignore when they attempt to provide understandings of the idea of the nature of ethnic groups. The importance of this analysis, if it goes through, is that it provides an analysis of ethnicity which states that ethnic groups must involve existential connections, as well as genealogical ties between members of the groups. In this way, genealogical and existential ties become the essences of ethnic groups. Therefore, it is not conceptually absurd to imagine a non-hierarchical ethnic essentialism that evades the difficulties posed to race essentialism by Naomi Zack.[12]

Thus whether the question is one of African American, Latino Ameri-

---

11. Appiah, "But Would That Still Be Me?" p. 498.
12. Zack, *Race and Mixed Race,* pp. 15–17; "Race and Philosophical Meaning," pp. 14–15.

can, Asian, Irish, or another ethnic group, (1) and (3) seems to capture, in a *preliminary* way, the nature of ethnicity.[13]

Objections to the Genealogical-Experiential Analysis of Ethnicity and Replies

There are a number of important objections that must be faced by the genealogical-experiential analyses of ethnicity: the arbitrariness objection, the incompleteness objection, and the insignificance objection. Let us consider them in turn in order to test the plausibility of this analysis. For it does not follow that, even should primitive race theories fail, that the genealogical-experiential analysis of ethnicity is either theoretically adequate or plausible.

Against the proposed analysis of ethnicity, one might argue that a family resemblance view of ethnicity is plausible, one which states that even though there are no essential features of, say, African Americans, a cluster of features are shared by members of the group. In-group members are identified by themselves and out-group members by the extent to which they share some of these features.

Zack argues that such a view of ethnicity is problematic because "it does not preserve the *intention* behind American racial designations."[14] However, a speaker's intention is not always decisive in determinations of linguistic meaning. I can use "good" in reference to a crooked politician, intending "good" to mean "evil" in reference to her. Likewise, I can refer to a good politician as "evil," intending that "evil" carry the same informational content as "good." The point is that the intentional use of language does not tell the entire story of language usage. For one can use a term in a confused or incorrect way. Thus, that U.S. citizens do not intend to use ethnic terms in a family resemblance fashion should in no way count against such language use.

---

13. This is not to deny, as Linda Alcoff astutely avers, that "an attempt to compare racism and sexism assumes their separability and thus erroneously suggests that sexism can be described and analyzed without addressing racial differences among women" (Linda Alcoff, "Racism," in *A Companion to Feminist Philosophy*, ed. Alison Jaggar and Iris Young, p. 475 [London: Blackwell, 1998]). Nor is it to deny Richard Wasserstrom's equally astute caution that "much of the confusion in thinking and arguing about matters concerning race and sex and in trying to determine which institutions, practices, attitudes, or beliefs are either racist or sexist results, I believe, from a failure to see that there are different domains of inquiry within which any of these matters can be examined." Richard Wasserstrom, *Philosophy and Social Issues* (Notre Dame: University of Notre Dame Press, 1980), p. 11.

14. Zack, "Race and Philosophical Meaning," p. 16.

But there is a more convincing objection to the family resemblance theory of ethnicity. What is in dispute for purposes of this project is whether or not there are conditions shared by members of an ethnic group, not whether or not such groups really exist. Thus a family resemblance objection to (1) and (3) confuses two different questions related to ethnicity. One is the question of which features are necessary and sufficient to make one a member of an ethnic group. The other is the question of whether or not there are ethnic groups that satisfy those conditions. If the family resemblance theory of ethnicity seeks to provide an answer to the latter question, it seems plausible. But to the extent that it wants to give an answer to the former question, it is found wanting. The plausibility of the family resemblance notion of ethnicity is contingent on the logical impossibility of there being an adequate analysis of ethnicity. To the extent that the genealogical-experiential analysis of ethnicity set forth herein is plausible, the family resemblance view is unneccesary. Thus it is important to consider additional objections to (1) and (3), respectively, in order to discern the plausibility of the genealogical-experiential analysis of ethnicity.

Another objection to genealogical-experiential analysis of ethnicity is that the experiential condition is not a necessary condition of ethnicity. Suppose, the objection goes, that S is born of parents X and Y, but that just after birth S is transferred to an island where S is alienated from any social interaction for the remainder of S's life. Under such conditions, it is not possible for S to acquire or share a language, a culture, or any other experience with those to whom S is genealogically tied. Yet it would be incorrect to hold that S has no membership in some ethnic group, and equally incorrect to say that S belongs to the ethnic group to which X and Y belong. The requirement of having a shared experience is not possible in S's case. How, then, does the genealogical-experiential analysis classify the ethnicity of S?

Although the genealogical-experiential analysis of ethnicity admits of degrees to which one belongs to an ethnic group, the concept of degrees of group membership does not assist in evading this criticism. However, a genealogical-experiential analyst may reply in the following way: there is nothing inherent in the genealogical-experiential analysis that requires that all humans belong to an ethnic group. In the case of S, it might be said that S has no opportunity to qualify as an ethnic group member. For S cannot, because of circumstance, intentionally share an ethnic experience with others. That there is no conceptual absurdity in this reply enables the genealogical-experiential analysis of ethnicity to evade the objection of isolated humans and the challenge to intentionally shared experience as a necessary condition of ethnicity.

A general objection to the genealogical-experiential analysis of ethnicity is that it falls prey to the objections to primitive race theories discussed above: such analyses, it might be argued, are arbitrary, incomplete, and insignificant. More specifically, the same method used to identify "races" in an arbitrary manner is used by genealogical-experiential analysis of ethnicity. That is, it is unclear, the objection goes, precisely how genetic arbitrariness is avoided in the case of genealogical-experiential analyses.

Here it is vitally important to clarify the primary difference between the genealogical-experiential analysis of ethnicity and primitive race theories. The difference between these two views is that primitive race theories, in their attempt to categorize humans into "races," employs *genetic* criteria to differentiate members of such "races" by *morphological traits* possessed by members of each group. Thus, according to primitive race theories, all "Negroids" (or "blacks," or in the United States, "African Americans") belong to such a "race" by virtue of their possessing certain morphological traits that are passed down *genetically* from one generation of members of the group to another. And the same holds true for each "racial" group. Morphological "markers" are passed on genetically from one member of the group to his or her offspring, according to primitive race theories.

Contrary to primitive race theories, the genealogical-experiential analysis of ethnicity does not characterize persons into genetically inherited properties or morphology. For that method of human categorization admits too many unnecessary complications—even errors. For instance, not all African Americans possess the same morphological features, and the same problem arises within other ethnic groups. Instead of such alleged genetically inherited morphology being used to categorize humans, the genealogical-experiential analysis of ethnicity holds that one belongs to an ethnic group to the extent that she is genealogically and experientially tied to it. But saying that one is genealogically tied to a group says nothing in particular about her morphological traits, whatever they might be. For she may or may not appear to be ("look like") her parents. More precisely, some members of a particular ethnic group may possess more genetic traits than others.

But it is the genealogical and experiential tie to the group, not the possession of genetic traits, that counts in determining ethnic group membership, according to the genealogical-experiential analysis of ethnicity. To insist otherwise would seem to court the conceptual disaster of holding that group membership is determinable by way of how someone *appears* physiologically, or morphologically.

In sum, I have raised objections to primitive race theories that call into question the very basis of folk conceptions of humans as racially categorized beings. Following this, I set forth a genealogical-experiential analysis of ethnicity. I then defended this analysis against criticism. If the arguments of this chapter go through, then a new paradigm of how humans ought to be categorized, if they are to be categorized at all, begins to emerge. It evades many of the problems of primitive race theories and seems to provide a more holistic conception of humans as evolving and complex beings.[15]

However illuminating the genealogical-experiential analysis of ethnicity is, it provides what appears to be just a hint at an adequate account of the conditions of ethnic group membership. Although it appears to provide the foundations of a metaphysical conception of ethnicity, it does not appear to serve well as a means of ethnic identification for purposes of public policy administration, such as affirmative action programs, reparations policies, and medical research. For ethnic group membership criteria seem to require a more robust articulation, one that would provide means by which persons can identify themselves accurately for purposes of public policy administration. Thus if the concept of race is empty, and if it is to be replaced by some notion of ethnicity, then precisely what conception of ethnicity is the most viable for the purposes stated, and why? What conditions, if satisfied, make one a member of this or that (or more than one) ethnic group for purposes of public policy administration?

In the following chapter, I articulate and defend an analysis of Latino identity as an instance of ethnic identity. The aim of the analysis is to provide conditions under which one is properly classified (by herself or others) as a member of the ethnic group, Latinos. This analysis can be used for other ethnic groups, so long as it is understood that it is not a metaphysical analysis of ethnicity, but rather an ethical one geared toward the accurate (though not overly complex) identification of persons into ethnic groups for purposes of determining who might qualify for affirmative action programs, other governmental allocations of resources aimed at members of certain ethnic groups (based on, say, historical oppression or the interpretation of medical research data), and for self-esteem or group solidarity purposes. All the while, my analysis will remain sensitive to the fact that policies such as the "one-drop rule" have used race for negative purposes.[16]

15. The account would also take into consideration the vast and complex political dimensions of race, as discussed in Goldberg, *The Racial State.*

16. Zack, "Race and Philosophical Meaning."

2

What Is Latino Identity?

Moral, social, and political philosophy is replete with issues of great importance, including those of racism, affirmative action, and the rights and duties of various "minority" groups.[1] In recent years, some have argued that the United States Census should begin to take into account a broader array of ethnic categories, including those of "mixed" ethnicity.[2] Accurate information about ethnic group membership or identification is essential for the equitable distribution of federal institutional entitlements or resources. But these and certain other matters assume that it makes sense to speak of racial or ethnic groups at all. Do not most accounts of racism and affirmative action assume that such practices target members of certain racial or ethnic groups? Do not most discussions of racism[3] assume that there *are* such groups, and that classification of persons into such groups makes sense, if only conventionally? Even discussions between po-

1. Will Kymlicka, ed., *The Rights of Minority Cultures* (Oxford: Oxford University Press, 1995).

2. Nathan Glazer, "The Hard Questions: Race for the Cure," *New Republic* (October 7, 1996), p. 29. I use "ethnicity" and its cognates rather than "race" and its cognates because of the conceptually problematic nature of the latter. See chapter 1.

3. Anthony Appiah, "Racisms," in *Anatomy of Racism,* ed. David Goldberg, pp. 3–17 (Minneapolis: University of Minnesota Press, 1990); Lawrence Blum, *I'm Not a Racist, But . . .* (Ithaca: Cornell University Press, 2001); J. Angelo Corlett, "Analyzing Racism," *Public Affairs Quarterly* 12 (1998): 23–50; Jorge Garcia, "Current Conceptions of Racism: A Critical Examination of Some Recent Social Philosophy," *Journal of Social Philosophy* 28 (1997): 5–42; "The Heart of Racism," *Journal of Social Philosophy* 27 (1996): 5–45.

litical liberals[4] and communitarians[5] about whether or not minority (numerical) cultural, racial, or ethnic groups have particular moral rights and thus are entitled to corresponding legal rights assume that the language of ethnic categorization makes adequate sense. But philosophers have tended to forego discussions of deeper questions about the nature of ethnic identity in favor of broader questions of ethnic group rights, duties, and other subjects. What is needed in order to bring conceptual clarification to these and other important matters is a philosophical analysis of ethnic identity that serves as at least a partial foundation for these and related discussions. One task of the philosopher, then, is to analyze the nature of ethnic groups. In so doing, she can provide substance for discussions that either explicitly or tacitly assume that talk of ethnicity makes sense, or is at least not akin to the parable of the emperor's new clothes.

Having in the previous chapter dispensed with primitive race theories, my current task is to provide a philosophical analysis of the nature of a specific ethnic group (or cluster of related ethnic groups): Latino. And I do so with full recognition that some of us who are Chicanos,[6] along with certain others of us, might very well disagree with the use of "Latino" in reference to various peoples having some Iberian descent.[7] Indeed, I use the category "Latino" as an inclusive one to refer to a number of ethnic groups such as Mexicans, Dominicans, Cubans, Puerto Ricans, Central and South Americans, and other of us folk who are in some way descendants of (and including) the Spanish and the Portuguese. However, I intend to use "Latino" and its cognates in ways that do *not* ignore the important historical and otherwise important sociological distinctions between such groups. In my usage, "Latino" stipulates a cluster or family of ethnic groups that are typically related in various ways such as language and culture, but

4. Ronald Dworkin, *Freedom's Law* (Cambridge: Harvard University Press, 1996); *Taking Rights Seriously* (Cambridge: Harvard University Press, 1978); John Rawls, *Justice as Fairness: A Reconsideration* (Cambridge: Harvard University Press, 2001); *The Law of Peoples* (Cambridge: Harvard University Press, 1999); *Political Liberalism* (New York: Columbia University Press, 1993); *A Theory of Justice* (Cambridge: Harvard University Press, 1971); Jeremy Waldron, *Liberal Rights* (Cambridge: Cambridge University Press, 1993).

5. Michael Sandel, *Liberalism and the Limits of Justice* (Cambridge: Cambridge University Press, 1982); Will Kymlicka, *Liberalism, Community, and Culture* (Oxford: Oxford University Press, 1989); *Multicultural Citizenship* (Oxford: Oxford University Press, 1995).

6. For a historical study of Chicanos, see Rudolph Acuña, *Occupied America* (New York: Harper Collins, 1988).

7. For an incisive philosophical treatment of arguments against the use of "Latino" and "Hispanic" as names for who we are, see Jorge J. E. Gracia, *Hispanic/Latino Identity* (London: Blackwell, 2000). Also, I use "Latino" as an inclusive umbrella category to include such ethnic groups as Cubanos, Puerto Ricans, Costa Ricans, Mexicanos, Colombians, Brazilians, and so on, even though many such persons would not refer to themselves as "Latino."

which have distinct historical roots. In stipulating the definition of "Latino" thusly, I attempt to minimize some difficulties that have arisen in the use of "Hispanic." It seems to have been a name invented by out-group members for purposes of public policy enactment.[8] In the United States, that umbrella term was adopted to refer to a cluster of ethnic "minority" groups to which many of us Latinos ourselves refer, self-referentially, as "Latino." Although the devising of ethnic or racial categories is not intrinsically a bad thing,[9] this practice can further alienate and disempower ethnic groups (to the extent that an ethnic group's being able to name and define itself is empowering),[10] especially ones that have a history of being disrespected. Whether we refer to ourselves as "Latino," or "Hispanics," or by some alternative category of unity within our diversity ("pan-Latino"?) we should wear our ethnic label with pride, even if, as Jorge J. E. Gracia notes, many out-group members construe our name(s) pejoratively: "We need to change people's attitudes toward us; a name is only an instrument of this task."[11]

In light of the foregoing, then, it is perhaps more appropriate to say that my task is to analyze philosophically the nature of those ethnic groups which, cumulatively and according to ordinary discourse, fall under the category of "Latino." But I must become even clearer, conceptually speaking, about my current project's aim. The question I seek to answer, at least in part, is not "*How* does one identify a Latino *group?*" Nor is it "What are the properties necessary to make a person *at different times* a Latino?" The latter question, of course, concerns continued Latino identity over time. The question I seek to answer is "What is the nature of a *Latino* person?" or "What are the necessary and sufficient conditions that define member-

8. Suzanne Oboler, *Ethnic Labels, Latino Lives* (Minneapolis: University of Minnesota Press, 1995), chapter 1. Actually, there is much more to the etymologies of "Hispanic" and "Latino" than what I have articulated. Jorge J. E. Gracia explains the rather historically complex evolutions of senses of these respective terms. See Gracia, *Hispanic/Latino Identity*, chapter 2. In light of this, my understanding of "Latino" is meant to capture Gracia's definition of "Hispanic": "Hispanics are the group of people comprised by the inhabitants of the countries of the Iberian peninsula after 1492, of what were to become the colonies of those countries after the encounter took place, and by descendants of those people who live in other countries (e.g., the United States) but preserve some link to other Hispanics" (p. 59). In light of the etymology of "Latino," then, I should reemphasize that my definition of the category is somewhat stipulative. I use "Latino" in light of the problematic nature of the category, etymologically speaking.

9. Oboler, *Ethnic Labels, Latino Lives*, xvi.

10. Coincidentally, Gracia makes a similar point concerning the political significance of self-naming when he argues that "everyone should be allowed to choose his or her name; for names have serious consequences. Some of them disempower those who have them in ways that have serious repercussions for their lives" (Gracia, *Hispanic/Latino Identity*, chapter 1). I would add, however, that self-empowerment by way of self-naming affords social/psychological benefits as well.

11. Gracia, *Hispanic/Latino Identity*, chapter 3.

ship in a Latino group, ethnically and ethically speaking?"[12] The aim of my analysis is not to analyze the nature of us Latinos in some metaphysical sense only. Rather, it is to provide a rational and reasonable means by which Latinos can be accurately categorized as such for *positive* aims of public policy administration, self-esteem, group solidarity, and the like. This is the ethical aim of the analysis. Moreover, the analysis of Latino identity is intended to be generalizeable to other ethnic groups insofar as ethnic group identification is concerned. The analysis is a realist one in regard to the stated ethical purposes, though it is not committed to any form of racial or ethnic realism, metaphysically speaking. Thus the analysis is ethically realist, but metaphysically antirealist, a distinction that philosophers do not seem to have made in the more recent literature on racial or ethnic identity theory.

Latino Identity

Prior to discussing the nature of Latino identity for purposes of public policy administration, it is important to delineate some desiderata of a theory or analysis of Latino identity. First, a theory of Latino identity should be able to distinguish members of the group, or cluster of such groups, "Latino," from other ethnic groups with as little ambiguity as possible while recognizing that differences exist between various Latino groups. This feature of the analysis allows for reasonably accurate identification of us Latino for positive aims of public policy administration. Second, a theory of Latino identity ought to identify Latinos according to standards that are used generally for the identification of members of other ethnic groups. In other words, what makes someone a Latino should not differ markedly, insofar as basic conditions of categorization are concerned, from what makes one, say, an African American or a Native American. The reason for these first two desiderata is that it is a good thing to seek to minimize arbitrariness in the categorization of us as members of ethnic groups.

Third, a theory of Latino identity should separate the question of the nature of Latinos from any moral evaluation of Latinos. This precaution guards against the use of identifying ethnic group membership for racist reasons, as has been done in the past (and is being done so now, for that matter) on various occasions. Fourth, a theory of Latino identity ought not to provide criteria that would politicize the conditions of what counts as being a Latino. This desideratum seeks to separate the question of the

---

12. Gracia refers to this kind of analysis as an "achronic" analysis. It also qualifies as being an ontological, rather than a discernibility, analysis.

nature of a Latino from the question of a Latino's particular standpoint on politics. It assumes, among other things, that the nature of ethnicity is not wholly a matter of social construction. If political affiliation or standpoint is permitted to enter into the analysis of Latino identity (or, more generally, ethnic identity), then groups targeted for positive purposes of public policy administration would include only those ethnic group members with particular political views. However, this would be absurd as any sizeable ethnic group will have members from a fairly broad spectrum of political, moral, and religious beliefs, none of whom ought to be disenfranchised for epistemic or doxastic reasons.

Furthermore, it is desirable that a theory of Latino identity recognize differences between aims of variant conceptions of Latino identity. Otherwise, confusion may result from the lack of this recognition. Most accounts of Latino identity end up being metaphysical ones, but ones that hardly end up providing useful guidelines for public policy. In fact, most philosophers writing on the topics of race and racism seem to be rather skeptical about the idea of classifying people into different ethnic groups. Yet such views imply that the employment of ethnic classification even for affirmative action aims is unjustified because it is arbitrary or capricious. I draw a distinction between positive and negative, metaphysical and ethical views of ethnicity. Positive analyses of ethnic group identity are those which hold that ethnic groups do exist while negative (say, skeptical or nominalist) accounts of ethnicity deny this. There are metaphysical positions that tend to focus on the issue of whether or not there are racial or ethnic "essences," as well as ethical views about ethnicity that tend to place value judgments on the employment of ethnic (or "color") categories for whatever reasons. I am an antirealist concerning the metaphysics of race and ethnicity, though I am a realist concerning the ethics of ethnicity. I have argued against primitive race theories taken as metaphysical dogmas,[13] though I believe certain moral and legal considerations behoove us to attempt to develop plausible conceptions of ethnicity. Racist harms of great magnitude ought not preclude justice to groups against whom such racism is perpetrated. And if justice to members of certain ethnic groups is to be minimally arbitrary, it must be grounded in plausible conceptions of ethnicity.

13. Indeed, I am a race eliminativist insofar as I see no good reason to retain the language of race in that it can be replaced with a plausible notion of ethnicities. So we ought to eliminate race-talk because it is problematic in fundamental ways, conceptually speaking (and perhaps even in light of the role it has played and continues to play in racism). But a more refined conception of ethnicity, such as the one set forth and defended in this chapter, can enable governments to rectify racist wrongs in a significantly less arbitrary manner than they can achieve by using categories of race (given its problematic nature as discussed in chapter 1).

Moreover, a theory of Latino identity should reflect an in-group perspective of what counts as being a Latino. Such a theory ought not to be developed by out-group members, no matter how well meaning they may be. Part of the project of defining or identifying who and what we are as Latinos is the ethnic pride that comes with naming and celebrating who and what we are, ethnically speaking. And identifying who and what we are as Latinos is, among other things, a process of self-empowerment. The act of identification, especially self-identification, empowers the self, and this self-empowerment can be either individual or collective. Although out-group members ought not to be allowed to decide who is or who is not a Latino, in-group experiences with out-group members may be part of what counts toward defining us Latinos. Finally, a theory of Latino identity should be sensitive to the ways in which history has, does, and will continue to shape what counts as a Latino from one generation to the next. This ought to give pause to those who believe that they are able to provide a decisive and complete account of who is or who is not a Latino.

Having articulated some desiderata of a theory of Latino identity, it is important to consider one of the leading theories of what counts as a Latino. Gracia has devoted significant philosophical energy to the task of identifying us Latinos. Concerning Latino identity, he writes that "there is no property, or set of properties, that characterizes all Hispanics at all times and in all places, but there are relations that tie them." Gracia goes on to argue that

> at any particular time and place, there are familial relations that Hispanics share and which both distinguish them from non-Hispanics and are the source of properties that also can be used to distinguish them from non-Hispanics. Particular physical characteristics, cultural traits, language, and so on, can serve to distinguish Hispanics in certain contexts, although they cannot function as criteria of distinction and identification everywhere and at all times.

This view of Latino identity is a nonessentialist one. It serves as a bold recognition of the Herculean task one faces in trying to define "Latino" in terms of, say, necessary and sufficient conditions. I concur with the admonition that it is problematic, if not "absurd," to discuss the plausibility of affirmative action for Latinos if the concept of Latino identity is defined arbitrarily.[14] Thus the importance of defining the boundaries of who counts as a Latino is important for at least purposes of public policy.

---

14. This point is made independently in J. Angelo Corlett, "Latino Identity," *Public Affairs Quarterly* 13 (1999): 273–95.

But it seems difficult to reconcile the view that

even though Hispanics do not constitute a homogeneous group, then, particular properties can be used to determine who counts as Hispanic in particular contexts. Hispanic identity does not entail a set of common properties which constitutes an essence, but this does not stand in the way of identification. We can determine who counts as Hispanic in context[15]

with the notion that Latino identity should not be unacceptably arbitrary and can be useful for purposes of public policy administration. For the same arguments that are leveled against Latino identity essentialism globally count also against any attempt to delineate "Latino" more locally. Thus contextualizing Latino identity, as Gracia argues that we can do, does not escape the full force of his own antiessentialist arguments.[16]

Not only are there conceptual problems with the contextualization of Latino identity, this conception of Latino identity will not suffice for purposes of determining wronged parties in cases of racist harms, nor will it make public policy administration likely to succeed in, say, awarding affirmative action benefits to Latinos (or to members of certain other ethnic groups, for that matter). For example, precisely how would a governing body determine who counts as a Latino in terms of criteria such as Latino culture, morphological characteristics, and language? Exactly which morphological characteristics would count as being adequately Latino? And just which cultural traits would count? And what level of competency in which Latino language or dialect would count for such purposes of public policy administration? It is dubious whether these and related questions can be answered in a nonarbitrary way. Yet the plausibility of any analysis of Latino identity is contingent on its being as nonarbitrary as possible.

It would appear, then, that a significantly more workable conception of Latino identity would be one that seeks to define the boundaries of Latinohood in some property or cluster of properties that the current U.S. law (or any other legal system, for that matter) can, in principle and in practice, verify or falsify empirically: for instance, genealogical ties. On such a conception, one is a Latino to the extent that he has a genealogical bond to those who are Latinos. This anchors Latino ethnicity in Latino genealogical lineage. Yet it hardly ignores the importance of Latino culture,[17] language, names, and other factors in determining the extent to

15. In Jorge Gracia, "Affirmative Action for Hispanics: Yes and No," *Hispanics/Latinos in the United States*, edited by Jorge Gracia and Pablo DeGreiff (London: Routledge, 2000), p. 205.
16. Such anti-essentialist arguments are found in Gracia, *Hispanic/Latino Identity*.
17. The significance of Latino culture for Latino identity is emphasized in Richard Del-

which one is a Latino.[18] This kind of view of Latino identity makes easier public policy decisions concerning ethnic groups such as Latinos. It also evades certain difficulties faced by competing conceptions. First, it would appear that on some views, it would make sense to say of a European American child who was adopted and raised in a Latino context that he is a Latino. Yet this seems just as counterintuitive as it would be to argue that I am an African American to the extent that I was raised around African Americans, yet having no genealogical tie to them.[19] Perhaps such a person is, say, a Latino in some cultural sense of her living as a voluntary and intentional participant in a Latino context. But recall that the analysis of Latinohood at issue here is one that, among other things, is workable in terms of public policy administration. Thus a "cultural Latino," if I may coin a term, should not count as a Latino for purposes of public policy. For there seems to be no adequate method by which "cultural Latinos" can be readily verified. A genealogically based analysis of Latinohood, on the other hand, provides the law with a way of supporting public policies seeking to uphold distributive and corrective justice for Latinos?[20]

Second, some conceptions of Latino identity appear to make room for the possibility that the offspring of two Latino parents, having been adopted by European American parents and raised apart from Latino culture, would no longer be a Latino. Yet this too is counterintuitive. As I have argued in chapter 3, though ethnicity is not a natural kind, it is not completely a matter of social convention either. One cannot lose that to which one is genealogically bound. Insofar as one's ethnicity is contingent on one's genealogy, one cannot lose one's ethnicity. This holds true for each ethnic group to which one is genealogically bound.

One could insist, even in light of the aforementioned considerations, that a cultural understanding of Latinohood is superior to a genealogical one, even for public policy administration. But how would a government effectively remedy or rectify Latinos for anti-Latino racist harms?[21] As we

---

gado and Vicky Palacios, "Mexican Americans as a Legally Cognizable Class," in *The Latino Condition: A Critical Reader,* ed. Richard Delgado and Jean Stefancic, pp. 284, 286 (New York: New York University Press, 1998).

18. This analysis of Latino identity is set forth and defended in Corlett, "Latino Identity." Similar conditions of Latino identity are recognized in Delgado and Palacios, "Mexican Americans as a Legally Cognizable Class," p. 284.

19. This point is echoed in Delgado and Palacios, "Mexican Americans as a Legally Cognizable Class," p. 285.

20. Thus a child of Italian immigrants to, say, Brazil, being brought up as a Brazilian, would be a "cultural Latino" (perhaps even a Latino in a linguistic sense). However, for purposes of public policy administration, this sense of being a Latino is insufficient for her to qualify as a Latino.

21. Assumed here is the plausibility of the notion of collective rights, as articulated and

have seen, without a clear and unambiguous idea of the nature of Latino-hood, public policies aimed at distributive or corrective justice for Latinos become unacceptably arbitrary. A purely cultural definition of "Latino" is insufficiently precise to distinguish us Latinos from those who are not. On the other hand, a conception of Latino identity anchored in Latino genealogical bonds, along with Latino cultural, linguistic, and other factors, seems to be a more promising foundation for the identification of us Latinos for purposes of administering public policy. Moreover, the genealogically based conception of Latino identity need not and ought not to be determined by out-group members. For ethnic identity requires a group's *self*-identity in order for it to exercise self-empowerment.

Thus the genealogical conception of Latino identity serves better the interests of public policy in identifying individuals belonging to an ethnic group deserving of instruments of distributive or corrective justice within the current U.S. legal system. This implies that the genealogical conception of Latino identity best enables government agencies in identifying those Latinos who qualify for affirmative action programs and/or reparations.

Models of Ethnicity

Ethnically and ethically, what is a Latino? There are various models of ethnicity that might in turn be taken as models of Latino identity.[22] A *relational model* of ethnicity describes ethnicity as the communication of difference by a group that perceives itself and is perceived by others as culturally distinct from members of other groups. On this model, culture plays no role in the description of ethnic groups such as Latinos. On a *shared culture model* of ethnicity, a description of an ethnic group is on the basis of its common cultural features, such as language, myths, and symbols (religious or otherwise). An *epistemic model* of ethnicity describes an ethnic group on the basis of its subjective beliefs about its common descent. The analysis of Latino identity that I develop and defend in this chapter seeks to include some elements of each of these models of ethnicity.

Prior to my proffering an analysis of Latino identity, it is important to consider a certain (metaphysical) view of ethnic identity that is often assumed or argued for by many academicians and non-academicians alike.

---

defended in J. Angelo Corlett, "The Problem of Collective Moral Rights," *Canadian Journal of Law and Jurisprudence* 7 (1994): 237–59.

22. These models are borrowed and adapted from Raymond Belliotti, *Seeking Identity* (Lawrence: University Press of Kansas, 1995), pp. 164–65.

According to what I shall refer to as "ethnic identity essentialism," to ask the question, "What is a Latino person?" is to query, positively, the necessary (and for most such essentialists, sufficient) condition(s) of Latino identity or personhood. It is to ask about the precise nature of the boundaries of membership in a Latino group, taken as a whole. Of the various ways in which the nature of Latino ethnic group membership might be construed on this account, one might adopt a naive essentialist view of Latino ethnicity according to which what is necessary and sufficient for membership in a Latino group is, for instance, one's *simply* being born into a Latino family (i.e., having Latino parents). But there are problems with this position. One is that it really never answers the question of what constitutes one's being a Latino. What it needs to do is to answer the deeper question as to what makes the putatively Latino person's *parents* Latinos. If the answer given to this problem is that the parents' parents are Latinos, then the regress argument continues to query what indeed makes the grandparents Latinos, metaphysically speaking. Somewhere along the line of argument the regress, though finite, must answer plausibly the fundamental question of Latino identity. Another problem with the naive view is that it assumes without supporting argument that factors such as culture play no role whatsoever in defining the content of expressions such as "Cesar Chavez is a Latino." One would think that, as Ruth Benedict argues, culture has very much to do with race and ethnicity.[23] If this is true, then there is good reason to think that one's genealogical tie to a certain ethnic group of people is not the only relevant factor for what counts toward membership in an ethnic group. (After all, ethnic categories such as "Latino," I argue, are *un*like racial ones in that the former include social factors as conditions of group membership such as language proficiency, name(s) and culture, while racial categories do not.) And this seems to hold true for us Latinos just as it would be true for members of other ethnic groups.

However, there is a more important reason why ethnic identity essentialism of the naive variety is problematic. Not unlike primitive notions of race discussed in the previous chapter, ethnicity is *not* purely a natural kind. By this it is meant that the term *ethnicity* does not "pick out" anything in the world, naturally speaking. Rather, ethnicity is to some extent a social convention, the meaning of which is at least somewhat determined by social groups, either over time or from generation to generation, from context to context.[24] Thus, whatever the general properties of Latinohood

23. Ruth Benedict, *Patterns of Culture* (Boston: Houghton Mifflin, 1934).
24. "Ethnicity is a primary focus of group identity, that is, the organization of plural per-

amount to, each such property may be given a different emphasis, contingent on the variations of what is construed as importantly Latino from one geographical location to another. In fact, "many of the puzzles presented by ethnicity become much less confusing once we abandon the attempt to discover the vital essence of ethnicity and instead regard ethnic affiliations as being located along a continuum of ways in which people organize and categorize themselves."[25] If this is true, then perhaps a different approach than the naive ethnic essentialist view must be taken, one which construes ethnic groups such as Latinos in terms of a cluster of concepts,[26] each of which is attributed to members of the group "Latino" by oneself, in-group and/or out-group members. This just is to make the nature of Latino identity largely sociological in nature,[27] though philosophical analysis is needed to bring conceptual clarity to the discussion of the nature of Latino identity. Although "Latino" is not merely a natural kind category, it might admit of definitions in terms of necessary/sufficient conditions.

However, it is important to note that the analysis of Latino identity for which I shall argue is *not* one of an identity relation, strictly speaking. For as Gracia points out, *X* is identical with *Y* *if and only if* there is nothing that pertains to *X* that does not pertain to *Y*, and vice versa, and *X* is identical to *Y* with respect to a particular property *if and only if* there is nothing that pertains to that particular property in *X* that does not pertain to that particular property in *Y*, and vice versa.[28] This is *not* the sense of "Latino identity" I seek to capture in my analysis. Instead, I seek to articulate and defend

---

sons into distinctive groups and, second, of solidarity and the loyalties of individual members to such groups" [Talcott Parsons, "Some Theoretical Considerations on the Nature and Trends of Change in Ethnicity," in *Ethnicity: Theory and Experience*, ed. Nathan Glazer and Daniel P. Moynihan (Cambridge: Harvard University Press, 1975), p. 53]. That Latino identity is contextually contingent provides meaning to the fact that being Latino in East Los Angeles, for instance, is different from being Latino in, say, Brazil or Cuba. For the context of Latino identity, like ethnicity more generally, differs to some extent dependent on an array of diverse influences on each particular Latino group's culture, language, and the like. This is consistent with the claim that "a single individual's racial identity can change across communities, and a family's race can change across history" (Linda Martín Alcoff, "Mestizo Identity," in *American Mixed Race*, ed. N. Zack [Lanham: Rowman and Littlefield, 1995], p. 274).

25. Donald L. Horowitz, *Ethnic Groups in Conflict* (Berkeley: University of California Press, 1985), p. 55.

26. What this amounts to is akin to Ludwig Wittgenstein's notion of "family resemblance" categories, ones that are defined in terms of a criss-crossing and overlapping set of characteristics shared by members of a class. See Ludwig Wittgenstein, *Philosophical Investigations* (New York: Macmillan, 1958), pp. 31f.

27. By this I mean what Thomas Hobbes meant when he argued that words are given their meanings by way of social convention.

28. Gracia, *Hispanic/Latino Identity*, chapter 1.

what Gracia sets forth as a *similarity relation,* where X is identical to Y *if and only if:* (1) there is at least one property that *is* shared by both X and Y, and (2) there is at least one property that is *not* shared by both X and Y.[29] In other words, my analysis of Latino identity seeks to define us Latinos in terms of a cluster of ethnic groups that share a particular property in common (namely, a Latino genealogical tie), while there are other properties (language[s], name[s], culture[s], to name the most obvious) deemed important for Latinohood that are not shared by all Latinos, where Latinohood is a matter of degree to which a Latino possesses such properties. Thus my analysis of Latino identity requires a measure of difference between us Latinos, recognizing the variances between Latino cultures, languages that exist between, say, Mexicanos, Cubanos, Brasilians, and Colombians. On the other hand, my analysis recognizes the blending of ethnicities that instantiates itself with mixes between Latino groups and others. Cubanos are precisely such an example, being a wonderful blending of Latino groups and African ones, among others.

Moreover, my analysis of Latino identity sees the nature of Latinohood as both a cluster concept and as a degree-laden one, where a cluster concept is, roughly, one under which fall closely related kinds having no single property in common, and where each of the properties that a Latino possesses admits of a certain degree to which that Latino possesses the properties. The remainder of this chapter is devoted to clarifying which properties count toward Latino identity for purposes of public policy administration, medical research data, and self- and group-esteem.

One might think that if ethnic categories such as "Latino" are not purely natural kinds, then there arise difficulties with social policies such as affirmative action, which award benefits to members of disadvantaged or wronged ethnic groups qua members of such groups. For if there are insuperable barriers to understanding the concept of ethnic identity, would this not pose problems for such policies? Would not the boundaries of ethnic group membership become so blurred that to carry out the policies would become exercises in moral arbitrariness? Are not such policies contingent on the ability of us to make conceptual sense of the notion of an ethnic group? Thus, for instance, if I as a Latino person am a beneficiary of an affirmative action program, would it not make sense to think that there need to be criteria for ethnic membership in Latino groups in order for the program to be well administered, even morally justified?

It becomes a challenge, then, to analyze the notion of Latino identity in such a way as to do no significant damage to ordinary usage of concepts

29. Ibid.

of Latino identity (on the one hand), and so that thinking about certain social policies rests on some sensible conceptual ground (on the other hand). Moreover, it is helpful to construe Latino identity as being a matter of degree. This implies that whatever qualities might be necessary and/or sufficient for Latino identity, a Latino person will *more or less* fall under the category: Latino. Let us consider a number of putative properties of Latino identity in order to establish, if we can, the nature of it. In so doing, I will begin to construct philosophically the foundations of a more plausible analysis of ethnic identity.

The Genealogical Conception of Latino Identity

Having noted some of the various problems facing a metaphysical analysis of Latino identity in particular and of ethnic identity more generally, it is important to investigate whether or not there is, at some level, meaningfulness in the categorization of ourselves into ethnic groups.[30] Continuing to use "Latino" as the example of an ethnic group, let us see if a philosophical analysis can be devised that proves useful and plausible, if not metaphysically, then perhaps for some other reason or purpose.

Genealogical Tie(s) to a Latino Group

Most would argue that one's genealogical tie to members of a Latino group is a sure sign of one's membership, at least to some extent, in it. But is this view plausible? Perhaps it depends on whether or not one takes ethnic group membership in either a narrow or a broad sense. For one might argue that to be a Latino in a narrow sense is to satisfy a certain set of conditions and to a strong degree. For instance, a species of this position might argue that a Latino person is one who has strong genealogical ties to a Latino group, that is, has two Latino parents, understands or speaks Spanish fluently, has a Latino surname, and participates willfully and often in Latino culture. More precisely, the narrow conception of Latino identity

---

30. For a social scientific analysis of Latino identity, see Teresa Sullivan, "A Demographic Portrait," in *Hispanics in the United States*, ed. Pastora San Juan Cafferty and William C. Mc-Cready, p. 12 (New Brunswick, N.J.: Transaction Books, 1985). Sullivan analyzes various proposed properties of Latino identity: country of birth, Spanish surname, Spanish language fluency, and Latino self-identification. That such characteristics have so often in the past been used to categorize us Latinos lends evidence regarding the importance of becoming conceptually clear about what ought and what ought not to count as being a Latino. Hence the significance of this project's aim, which is to analyze philosophically the plausibility of these and other related putative properties of Latinohood. Various criteria for *racial* identity are discussed in Charles Mills, *Blackness Visible* (Ithaca: Cornell University Press, 1998), pp. 50–54.

states that there is a set of conditions, *C*, commonly appealed to when identifying a person, *X*, as a member of a Latino group, *L*, and *X* is a member
of *L* only if *X* satisfies *all* of those conditions in *C*. This view of ethnic group
membership is reluctant to allow into the ranks of Latinos those who, for
instance, are acculturated "out of" Latinohood as Latinohood is construed
by the core members of the group. This view might also be reticent concerning the plausible membership status of certain of those who are said
to "pass" as members of non-Latino groups. However, this conception of
Latino identity is contingent on the plausibility of there being a range of
conditions in *C* that constitute necessary and sufficient conditions satisfied
by all Latinos. The plausibility of such a position will be tested below.

On the other hand, a broad view of ethnic group membership would be
more permissive concerning who qualifies as a Latino person. Perhaps it
would agree that certain folk who fit a narrow description, socially construed, lie at the core of some Latino group, while those of us who "pass"
might be considered as part of the periphery of that group, perhaps largely
contingent on our self-conception as Latino persons.[31] The broad conception of Latino identity states that there is a set of conditions, *C*, commonly appealed to, and *X* is a member of a Latino group, *L*, when there is
some member of *C* that is satisfied by *X*. This view of Latino identity might
appeal to those who are tempted to think that, for example, some person
having a traditionally construed Latino surname is a Latino, even though
nothing else about that person's ethnicity is known. Below we shall see,
however, whether or not one's having a traditionally construed Latino surname is either a necessary or sufficient condition of Latino identity.

At issue between the narrow and broad views is whether or not one's genealogical tie to a Latino group is sufficient, necessary, or neither necessary nor sufficient, for Latino identity. While both views affirm that some
significant Latino genealogical tie is necessary for Latino identity, the narrow view will argue that strong genealogical ties to Latino groups are, along
with strong degrees of Spanish language fluency, Latino cultural experience, and having Latino names, necessary and jointly sufficient conditions
of Latino identity, while the broad view affirms varying degrees of each of
these conditions as being necessary for Latino identity on the grounds that
ethnic identity is not simply a natural kind and that ethnic group membership is largely, at least, conventional. So whereas the narrow view of
Latino identity construes Latinohood as an all-or-nothing category, the

---

31. This notion is consistent with the idea that "ethnic groups can become more or less
inclusive," by way of, say, assimilation and differentiation (Horowitz, *Ethnic Groups in Conflict*, pp. 64f.).

genealogical view sees Latino identity as a degree-laden concept. Thus both views hold that membership in a Latino group *is* contingent on one's being born into some such group.[32] Otherwise, one who has absolutely no genealogical ties to Latinos would qualify as a Latino, which is counterintuitive. Therefore, genealogical ties to Latinos are necessary for Latino identity. But are such ties sufficient for Latino identity?

On the genealogical conception of Latino identity, genealogical ties to Latinos might be construed as being both necessary and sufficient for Latino identity in at least the sense that one person's possessing such properties would satisfy *some* significant condition of membership in a Latino group. Remember that Latino identity is a matter of degree on this account. However, on the narrow account, Latino identity entails more than Latino genealogical ties. It involves one's significant command of Spanish (or its dialects), having a Latino name, and willfully and voluntarily participating in Latino culture. Let us examine each of these putative conditions of Latino identity in order to determine the philosophical fate of the narrow conception of it.

Spanish Language(s)

If, as the narrow view has it, genealogical ties to the cluster of Latino groups are necessary for membership in them, then what, in addition to Latino genealogical ties, might be sufficient for Latino identity? What, in addition to Latino genealogical ties, defines the boundaries of Latinohood? It might be argued that one's ability to understand or speak Spanish (or a dialect thereof) is necessary and/or sufficient for membership in the cluster of Latino groups. Although it is natural to recognize many folk as being members of a certain ethnic group by way of the language(s) they speak natively, language in itself is not a necessary condition of one's being a Latino for the following reason. Someone (such as the famous rock and roll musician Richard Valenzuela, aka, Ritchie Valens) might be born into a Latino family, maintain many Latino traditions, yet lack a fluency in Spanish. The reasons for this might include the desire to survive and assimilate into a society as anti-Latino as the United States. Yet it would be implausible to think that simply because such a person did not understand or speak a Spanish dialect (in Valenzuela's case, until he began to learn and speak it as an adult, and even then, rather infrequently) that he was not a Latino, if even in a broad sense. Thus one's ability to understand or speak Spanish natively is not a necessary condition of membership in a Latino group. This is a rather

---

32. More generally, "ethnicity is connected to birth and blood, but not absolutely so" (ibid., pp. 51–52).

crucial point concerning U.S. public policy administration. For as things currently stand, it is permissible for affirmative action decision-makers to consider for hire only those who demonstrate a command of the language (or dialect) of the ethnic group to which the candidate for hire belongs. But it is racist to think that only Latinos who have a command of, say, Spanish are the only "genuine" Latinos for such purposes. It is to stereotype all Latinos as speaking a certain language, as if "authentic" Latinos are ones for whom English is a second language rather than their native tongue.

Moreover, having a command of Spanish is not sufficient for Latino identity either. For one can imagine a European American or African American with no Latino genealogical ties, yet who has mastered the speaking, reading, and writing of Spanish. Such a person, however expert she is in the use of the language, hardly qualifies as being a member of a Latino group, even in a broad sense. Thus something more than one's genealogical tie(s) and ability to understand or speak Spanish is needed for Latino identity.

Latino Name(s)

If it is true that persons' names usually serve as indicators of ethnic group identity,[33] then one might argue that a person's having a Latino name is an indicator of one's being a member of a Latino group. However, we would then want to ask whether or not one's having, for example, a Latino surname is necessary and/or sufficient for membership in a Latino group. Consider the tradition (in some cultures) of a woman's giving up her surname in marriage in order to take on the surname of her husband. In such cases, a woman's surname might change from Jimenez to Jones, or from Rodriguez to Robertson. Yet would we want to infer that the woman has somehow lost her Latino heritage with such a name change? Thus one's having a Latino name is unnecessary for Latino identity.

But it is also insufficient, and for the following reason. Consider the case of a European American member of the Ku Klux Klan, rather proud of her membership in the KKK and of her "pure white race," who in an inebriated state marries a Latino, with the traditional name change accompanying her marriage to him. In marrying the Latino gentleman, who himself very likely had more than a bit of alcohol to consume while marrying the Klanswoman, the Klanswoman has taken on the Latino surname of her husband. Yet common sense would tell us that the Klanswoman is anything but a member of a Latino group. In fact, though she now bears the surname of her Latino husband, she is an enemy of Latinos, at least, insofar

33. Harold R. Isaacs, "Basic Group Identity," in *Ethnicity: Theory and Experience*, p. 50.

as I am aware of the KKK's views on the nature and value of us Latinos. Perhaps she does not even understand or has not heard of the differences between Mexicans, Dominicans, Puerto Ricans, and other Latino groups. For we all look somewhat "Mexican" to the KKK. The fact is that a simple change of a name is insufficient to qualify or disqualify one as a member of a Latino group.

Latino Culture(s)

If genealogical ties to the cluster of Latino groups, having the ability to use and understand Spanish, and having a Latino name are not necessary for Latino identity, then might cultural ties help define the boundaries of membership in a Latino group? Ethnic groups, argues Donald L. Horowitz, are said to be based on shared cultures.[34] By "culture" is meant what Benedict means when she writes that "what really binds men together is their culture,—the ideas and the standards they have in common."[35] Myth, legend, and ritual are also often traits of an ethnic group's culture, whether or not they have a familial basis. Moreover, the culture of an ethnic group often, if not always, entails some sort of metaphysical standpoint, whether religious or otherwise. Such a conception might involve a group's understanding of itself, rightly or wrongly, as having a specific role in the world, such as its being "God's chosen people" or the like, as in certain Semitic cultures. With us Latinos, it might involve the emphasis on the vitality of familial life, or (for many Latinos) the importance of traditional Roman Catholic mores. But it is crucial to see that even such metaphysical conceptions are, however gradually, subject to evolution. So it appears that culture may involve an element of an ethnic group's metaphysic, and this may well be true in the case of Latino identity. Yet, as Horowitz argues, "Culture is important in the making of ethnic groups, but it is more important for providing *post facto* content to group identity than it is for providing some ineluctable prerequisite for an identity to come into being."[36] But what are the arguments in support of such a claim?

It is easy to imagine a Latina person who has been acculturated into the European American ways of the United States such that she no longer participates in any meaningful way in the culture of her Latina heritage. This reluctance of hers might be out of fear in the face of perceived or actual anti-Latino racism should she attempt to participate in her Latina culture, or it might be that she has, on due reflection, disavowed her Latina culture.

34. Horowitz, *Ethnic Groups in Conflict*, p. 73.
35. Benedict, *Patterns of Culture*, p. 16.
36. Horowitz, *Ethnic Groups in Conflict*, p. 69.

Yet it is unclear that she has therefore placed herself outside of every Latino group. It is not obvious that she has placed herself outside of the pale of Latinohood simply because she knowingly disavows much or all of Latino culture. Perhaps she disavows the dominant forms of religion of her culture, believing, in light of her considered judgments, that such rites and rituals are superstitious or evil or are in some other way bad. Is she not a Latina, given that, say, she has Latino genealogical ties? This example is intended to show that participation in Latino culture is unnecessary for one's being a Latino.

But consider another example, one of a cocaine addict, Carlos, who himself having both a Latina mother and a Latino father, and who until his teens willingly and intentionally participated in Latino culture, yet was a cocaine addict from his late teens until he was about thirty years old. Suppose further that Carlos did not participate in the culture of his youth while he was on drugs. Thus for more than a decade, Carlos was for all intents and purposes alienated from his culture, just as cocaine addiction can alienate addicts from various persons and things. The question here is not so much one of qualitative identity of Carlos from his youth to his post-addictive years, but one of numerical identity, as Derek Parfit might put it.[37] Clearly, at thirty years of age, Carlos is not the same person he was as a youth. We are concerned with whether or not he is still a Latino given his long-term drug addiction, which contributed to his being alienated from Latino culture for such a length of time. Should we say that during the time of Carlos's addiction, and consequent alienation from Latino culture, that he was not a Latino? Such an inference seems counterintuitive given his Latino genealogical ties. Thus we may conclude that one's being active in Latino culture is not a necessary condition of Latino identity.

This kind of drug addiction case also serves as a counterexample to the claim that a person's participation in a Latino culture is necessary for Latino identity. Furthermore, the fact that certain European American scholars can and do study, know, and understand much of Latino culture, and participate in many Latino cultural activities even though they are not Latinos in any meaningful sense, is enough to show that participation in Latino culture is not sufficient for Latino identity.

Based on the foregoing analysis, it would appear that the genealogical conception of Latino identity is correct when it says that ones having a Spanish surname, fluency in Spanish (or a dialect thereof), and/or participation in Latino culture are each neither necessary nor sufficient for

---

37. Derek Parfit, *Reasons and Persons* (Oxford: Oxford University Press, 1984), p. 201.

Latino identity. *Ethically speaking,* what is necessary and sufficient for Latino identity is that one has the relevant genealogical connection to, generally, Latinos. But more specific Latino identities are needed, as within the stated notion are hidden Latino groups who are, on the one hand, perpetrators of evils (historically, the Spanish and Portuguese governments, for instance) against other Latino groups (currently, it might be argued, the Basque separatists, for example). This ethical sense of "Latino" is to be read into my use and mention of the term. It should be noted that this definition of "Latino" preserves the notion that one's genealogical tie to Latinos is both a necessary and sufficient condition of Latino identity.

In Defense of the Moderate Conception of Latino Identity

Now the defender of the narrow conception of Latino identity might remind us that her position is not that any one of the above conditions *alone* is necessary for Latino identity, but that Latino genealogical ties, understanding or speaking Spanish (or a dialect thereof), having a Latino name, and willful and voluntary participation in Latino culture are necessary and *jointly* sufficient conditions of Latino identity, while genealogical ties are merely necessary but not sufficient conditions.

To this line of argument the proponent of the genealogical conception of Latino identity might argue that it hardly follows from the previous analysis that Latino genealogical ties, use of one's native Spanish language, the having of a Latino name, and willful and voluntary participation in Latino culture do *not* serve as a cluster of attributes which, when held in some combination and to some significant degree, serve to identify one as being more or less a Latino. Ethically speaking, it would seem quite problematic to implement the narrow conception of Latino identity when it comes to public policy administration. For how would it be determined how much cultural participation, language mastery, or which names count as making one a Latino (or, more generally, a member of this or that ethnic group)? In addition, factors such as Latino self-perception are also important, as is the identification both of some members of a Latino group, and of out-group members of one as being Latino in some meaningful way. Yet even these factors are neither necessary nor sufficient for Latino identity. For one can, out of self-deception, identify or misidentify oneself as a Latino, and others may do the same, out of mere ignorance of a person's ethnicity-related characteristics, or out of racism or political dogmatism. For example, some might—out of a politically ideological motivation—deem anyone who is not a Chicano *not* a Latino because such persons do not subscribe to certain political views. Yet it would appear that political standpoint or worldview hardly serves as either a necessary or sufficient condition of ethnicity, normatively speaking. Otherwise, those who have Latino genealogical ties but who did not hold such political views would not qualify as Latinos, and those who did hold such political views but lacked any Latino genealogical ties would qualify as Latino. In either instance, however, there are counterintuitive results. Thus one must be careful to not give too much weight to the judgments of others where ethnic identification is concerned. And the very same thing is true of Latino identity. Otherwise, we might fall prey to thinking, as some rather confused or misguided, though well-intentioned, persons do, that certain assimilated or acculturated Latinos are not "really" Latinos, a categorization based on their respective political and social views. The fact is, however, one's ethnicity has nothing to do with one's personal political views or commitments. Even if one's political and social views did legitimately count toward the categorization of some of us Latinos, for instance, Chicanos, it would not necessarily follow that one's views about politics would serve as a necessary/sufficient condition of membership in a Latino group. For it might be that a radical Chicana would be considered a Latina, as would a politically conservative Latina. So there might well be several kinds or degrees of us Latinos having various belief-systems and cultural mores. Yet we are all Latinos nonetheless. Perhaps only an exclusivistic ideological dogmatism would, lacking adequate supporting argumentation, deny such a claim's plausibility. For such categories can and do make room for diversity within ethnic groups.

Although the genealogical ethnic tie is not all there is to say about ethnic identity, it at least serves as somewhat of an anchoring concept so that political and moral views do not define who is or who is not a member of a Latino group. But to allow genealogical ethnic ties to play the defining role in Latino identity would be to miss out on the linguistic and cultural elements that have proven our Latino heritage, or at least much of it, so meaningful and worthwhile; yet to permit the judgments of in-group or out-group members to determine Latino identity would be to court a kind of hyperbolic form of Latino identity as being *nothing but* a social construct or convention, mutable at the whims of some powerful or even ill-motivated individuals.

Furthermore, it might be argued that the foregoing analysis of Latino identity is problematic in that, contrary to either the narrow or broad versions of ethnic group membership, one's having a genealogical tie to an ethnic group is unnecessary for one's ethnicity. Consider William and Kimberly Anderson, a European American couple who decides to move to and settle in the heart of East Los Angeles. They bear a daughter, María, who grows up and resides in the area for her first twenty years, voluntarily and frequently associating with other children and youth in the area, becoming aware of various features of Latino culture. She learns to speak Spanish at a very young age, and speaks it regularly when she is around other Spanish speakers. María willfully participates in various cultural events in the neighborhood area(s). Those who meet María for the first time see her as being a Latina. Moreover, María has a Latina consciousness, socially and politically. In fact many Latinos and non-Latinos see her as being a Chicana. Is not María a Latina? Yet she has no genealogical tie(s) to Latinos. This example shows, it might be argued, that genealogical ties to an ethnic group are not necessary for ethnic group membership. More specifically, Latino genealogical ties are unnecessary for Latino identity.

In reply to this objection, it might be argued that the example of María merely emphasizes the importance of socialization as it pertains to ethnic identity. Yet it hardly shows that ethnic identity is *merely* socialized, having nothing at all to do with genealogical ties one might have to a particular ethnic group. Moreover, if the example of María were taken to show that genealogical ethnic ties are not necessary for ethnic group membership, then at least two questionable points seem to arise concerning the counterclaim that genealogical ethnic ties are unnecessary for ethnic group membership. First, if true, the proposition would suggest that ethnicity is totally voluntary. This implies, among other things, that María can change her ethnicity from Latina to African American by simply resocializing herself, by, say, relocating and settling into certain areas of nearby Compton, California. Yet regardless of how much African American culture and consciousness María absorbs (however willfully and permanently), it would be counterintuitive to suggest that María's ethnicity amounts to only what she experiences in the moment, ignoring her history as an alleged Latino person. Second, to ignore María's genealogical tie(s) seems to imply that we need not consider her to be a European American *at all*, which is equally counterintuitive. Thus one can agree that the case of María shows the significance of socialization for ethnicity and Latinohood. But the example of María fails to defeat the claim that ethnic genealogical ties are necessary for ethnicity, and that, more specifically, Latino genealogical ties are necessary for Latino identity.

It might also be argued that the genealogical conception of Latino identity falls prey to the first objection raised against the naive variety of ethnic identity essentialism, namely, that it begs the question of what counts as one's being a Latino, and never really defines "Latino." However, this criticism overlooks the fact the genealogical conception of Latino identity does provide a significantly more robust notion of the kinds of categories *relevant to* the *extent* to which one might be a Latino, which is more than what the naive version of ethnic identity essentialism does. So the account of the nature of Latino identity found in the genealogical conception of Latino identity is less viciously circular than the account provided by naive ethnic identity essentialism. Moreover, it is hardly an uninformative analysis, as it excludes certain peoples who in fact do not qualify as Latinos, demarcating a specific cluster of ethnic groups as falling under the stipulatively used category Latino. Furthermore, that the genealogical conception of Latino identity is more plausible than naive ethnic identity essentialism is also clear in that the latter falls prey to the natural kinds objection (that Latino ethnicity is not purely a natural kind), while the genealogical conception of Latino identity does not. So the genealogical conception of Latino identity is the more plausible of the competing conceptions of Latino identity. Finally, the objection in question fails to take into account that the *ethical aim* of my analysis provides an overriding context according to which the genealogical conception of Latino/a identity sets forth the most plausible account of ethnic identity for purposes of public policy administration. For the most promising indicator of ethnic identification that guards best against arbitrary ethnic identification is the genealogical conception of Latino identity, not one based on *mere* social construction and metaphysics.

More on the Genealogical Conception of Latino Identity

Having considered and rejected a naive variety of ethnic group essentialism, I have provided reason for us to think that Latino identity is somewhat of a social construct rather than being a natural kind category. Moreover, against a narrow conception of Latino identity, I have argued that Latino identity, like ethnic identity in general, is a matter of degree. The concept of there being degrees of Latino ethnicity makes room for the fact that all or most people belong to more than one ethnic group, contrary to those who hold to a view that there exist pure races or ethnic groups. Yet even though most or all of us belong to more than one ethnic group, and some to more than one *Latino* ethnic group, this leaves room for the common sense judgment that most or all of us belong to one or more such groups *predominantly*. That one is a member of a Latino group is a function of the degree to which one: (1) has genealogical ties to others who are Latino (a necessary and sufficient condition); (2) has some command of and respect for the Spanish, Catalonian, Castillian, and other Spanish-related languages, or their respective dialects; (3) has and respects his or her Latino name(s), should he or she have some; (4) respects and engages in some significant elements of Latino culture(s), however that is defined socially; (5) perceives himself or herself to be a Latino, while not doing so to deceive himself, herself, or others of his or her ethnic identity; (6) is perceived by other Latinos as being a Latino; and (7) is perceived by non-Latino as being a member of a Latino group. Although only Latino genealogical ties are necessary and sufficient for Latino identity on this moderate view, none of the remaining "cluster" conditions are alone either necessary or sufficient, though each is, to some extent and in combination with others, sufficient to determine the *degree* to which one is a Latino. Those who are at the core of Latinohood would satisfy all of the above conditions robustly, while those who satisfy the conditions to lesser degrees will occupy a place in Latinohood between its core and its periphery, contingent on the extent to which they satisfy each of the conditions (1)–(7). I refer to the former Latinos as being Latinos in a strong sense, while I refer to the latter Latinos as being Latinos in a weaker sense. This is what I have referred to as the "genealogical conception of Latino identity." It evades the problem confronting the narrow conception of Latino identity, which sets the standards for Latino identity too high, disallowing several folk who are genuinely Latinos from belonging to the category "Latino." On the other hand, the moderate view evades the problem facing the broad conception of Latino identity, namely, that of allowing into the ranks of Latinohood those who truly do not belong (such as those possessing merely a traditionally construed Latino surname). In evading the respective problems facing the narrow and broad views, the genealogical conception of Latino identity is both narrow and broad in that it both grounds Latino identity in a Latino genetic tie and a cluster of properties, where the possession of any of these properties is a matter of degree.

The genealogical conception of Latino identity differs from Gracia's analysis of "Hispanic" identity. While each analysis denies that fluency in Spanish, Catalonian, Castillian, or their respective dialects and having some Latino name(s) or involvement in Latino culture(s) are necessary or sufficient conditions of identity of the cluster of groups in question, the genealogical conception of Latino identity articulates a degree-laden notion of ethnic identity according to which a person is a Latino to some extent. Additionally, the genealogical conception of Latino identity anchors Latino identity in the notion of Latino ancestral (or genealogical) ties as a necessary and sufficient condition of Latino identity, while Gracia argues that there are no properties that all "Hispanics" share in common. Thus while Gracia's neo-Wittgensteinianism concerning Hispanic identity is pervasive concerning any putative property of Hispanic identity, a more limited notion of Ludwig Wittgenstein's concept of "family resemblance" is employed by the genealogical conception of Latino identity. For the latter analysis, the family resemblance or cluster concept notion applies *after* arguing that Latino genealogical ties are both necessary and sufficient for Latino identity. At least, this holds true insofar as public policy administration is concerned.

The genealogical conception of Latino identity might also be compared to the conception of ethnicity articulated by Raymond Belliotti in his discussion of various dimensions of ethnicity:

> A robust ethnicity includes several dimensions: *ethnic ancestry,* beliefs about the origins of one's ancestors; *subjective acceptance,* one's self-identification as an ethnic; *ethnic behavior,* experiential expression of identity; and *salience,* the felt intensity and associated relevance of ethnic identity and behavior in a variety of social settings. Ethnic ancestry unaccompanied by subjective acceptance of ethnicity and salient ethnic behavior is empty. Ethnic ancestry and subjective acceptance of ethnicity without salient ethnic behavior is an effete form of symbolic ethnicity that lacks cultural content. Ethnic behavior unaccompanied by subjective acceptance of ethnicity is experienced as cultural limitation, even self-hate.[38]

Belliotti's characterization of a robust ethnicity is indeed helpful, though I might add that subjective acceptance of ethnicity, ethnic behavior, and salience without ancestry (genealogical ties) falls short of membership in an ethnic group (a claim that Belliotti can accommodate, logically speaking and for all he says). And this must be true, especially of robust ethnicity. It is important to note the similarities between Belliotti's description of a robust ethnicity and the genealogical conception of Latino identity. Both conceptions agree that genealogical ties are important for ethnic identity. Both agree that ethnic self-identity is important. Moreover, the importance of what Belliotti refers to as "ethnic behavior" and "salience" is meant to be captured by what I refer to as "culture," just as what I call the "language" criterion is captured by what Belliotti refers to as "ethnic behavior." Belliotti does not seem to attach *as much* importance to ethnic names as I do, though I should point out that I do not mean to attach much importance to them either, as my arguments indicate.

The differences between Belliotti's characterization of robust ethnicity and the genealogical conception of Latino identity are crucial. First, for all he says, ancestry is not a necessary condition of ethnic group membership (despite his claim, quoted above, that "ethnicity is neither merely a freely

38. Belliotti, *Seeking Identity,* p. 175.

chosen social construction nor merely a fact of ancestry"), whereas on my account of Latino identity genealogical ties are necessary for Latino identity. Second, though Belliotti's construal of ethnic identity incorporates, even requires, ethnic self-identification, my analysis of Latino identity also sees in-group and out-group identification of persons as relevant to Latino identity in particular, and for ethnicity in general.

Perhaps the most important way in which the genealogical conception of Latino identity differs from both Gracia's and Belliotti's respective views concerns the former's insistence on Latino genealogical ties as being necessary and sufficient for Latino identity over against Gracia's and Belliotti's denials of this claim. But I would hasten to point out some of the implications of their respective analyses. If there are no properties that are shared in common by all Latinos and if we cannot know what they are, then this poses a fundamental difficulty for the understanding of who we are as a cluster of ethnic groups. In turn, this poses significant problems for any social programs designed to target certain members of particular ethnic groups such as us Latinos. After all, if it is too difficult to define the intended beneficiaries of, say, affirmative action programs, then arguments in favor of affirmative action (forward or backward-looking) will be significantly problematic. Considerations of justice, whether distributive or retributive, are based on assumptions that certain names have referents. Where they do not, then policies based on such arguments can be dismissed as being implausible (here I assume that such social policies are group-based and not individual-based). Thus the genealogical conception of Latino identity, while it is not motivated primarily by an attempt to justify public policy, seems nonetheless to lend a certain credence to our commonsense notions of Latino. For this reason, among others, the genealogical conception of Latino identity enjoys a certain level of support from our intuitions about Latino identity and public policy administration, normatively speaking.

I argue, then, that the genealogical conception of Latino identity is a plausible way in which we ought to *begin* to conceptualize Latino identity. That is to say, I believe that this conception of what counts as a Latino is a plausible and helpful propadeutic for further and sustained philosophical discussion of us Latinos.

Much more needs to be said about this crucial topic. Several questions remain unanswered. For instance, what constitutes a Latino "genealogical tie"? Is it one's having at least one fully Latino parent? How "mixed" or partial may one's Latino genealogical tie be before one is rightly said to not belong to a Latino group? What ought we to say in such cases where one is, say, of "mixed" ethnicity, genealogically speaking? Take an instance of

Jaime, who has one Latino parent and one European American parent. In such a case, Jaime's genealogical ties alone, lacking further information about the genealogical ties of each of his parents, might not tell us enough about the ethnic group to which Jaime belongs for purposes of, say, public policy administration. Actually, we might well say that Jaime is both Latino and European American, genealogically speaking. Although genealogical ties constitute, on my view, an anchoring consideration in ethnic categorization, cases of "mixed" ethnicity (by far the largest class of cases of ethnicity) will require us to delve deeper into Jaime's cultural ties, language use, and name(s) in order to make a determination as to whether he is more Latino than European American, all things considered. And when these other nongenealogical factors are considered, we must realize that Jaime's ethnicity might to some extent change from one period of his life to another, and from context to context, as Jaime adjusts and readjusts himself to life's mutable circumstances. For example, in many contexts in the United States, Jaime might find the attitudes of anti-Latino racism so great that he chooses to assimilate in order to survive, while if he moves to a Latin American country, Jaime might well feel much less reticent to embrace his Latino heritage more fully than he might want to in the United States.

It might be asked precisely what percentage of genealogical or "blood" tie(s) one must have to be rightly considered to be a Latino. The answer to this, it seems, will always be at least somewhat arbitrary, that is, if one seeks to answer with a specific percentage, such as one-eighth, or one-fourth, one-half. But a rather different answer is available to us on the genealogical conception of Latino identity. Instead of having to provide a universal answer to the question of how much Latino genealogical ties one must have in order to be a Latino, we can reply that, in general, what one is mostly, ethnically speaking and for purposes of public policy administration, is what one is (predominantly). For example, if one is one-eighth Hopi, one-eighth African American, one-fourth European American (perhaps Germanic), and one-half Latino, then she is a Latina, especially if her nongenealogical factors (language/name(s)/culture) support in some important measure her Latina identity. And when, as in some cases, her ethnicity is evenly divided among a set of ethnic groups, genealogically speaking (say, if she is one-fourth Seneca, one-fourth European American, one-fourth Asian and one-fourth Latina), then an evaluation of her nongenealogical factors will determine the extent to which she is a Latina. Thus for purposes of public policy administration, one is a Latina to the extent that she has a Latina genealogical tie, and to the extent that her genealogical tie is equal to or dominant over her genealogical ties to other ethnic groups, and to the extent that her nongenealogical factors of ethnicity support her being classified as a Latina. Although one can deny or attempt to subsume one's predominant ethnicity under that of another she prefers to assimilate into, she cannot in reality do so. For her predominant genealogical tie(s) cannot be ignored, and ethnicity is not wholly a matter of voluntary socialization or resocialization. A person who seeks to completely opt out of what is clearly her genealogically based ethnicity is one who is engaged in self-deception, and some Latinos, like some African Americans, Asian Americans, and members of other ethnic groups are not immune to this unfortunate disposition. That genealogical ties are necessary for ethnicity, including Latino identity, implies that one cannot completely alienate oneself from one's ethnicity, though one can become less a member of one's ethnic group insofar as nongenealogical factors of ethnicity are concerned.

Also, to what extent must one understand and or speak Spanish, Catalonian, Castillion, or a dialect thereof to qualify as being a Latino? Precisely what counts as a Latino name? How important are traditionally Latino names along these lines? Or, is it that any name given to a child of Latino parents will do? Precisely what counts as Latino culture? Which one(s) qualify here? For surely there are interesting differences between the cultures of, say, Mexico, on the one hand, and Cuba, on the other. Even within regions of Mexico there are marked differences between subcultures. Furthermore, how long must one live in a Latino culture or in a Latino group to qualify as a Latino? Considering the fact that Chicanos, due to our assimilation into U.S. society, would in general fail to cut muster along many or all of these lines, we must be careful to not make the standards of Latino identity so high that such a group would fail to qualify as being Latino. For in the case of Chicanos, that would be tantamount to excluding from Latinohood one of its proudest subset members! Thus an adequate analysis of the nature of Latino identity must be broad enough to include assimilated Latinos, while not being so inclusive so as to include in the group of Latinos those without some significant Latino genealogical tie(s), where "significant" amounts to a person's having their strongest genealogical tie, whatever it is, as the Latino one. Finally, should the conditions of Latino identity (aside from genealogy) be ranked or articulated in lexical ordering? Do some such conditions admit of more importance than others in identifying in-group members? If so, then arguments need to be given in favor of some such conditions being weighted more heavily than others in analyzing the nature of Latinohood.

With the evolution of societies and cultures, each of these and other queries pose daunting questions for those of us who seek to delve deeper into concepts that often lie at the core of important political and moral dialogue.

3

Defending the Genealogical Concept of Latino Identity

Having in the previous chapter discussed desiderata of an adequate analysis of Latino identity, set forth the genealogical conception of Latino identity, and contrasted it to and with some competing conceptions of Latino and ethnic identity, I would like to elaborate and defend my analysis in light of some recently expressed concerns.

The problem of ethnic identity vexes a number of ethical issues, not the least of which include color-conscious versus color-blind attitudes underlying public policies such as affirmative action programs. But the problem of ethnic identity is also important for accuracy in interpreting medical research data gathered about certain health issues within ethnic groups, determining accurately census information for the redistribution of material resources (in the United States),[1] and self- and group-respect and esteem (assumed here is the plausibility of the claim that one's self-understanding contributes significantly to one's self-respect).[2] For these reasons, it is vital to articulate reasonably accurate terms that define ethnic categories. Assumed herein is what was argued in chapter 1, namely, the highly problematic nature of the traditional notions of races, or "primitive race

1. Vilma Santiago-Irizarry, *Medicalizing Ethnicity* (Ithaca: Cornell University Press, 2001), p. 25. For a philosophical discussion of some difficulties concerning the use of the concept of race in medical research, see Michael Root, "The Problem of Race in Medicine," *Philosophy and the Social Sciences* 31 (2001): 20–39.

2. Similar points are made in Michael Walzer, *On Toleration* (New Haven: Yale University Press, 1997), p. 104; and Lawrence Blum, "Ethnicity, Identity, and Community," in *Justice and Caring*, ed. Michael S. Katz, Nel Noddings, and Kenneth A. Strike (New York: Teacher's College Press, 1999), p. 127.

theories."[3] In their place, categories of ethnicity are used, ones that admit not only of degree of ethnic group membership, but of a greater number of categories of persons (and ethnic groups) than do primitive race theories. Moreover, whereas primitive race theories support a view of human groups as being natural kinds,[4] ethnic categories are not natural kinds, but are to some extent, if not wholly, social constructs. Finally, unlike primitive race theories, which tend to place a higher regard on a certain group (in the United States, typically "Caucasian" over "Mongoloid" or "Negroid"), the categories of ethnicity assume no such qualitative hierarchy among human groups. Furthermore, I believe that the strategy of employing ethnic rather than traditional racial categories will have the effect of reducing racist categorizations because ethnic terms, unlike racial ones, confer agency on members of ethnic groups and in-group members decide for themselves (on my view, in light of genealogical considerations) what makes them who and what they are.

Nonetheless, it is difficult to define precisely the conditions of ethnic group membership and hence a Herculean task to identify ourselves as being members of this or that ethnic group. This is essentially the primary problem of ethnic identity: the difficulty of defining in a plausible manner what it means to be properly classified as a member of an ethnic group. Construed thusly, ethnic identity (or Latino identity more specifically) is a matter of ethnic or Latino identification or classification. Although many social scientists use categories of ethnic identity in other ways, I shall use categories of ethnic identity to refer to ethnic classifications/identifications. After all, it does little if any good to discuss terms until we at least attempt to define them so they make sense and are of value in ordinary discourse. As we shall see, the manner in which this problem is approached reveals various sorts of motives or purposes. In fact, philosophical analyses ought to be aimed at or driven by a particular purpose.[5] Moreover, it should not surprise us if a construal of ethnicity turns out to be plausible given certain purposes, but problematic given others. From the outset of

3. J. Angelo Corlett, "Parallels of Ethnicity and Gender," in *Race/Sex,* ed. Naomi Zack (London: Routledge, 1996), pp. 83–93. For a discussion of various conceptions of race, see Linda Alcoff, "Towards a Phenomenology of Racial Embodiment," *Radical Philosophy* 95 (1999): 16f. For a racial realist position that differs from primitive race theories, see Linda Alcoff, "Philosophy and Racial Identity," *Radical Philosophy* 75 (1996): 5–14.

4. For interesting critical discussions of this point, see Daniel G. Blackburn, "Why Race Is Not a Biological Concept," in *Race and Racism in Theory and Practice,* ed. Berel Lang (Lanham: Rowman and Littlefield, 2000), pp. 3–25; Naomi Zack, ed., *American Mixed Race* (Lanham: Rowman and Littlefield, 1995); *Race and Mixed Race* (Philadelphia: Temple University Press, 1993); *Thinking About Race* (Belmont: Wadsworth, 1998).

5. Keith Lehrer, *Theory of Knowledge* (Boulder, Colo.: Westview Press, 1990), p. 5.

my own writings on ethnicity, I have been clear about the primary purposes that underlie my analysis of Latino identity.

The primary purpose of my analysis is to accurately classify people into categories of ethnicity[6] for purposes of justice under the law. Should it turn out that ethnic classifications make no sense at all, then it would seem to follow that programs of affirmative action or policies of reparations would be unjustified. It would also imply that medical research statistics regarding ethnic groups are quite confused, being based on empty concepts. Moreover, if the concept of ethnicity is null and void, those who invest themselves in notions of ethnic pride are deluding themselves. But if this conclusion is inferred, it ought to be the end result of a protracted philosophical investigation that is not motivated by partisan politics. Thus it is clear that my analysis of Latino identity is intricately tied to public policy considerations, rather than being a purely metaphysical dogma divorced from the very considerations which would (and should) inspire the discussion in the first place: a search for our Latino selves in a society[7] that commits injustices against us.

In proffering my analysis of Latino identity, I make at least the following assumptions. First, I assume that the problems of Latino and ethnic identity fall under the more general problems of personal and/or group identity. That is, whatever turns out to make me a Latino, for instance, is part of what turns out to make me who and what I am more generally, for example, as a person. And this is true whether or not I recognize this (ethnic) fact about myself. Indeed, this holds true whether or not others recognize me as a Latino. Just as there are other aspects of my being of which for whatever reason I am (or others are) unaware, I (or others) might be unaware that I am a Latino, yet I might be one nonetheless. This implies, of course, that ethnic self-identification (or even out-group ethnic identification) is not necessary for ethnicity, points to which I shall return below. This in turn implies that ethnicity is not totally a matter of social construction, something which I have taken great pains to argue in the previous chapter. Second, I assume that matters of public policy are important.[8] By "public policy," I mean, for example, affirmative action programs

---

6. This is what Lawrence Blum refers to as a "classificatory group" (Blum, "Ethnicity, Identity, and Community," p. 134).

7. I have in mind here U.S. society.

8. As Ofelia Schutte argues, "At the level of policy making, our society needs to be concerned with the balance of group representation, and to make sure that leadership positions in civil society and the state are not only open to, but also filled by, members of 'underrepresented groups'" (Ofelia Schutte, "Negotiating Latina Identities," in *Hispanics/Latinos in the United States*, ed. Jorge J. E. Gracia and Pablo DeGreiff, [London: Routledge, 2000], p. 62).

of various sorts. Because this is such a controversial and complicated matter, I shall not undertake a discussion of such policies here. Elsewhere I have argued that such programs might be justified, but only if based on what groups deserve in light of their relative harms experienced, wrongly, at the hands of the U.S. government. In any case, such programs are only justified, if they are justified at all, according to backward-looking arguments and are never to be confused as replacements for reparations. In this chapter, I assume the justifications of such policies and programs. Third, I shall optimistically assume, though not naively, that philosophical analysis can make productive conceptual progress regarding the matter of ethnicity. However, I assume neither a skeptical, nominalist, nor a realist position on the nature of ethnic groups, though I do take a position regarding the nature of ethnic groups. My view is the result, I hope, of a fundamentally coherentist moral epistemology wherein my analysis of Latino identity makes best sense of some rather important moral considerations, mentioned above. Fourth, I do not rule out the fact that race is related to the notion of class, nor that ethnicity and class are related in important ways.[9] However, given the aim of my analysis, it is quite possible to discuss ethnicity without referring to class, though a full-blown account of the former would no doubt include a discussion of the latter. In admitting this, however, it does not follow that ethnicity is somehow dependent on the notion of class. Fifth, I assume that so long as we Latinos are the ones who are classifying ourselves, it is inconsequential whether we adopt the label "Latino" or "Hispanic" (or other inclusive labels). After all, Jorge J. E. Gracia has pointed out the problematic natures of "Latino" and "Hispanic"; neither label enjoys a substantial amount of favor over the other, historically and etymologically.[10] Whichever category we adopt, should we adopt one or the other of these two,[11] it is important that *we* adopt it as a people with a sense of pride and dignity.

9. Angela Y. Davis, *Women, Race & Class* (New York: Random House, 1981); Paul Lauter, "The Race for Class," in *Race and Racism in Theory and Practice*, ed. Berel Lang (Lanham: Rowman and Littlefield, 2000), pp. 243–52; Johnny E. Williams, "Race and Class: Why All the Confusion?" in *Race and Racism in Theory and Practice*, ed. Berel Lang (Lanham: Rowman and Littlefield, 2000), pp. 215–27.

10. Jorge J. E. Gracia, *Hispanic/Latino Identity* (London: Routledge, 2000). For discussions of the importance of Latino labels, see Suzanne Oboler, *Ethnic Labels/Latino Lives* (Minneapolis: University of Minnestoa Press, 1995); Ofelia Schutte, *Cultural Identity and Social Liberation in Latin American Thought* (Albany: State University of New York Press, 1993).

11. I adopt "Latino" for lack of knowledge of a better term inclusive of *all* of us who genuinely fall under the categories that attempt to identify us as such, ethnically speaking and with an aim toward positive public policy administration. But I am not conceptually wedded to this term. Nor does the content of either my argumentation or my analysis depend on my use of "Latino" for their plausibility.

In the previous chapter, I did not mention the possibility that Latino identity might entail some difference along gender lines. I simply assumed that what fundamentally makes someone a Latino was the same for both Latinos and Latinas. I maintain this position. However, I do want to recognize variant experiences between Latinos and Latinas, and along at least the following lines. One difference between Latinos and Latinas, on balance, is that although we Latinos are more often than not disrespected intellectually (and in various other ways) in U.S. society by out-group members (and at times even by other Latinos!), Latinas not only face this problem, but confront in-group traditions that discourage their intellectual growth and independence. This works against Latinas' self-respect in ways that are deeper than what the typical Latino faces. It is one thing to face out-group disrespect; it is quite another to experience not only out-group disrespect, but discouragement from within one's own group and family. Moreover, instead of being born with privileges as Latinos carrying the family name, Latinas must overcome parental expectations regarding traditional female roles. Whereas, then, Latinos are disrespected by out-group members, we enjoy a general in-group respect. But Latinas, on the other hand, experience disrespect by both out-group and in-group members. If it is true that we Latinos are disrespected in U.S. society, then it seems that Latinas are doubly disrespected. For even in the American world of feminism, Latinas are largely invisible or disrespected. This is not a novel point, as many writers have articulated Latina experiences along these and related lines in rather moving and impressive ways.[12] As Ofelia Schutte argues, "As Latina women, we have to negotiate our identity constantly in the midst of a complex of stereotypes that include masculine-dominant expectations (both Hispanic and non-Hispanic) as to what woman should do with her body, in addition to undertaking another whole set of negotiations with respect to what a woman will do with her mind and how she will apply her intelligence."[13] Further, some Latino cultures discourage Latinas from even considering the sorts of leadership roles in society that are "reserved" for Latinos.

Even though the double-disrespect problem is an important difference between Latinos and Latinas, it is not one that would justify distinct analyses of Latinos and Latinas, respectively. The concern of this project (thus far) is to analyze Latino identity. And in so doing, recognizing existential differences

12. Gloria Anzaldúa, *Borderlands: La Frontera: The New Mestiza* (San Francisco: Aunt Lute Books, 1987); Ana Castillo, *Massacre of the Dreamers: Essays on Xicanisma* (New York: Plume, 1994).

13. Schutte, "Negotiating Latina Identities," p. 70.

between Latinos and Latinas does not seem to suffice for distinct analyses of each category insofar as the analysis of Latino identity is concerned.[14]

However, if the point of discussion concerns the administration of public policies such as affirmative action programs, it might well be important, even necessary, to make gender distinctions within ethnic groups such as Latinos. In chapter 7, I will argue that based on a general notion of proportional compensation underlying affirmative action programs, which are distinctly backward-looking in their primary justifications, it is important to award benefits of such programs differentially based on the amount of harm experienced by group members (say, in U.S. society), past and present. On this construal, Native and African Americans would, given the arguments in chapters 8 and 9, receive not only adequate reparations from the U.S. government because of the evils experienced at its hands, but would also receive affirmative action differentially greater than any other groups in the United States. The reason why affirmative action would be morally justified in such cases is that, it is assumed, reparations would never suffice to compensate for the evils each group has experienced at the hands of the U.S. government. Moreover, using this differentialist model of proportional compensatory justice to ethnic groups that have experienced significant harms, it would seem to follow that since Latinas on average experience significantly more obstacles to equal opportunity than do we Latinos, then Latinas ought to receive greater affirmative action benefits than us Latinos. If this is plausible, then it is rather important to note and respect the existential differences between Latinos and Latinas, for public policy purposes. Thus while Latinas, relative to Latinos (among others), deserve greater compensatory benefits via backward-looking affirmative action benefits due to their experiencing greater racist harms at the hands of the U.S. government and its citizenry, it does not seem to follow that this difference in experience amounts to a difference in what makes one a Latino. This assumes, of course, the existence of groups, group harms, group desert, and group compensation.

As I have argued, genealogy is the necessary and sufficient condition of public-policy-oriented ethnic identity in general, and of Latino identity in particular. Although there are other qualities individually or collectively that might count toward the enhancement of Latino identity, it is genealogy that makes one a member of this or that Latino group. That Latino identity ought to be indexed to or grounded in a particular aim or purpose

14. These points are consistent with the one made about the underlying unity of Latinos and Latinas found in Schutte, "Negotiating Latina Identities," p. 72.

is consistent with the claim that ethnic categories are socially constructed. And as Linda Alcoff points out, "To say that an identity is socially constructed is to say not that it does not refer to anything in reality, but that what it refers to is a contingent product of social negotiations rather than a natural kind."[15] But one question here is whether or not, for purposes of public policy administration, such identities are total social constructions.

My genealogically based, public-policy-oriented analysis of the nature of ethnic and Latino identity (referred to in the previous chapter as the genealogical conception of Latino identity) attempts to answer the charge that "there is no internally consistent or coherent theory of ethnic or racial identity underlying the diversity of categorizations."[16] One challenge to analytic philosophy is that it attempts to provide precisely such an analysis. And it would seem premature to rule out our being capable of meeting the analytic challenge until and unless we have devoted sufficient time and effort in developing such analyses and critiquing them. For as with other areas of philosophy, the opportunities for conceptual progress are sufficiently probable to question a cynical skepticism along these lines. In other words, the rewards of attempting philosophical analysis here are too great for us to rule out a priori the possibility of conceptual progress. Given the importance of ethnic categories in our daily lives, the stakes are simply too high for intellectual cynicism to reign. This is precisely why I adopt, not uncritically, an optimistic stance regarding the use of analytical philosophy in our attempt to wrestle with the problems of ethnic and Latino identities.

However, there is another reason why I reject a completely social constructivist account of the nature of ethnicity. It is the epistemological problem of human fallibility. If ethnicity is purely a social construction, and if whatever ethnic group I belong to is simply the one to which I claim to belong, then it seems on the social constructivist account of ethnicity that I cannot be wrong about the ethnic group to which I belong. Yet this is counterintuitive in that it does not make adequate sense of various charges of out-group members trying to act or pass as in-group ones, as in the cases of various African Americans arguing that some European Americans try to act or pass as African Americans. If there is sense in these allegations, then it seems possible that one can be mistaken about one's own ethnicity.

Furthermore, not only can out-group members be mistaken about their own membership in a particular ethnic group, but in-group members can mistakenly accept or reject folk as members of their ethnic group, as in

15. Linda Alcoff, "Is Latina/o Identity a Racial Category?" in *Hispanics and Latinos in the United States*, ed. Jorge J. E. Gracia and Pablo DeGreiff (London: Routledge, 2000), p. 30.

16. Ibid., p. 31.

cases where, typically for ideological reasons, some Chicanos reject as pseudo-members of "La Raza" those who are not "Brown enough." Finally, out-group members can misidentify persons ethnically in at least two ways. First, they might refuse to admit that, say, a "mixed-race" person truly belongs to one of the ethnic groups to which she genuinely belongs (given the genealogical conception of Latino identity [or ethnicity] discussed in the previous chapter). This can occur when out-group members, because of racist ideology (typically leftist), *refuse* to admit that a person is a member of this or that ethnic group, perhaps because of masked stereotyping on their part. Or, they might mistakenly *include,* perhaps because of racist stereotyping (often based on rightist ideology), a person in an ethnic group to which in fact she or he does not belong.

The epistemic problem of human fallibility, then, poses serious difficulties for any conception of ethnicity that relies *solely* on self- or out-group identification as *the* mark of ethnic group membership or identity. To the extent that social constructivist accounts of ethnic identity are contingent for their plausibility on this factor, they are problematic as analyses of ethnic identity that can enable governments to award benefits to members of ethnic groups.

What, then, is my analysis of the nature of Latino identity? To summarize briefly what was argued in the previous chapter, the analysis concerns fundamentally public policy classification of us into the cluster of ethnic groups comprising "Latino." As with the Diné (otherwise known as the Navajo) of Window Rock, Arizona; the Maori of New Zealand; and various other indigenous peoples dealing with their respective colonial governments, genealogy is the basis of consideration. I argue that for public policy administration considerations, genealogy ought to be construed as both a necessary and sufficient condition of award or benefit. *Aside from public policy considerations,* however, factors that would go toward making one more or less a Latino may include the degree to which one knows and respects a Latino language or dialect thereof; possesses and respects a traditional Latino name; engages in and respects Latino culture or parts thereof; accepts and respects himself or herself as a Latino; is accepted and respected as a Latino by other Latinos; and is construed as a Latino by out-group members.[17] Like the genealogical condition, each of these conditions admits of degrees. Yet while the genealogical condition is both necessary and sufficient for Latinohood, neither of the other conditions is either necessary or sufficient to make one a Latino, that is, for one to be properly classified as a Latino.

17. See chapter 7 of this book.

Thus we can see that only genealogical considerations count as being necessary and sufficient for Latino identity when it comes to public policy matters. Otherwise, it would simply become far too difficult for governments, even well-intentioned ones, to administer public policy to us Latinos and other more or less deserving ethnic groups. And we need to understand that each of the conditions discussed admits of degrees, and the degree to which one is a member of a Latino group is the extent to which one deserves a benefit. This point is based on a simple matter of proportional compensation for harms experienced (or harms experienced by one's forebears). This assumes the plausibility of the notion of group-based harm, which would serve as at least part of the justification for ethnicity-oriented public policies.

Now that my analysis of the nature of Latino identity is articulated, I can begin to consider and reply to various concerns that have been raised about it in recent years.[18] Although Schutte argues that "it is in the best interest of Hispanics to retain our ethnic/cultural identifications and insist on some form of political representation based on group classifications," she cautions that

> the classification of individuals into groups for purposes of social policy control is subject to a number of significant objections, including the fact that group identifications are vulnerable to manipulation, are subject to easy stereotyping, and in fact can do violence to individuals who differ substantially from the mainstream members of their groups. A different kind of objection with which I sympathize is that if one classifies people according to their membership in groups, in a racist society this will result in dividing people racially.[19]

As insightful as her cautions are, I believe that there are plausible replies to Schutte's points. Although it is unclear exactly what sorts of manipulation, according to Schutte, to which we might be vulnerable in public policy contexts, it is possible that political powers might well use ethnic crime statistics, for instance, in rather selective ways to support or enact legislation that might not be in the interests of all citizens equally. Such selectivity might well lead to the passage of laws that would result in the

---

18. Jorge García, "How Latina? More Latina? In Debate with Angelo Corlett," *American Philosophical Association Newsletter on Hispanic/Latino Issues in Philosophy* 1 (2001): 93–97. See also Jorge García, "Is Being Hispanic an Identity?" *Philosophy and Social Criticism* 2 (2001): 29–43.

19. Schutte, "Negotiating Latina Identities," p. 65. See also Alcoff, "Is Latina/o Identity a Racial Identity?" p. 41, for support of Schutte's final point concerning the racialization of ethnicities.

persecution of certain ethnic groups, thereby creating an unfair advantage for others. Nonetheless, this is not the fault of ethnic classification per se, but of those in power who misuse the classifications. To blame ethnic classification itself for its misuse is akin to blaming gender classification for the wrongful treatment of women. Such classifications exist, plain and simple, as functions of our human cognitive architecture.[20] That they exist is a value-neutral fact about our cognitive selves. It is what is done with such classifications that is either good or bad, just or unjust. So that ethnic classification might well lead some to manipulate ethnic statistics is insufficiently good reason to not classify ourselves according to ethnicity.

What might be said concerning the problem of stereotyping due to ethnic classification? This difficulty is not faced by my analysis of Latino identity, as my analysis insists that it is a matter of genealogy, not skin color, or other morphological features, that makes one a member of this/that ethnic group/s. If my analysis were used in public policy administration, as it is in some contexts concerning indigenous peoples, then the diversity within each ethnic group would tend to vitiate against stereotyping. Either one is a member of this/that ethnic group/s or one is not, genealogically speaking. Once this is understood in public policy contexts, then the diversity within most ethnic groups will (should) eventually minimize stereotyping of the type that concerns Schutte (and the rest of us).

But violence might be done to those who, being recognized as members of an ethnic group, do not fit the mainstream image of what members of the group ought to look like or how they ought to behave. This is certainly a legitimate concern. However, my analysis of Latino identity is motivated in part by a rejection of stereotyping and in-group ostracization that can result from this. For what makes one a member of an ethnic group has nothing whatsoever to do with class, politics, religion, or other such ideologically based factors, thereby minimizing the extent to which ethnic stereotyping might obtain in public policy administration.

In short, the fact that ethnic classification might be used by many for racist injustice is not a good enough reason to prevent genealogy from forming the foundation of ethnic classification. For it is precisely such classification that can and should enable a society to use genealogy to award justice to deserving groups. Even if it were true that ethnic stereotyping will occur because of ethnic classification, I argue that these are risks that are worth the taking. After all, we have experienced (and continue to experience) just these kinds of problems, yet without sufficient justice based on adequate models of ethnic classification.

20. See chapter 4 for a discussion of human categorization in cognition.

This leads to Schutte's own concern with ethnic classification, namely, that in racist societies (I take it that this includes all societies, more or less), people will be divided along ethnic or racial lines. In response to this concern, it might be argued that "divided" is ambiguous. If it means that folk will simply be classified into different groups (a kind of division), then such division seems innocuous. But Schutte would appear to have something else in mind here. Perhaps she has in mind ethnic groups being divided for adverse purposes, such as discriminatory racism. And such racism might lead some societies to a kind of apartheid or segregationist system. While such systems perpetrate injustices against the more powerless in society, segregation is not necessarily a bad thing. In many instances, ethnic groups that are oppressed (or have been oppressed) have no desire to integrate with the powers that oppressed them. Nor should they. Thus ethnic classification that leads to racial divisions is not necessarily a bad thing, though it might be in some cases. And for all Schutte says, there is insufficient reason to think that a genealogically based conception of Latino identity or ethnicity is problematic.

Turning to García's probing discussion of my early work on Latino identity, it is essential that my use of the term *identity* be clarified in this discussion. The reasoning behind my use of the phrase, "Latino identity" when referring to the problem of how to classify us Latino is as follows. I take it that questions of identity are those that concern who or what makes me who or what I am as a person. Since ethnicity is part of what it means to be a person, then my ethnicity is part of what it means for me to be who or what I am. My ethnic identity is part of my overall identity. Thus my identity as a Latino is part of my overall identity since it is part of my ethnic identity and my ethnic identity is part of who and what I am, holistically speaking. "Latino identity" refers to that cluster of questions concerning who and what I am *as a Latino:* What does it mean to say that I am a Latino? What makes me a Latino? What are the conditions of Latinohood? and other related questions. I have focused my attention primarily on the conditions of the nature of Latinohood. For I hope that this set of conditions will provide policymakers with the means to adequately classify us as Latinos for positive purposes.

García raises some important concerns about my analysis, which I would like to address. I am a Latino to the extent that I am genealogically tied to a Latino group, ethnically speaking. But my genealogical tie to a Latino group is a matter of degree. For given my family tree, I might be one percentage or another Latino. As I argued previously and repeatedly, my genealogical tie to a Latino group is both necessary and sufficient for my Latino identity. The point at which I am not a Latino for purposes of public policy administration is an open question, and I see no unprob-lematic or nonarbitrary way by which to decide this matter. Nonetheless, a percentage can and should be adopted for reasons of compensatory jus-tice for racist harms. That the decision as to how much of a genealogical tie to a Latino group one must have in order to be a Latino is fraught with some degree of arbitrariness is not sufficient reason to refuse to decide whatever minimal percentage of Latinoness I need to qualify for affirma-tive action programs. Thus far my analysis remains unchanged from the way I have stated it previously.

But whereas previously I stated that the degree to which one is a Latino is the degree to which the other six conditions are satisfied, I would now reiterate that these secondary conditions are not applicable in public pol-icy contexts, as they are neither necessary nor sufficient conditions of Latinohood. Indeed, they would tend to fall prey to manipulation, stereo-typing, and such, the very concerns Schutte has when ethnic classifications are used in public policy contexts.

However, the six conditions other than genealogy may be construed as conditions of Latinohood *apart from public policy administration*. Each may serve as an "enhancing condition" of Latino identity, one that is neither necessary nor sufficient for Latino identity, but one which, to the extent that it obtains in a given case, serves as a secondary indicator of one's be-ing a Latino. Although these enhancing conditions ought not to be used to define Latino identity in public policy contexts, they may in some sig-nificant measure signify ones devotion (or lack thereof) to some Latino cultural traditions, for instance. I *am* a Latino based solely on genealogical considerations, yet my respect for and enjoyment of and identification with certain aspects of Latino music, art, dance, food, and language further identifies me as a Latino so long as I am a Latino in the requisite ge-nealogical sense. Thus my identification with and participation in various aspects of Latino culture "testifies" to my being a Latino on the condition of my being a Latino in the genealogical sense. This is the sense in which I mean to use the six conditions as enhancing ones: although they do not in any way affect my being a Latino (for aims of public policy administra-tion), they do signify the extent to which I identify as such, given the fact of my Latino genealogy.

Furthermore, as I have stated previously, *ethnicity is a matter of complexity and degree*. It is highly unlikely, if not impossible, that there is "purity" of ethnicity just as there is no such thing as a "pure race."[21] If this is true, then various possibilities emerge. One is that I might well be a member of more

21. Assumed here is the idea of a common human origin, evolutionary or otherwise.

than one Latino group, ethnically speaking. Another is that I might be a member of more than one ethnic group (Latino and, say, African American). Yet another possibility is that I might be a member of more than one Latino group and, say, a European American of some sort. With this sort of ethnic complexity, it is important that minimal genealogical qualifications be drawn (admittedly, somewhat arbitrarily) in order to enact and implement public policy targeting certain ethnic groups. I see no way to escape some degree of arbitrariness here, though percentages of one-eighth and one-fourth have been used by some governments in dealing with justice toward certain ethnic groups harmed by them. Perhaps these figures might prove useful for affirmative action purposes, so long as it is understood that the blood quantum is determined solely by genealogical considerations.

Given this degree of complexity concerning ethnic identity in general and Latino identity in particular, it makes good sense to think, though my being a Latino is a matter of degree only in the sense that I am this or that much Latino, genealogically speaking and in regard to public policy matters, my Latinoness might well wax and wane *beyond public policy* matters given how much I participate in, respect, and identify with, say, Latino culture. I see no problem with this concept of waxing and waning ethnicity so long as what is meant is that it is one's identification with Latino culture, for instance, that waxes and wanes, just as in a marriage it is not the fact of the (loyalty of the) marriage that waxes and wanes (until the point of legal divorce, of course), but the devotion each partner has for the other that sometimes waxes and wanes.

These answers are meant to address García's concerns about what he terms the "commensurability problem" with my analysis of Latino identity, according to which: "How *can L's* learning *any* amount of Spanish add some of what she lost in changing her name? What is the metric in which this sort of commensuration could take place? What could be the relevant unit of measure?"[22] My clarifications seem to evade the difficulties he notes, though I should point out that the problems he notes seem to face any positive account of ethnic identity. Nonetheless, I believe that it is important for me to defend my analysis against important concerns.

It is not, then, that my analysis of Latino identity is one that seeks to define Latinos across cultures and times. It is that, however we Latinos define ourselves in a particular historical and social context, public policy must base its understanding of what makes us who we are solely on genealogical considerations. Beyond that, enhancing conditions, when they obtain, may

22. García, "How Latina? More Latina?" p. 95.

tell us the extent to which one is a Latino in some traditional or mainstream sense, metaphysically speaking. But we need to be ever mindful of the fact that this schema for identifying Latinos is neither intended to be nor is unproblematic in that it can be used to ostracize those who do not fit the mainstream of what is Latino. Being attentive to this important fact, however, is a step in the right direction in ethnic relations.

Yet another concern with my analysis as it was initially articulated[23] is that it indexed the genealogical condition to geography by defining "Latino" as one whose genealogy connected to the Iberian Peninsula. I believe that this is a mistake because ethnic groups have mingled throughout the world in such complicated ways that it is simplistic to hold that any such group includes only those whose genealogical ties trace to a particular region.[24] This concept would be as problematic for Latinos as it would for most, if not all, other ethnic groups. Thus I no longer link the genealogical condition to some geographical one. This implies that the first generations of ethnic groups, like Latinos, remain undefined, just as it does for all other positive accounts of ethnicity. However, it does not logically follow from this intractable difficulty that ethnicities cannot be traced several generations backward (from the present day) in order to identify members of certain groups deserving of reparations and/or affirmative action benefits. Thus in this way, metaphysical problems do not stop ethics from legitimate inquiry into ethnic identity and public policy administration.

Nonetheless, it might be objected that for all I write about Latino identity, I never provide a complete definition of "Latino" beyond my arguing for its genealogical basis. Hence my use of such terms as "Latino identity," "Latino culture," and "Latino names," are problematic as they are undefined. This circularity objection has been raised previously, aimed at analyses that purport to provide a realist conception of Latino identity.[25] Of course, the circularity problem faces every positive analysis of Latino identity, and so it is not a unique problem for my analysis. Still, it is important to address this conceptual difficulty.

In reply to the circularity objection, it should be noted that, if William P. Alston is correct, circularity per se is not so much the problem, as there are, he argues, virtuous circles in philosophical analysis and argumentation.[26] Moreover, some contradictions are such that it is even rational to

---

23. Corlett, "Latino Identity."
24. I am indebted to Rodney C. Roberts for pressing this point.
25. Gracia, *Hispanic/Latino Identity*.
26. William P. Alston, "Epistemic Circularity," *Philosophy & Phenomenological Research* 47 (1986): 1–30.

believe them.[27] And if it is true that at some point and in some way each analysis of Latino identity falls prey to the circularity objection, then it would seem that the more virtuously circular ones would be those which provide the best account of what common sense would tell us about Latino identity. I submit that my analysis of Latino identity is superior to competitors because it not only recognizes the fact that ethnic identities are products of social construction, metaphysically speaking, but it provides—like no competing philosophical analysis or theory—an account of Latino identity that is useful by governments for positive purposes. Moreover, there is empirical evidence over generations that genealogically based accounts such as mine are indeed successful in providing government benefits to certain ethnic groups. So whether the issue is public policy in the form of affirmative action or reparations, or public policy regarding the rights of ethnic groups,[28] my analysis goes a long way toward providing the most robust philosophical account of who and what we are, ethnically speaking, for the purpose of improving the lots of increasing numbers of Latinos and other persons of color, say, in the United States.

For those who would still raise the circularity problem for my analysis, I would remind them that one of the desiderata of a theory of ethnic or Latino identity is that it recognize the distinction between metaphysical and ethical accounts of Latino identity. So whereas I acknowledge the problematic nature of metaphysical views to define adequately "Latino," orienting my analysis to public policy considerations just means that I have delimited the range of definitions of "Latino" to genealogical matters. This is hardly question-begging. Rather, it simply recognizes that given a certain purpose for the analysis, it makes best sense to ground the analysis in genealogical considerations. In the end, the circularity objection faces every notion of ethnicity. However, the genealogical conception of Latino identity provides a plausible philosophical basis for governments to award compensation to ethnic groups that have experienced the pain of racist harms.

27. Graham Priest, "What Is So Bad about Contradictions?" *Journal of Philosophy* 95 (1998): 410–26.

28. For some discussions of group rights, including ethnic group rights, see Judith Baker, ed., *Group Rights* (Toronto: University of Toronto Press, 1994); *Canadian Journal of Law and Jurisprudence* 4 (1991); J. Angelo Corlett, "The Problem of Collective Moral Rights," *Canadian Journal of Law and Jurisprudence* 6 (1993): 237–59; David Ingram, *Group Rights* (Lawrence: University Press of Kansas, 2000); Will Kymlicka, ed., *The Rights of Minority Cultures* (Oxford: Oxford University Press, 1995); John Rawls, *The Law of Peoples* (Cambridge: Harvard University Press, 1999); Ian Shapiro and Will Kymlicka, eds., *Ethnicity and Group Rights: NOMOS* 39 (New York: New York University Press, 1997).

It need not provide a *complete* genealogical history of ethnic groups in order to effect justice to groups in a reasonably fair manner. For it can take our current understandings of, say, Latinos and trace them *backward* in time for as long as we need to for purposes of rectificatory justice. The fact that our social constructions of "race" cannot, for at least the reasons noted, be grounded by perfectly accurate (e.g., complete) genealogical research in no way logically or conceptually precludes our tracing the genealogies of our existing social constructions of ethnicities sufficiently far back in history (a few generations or so, in most cases, several more in other cases) to serve as the moral basis of claims to rectificatory justice.

In sum, my analysis of Latino identity (or classification) is multitiered, respecting the distinction between metaphysical and ethical issues pertaining to the nature of us Latinos. The conditions defining the nature of Latinos for public policy or ethical concerns are not the same as those which might define us metaphysically. Indeed, there is good reason to be metaphysical skeptics about Latino identity, especially because of the regress problem of the origins of us Latinos (also known as the circularity objection), a difficulty facing the classification of every ethnic group, as well as other previously noted difficulties. However, leftists who favor affirmative action programs, for instance, face the problem of how to classify nonarbitrarily us Latinos (as well as other targeted ethnic groups) in order to fairly distribute affirmative action benefits to us. For this purpose, I proffer and defend a genealogical analysis of Latino (and ethnic) identity:

> For purposes of public policy, one is a Latino to the extent that she or he has a Latino genealogical tie, and to the extent that her or his genealogical tie is equal to or dominant over her or his genealogical ties to other ethnic groups.

This analysis has the benefit of prohibiting non-Latinos from qualifying for policies aimed at us Latinos, unless they are predominantly Latinos, genealogically speaking, relative to the other ethnic groups to which one belongs. For it is genealogy that, however hard to ascertain in many cases, stands as the most objective means of classifying persons ethnically. In order for this analysis to be utilized positively by governments, governments must begin to keep good genealogical records of ethnicity, perhaps working with duly elected and well-respected representatives of each ethnic group. This assumes, of course, a government that supports a society not unlike John Rawls's pluralistic society (including ethnic pluralism represented in its democratic structure).[29] For this would better ensure that records of ethnicity would not be misused.

One question remaining here is whether or not public policies ought to permit a person to identify oneself in terms of more than one ethnicity. The genealogical conception of Latino identity is not committed to a position along these lines. Although there are those who might insist that no one ought to be permitted to benefit "more than once" from group-oriented public policy programs, it might be countered that one ought to benefit from such programs *to the extent that* one genuinely qualifies for them, contingent on the degree to which one is indeed a member of this or that (or more than one) of the groups targeted for such public policy programs. This latter position holds that just as proportionality ought to play a primary role in which groups the members of which ought to receive differential benefits from public policy programs over others, so ought proportionality to play a primary role in the *extent to which* a person qualifies, genealogically speaking, for the benefits of such programs. More will be made of this point in chapter 7.

My conception of Latino identity serves more than any other philosophical conception of who and what we are as Latinos to assist governments in enacting and administrating positive public policies aimed at Latinos, and it leads us away from the despairing rubble of metaphysically based skeptical views with their negative implications for public policy administration. That ethnic categorization has in the past and continues to be morally problematic is an insufficiently good reason for us to forgo defining who and what we are so that the government can use our classification of ourselves for positive public policy administration. Perhaps metaphysics leads to a justifiably skeptical or nominalistic view of the nature of ethnic identity. However, if affirmative action policies are in some measure morally justified, then it behooves us to develop an analysis of Latino identity that is useful in legal contexts, and for positive (not negative) aims. I sincerely and respectfully hope that my analysis achieves this goal in some meaningful way. And I am grateful to García for asking a series of probing queries that have begun to test what appears to be the most plausible public policy-oriented philosophical analysis of who and what we are. I suspect that the discussion will continue, and that it should until even greater clarity

29. John Rawls, *A Theory of Justice* (Cambridge: Harvard University Press, 1971); *Political Liberalism* (New York: Columbia University Press, 1993); *The Law of Peoples* (Cambridge: Harvard University Press, 1999); *Collected Papers*, ed. Samuel Freeman (Cambridge: Harvard University Press, 1999); *Justice as Fairness: A Restatement* (Cambridge: Harvard University Press, 2001).

and plausibility is attained. In the end, should this discussion continue its course, it will be us Latinos who define ourselves. And if that alone is achieved and we end up in a quandary of skepticism or even nominalism with regard to Latino identity and public policy administration, that would be an improvement over the current situation wherein we are defined by others (and the U.S. government) and for not altogether positive purposes.

Now that the concept of race has been found to be empty, and now that there is, for purposes of public policy administration, a workable analysis of the nature of ethnicities, it is helpful to explore the basis of harms directed at individuals/groups on the basis of perceived race or ethnicity. What *is* racism? It is to this question that I now turn.

4

What Is Racism?

There are few words more misused than "racism," and few phenomena less understood than racism. Immanuel Kant's use of "races of mankind" (in German) was perhaps the first explicit use of "race" in this sense.[1] Basic to this view was the notion of distinct *genetic* groups with distinctive physical characteristics, along with the idea that such characteristics made for a hierarchy of racial groups. From this rather primitive idea of "racial groups" came the view that a racial group is "a social group which persons inside or outside the group have decided is important to single out as inferior or superior, typically on the basis of real or alleged physical characteristics subjectively selected."[2] Many contemporary cultural anthropologists have largely shied away from classifying humans in terms of different races. Instead, they have tended, for some time now, to classify humans in terms of one race (the human race), yet according to various and distinct *ethnic* groups. "Ethnic group" is used in the social sciences in two different senses: broad and narrow. Nathan Glazer describes the broad construal of this category as follows:

> Thus one possible position on ethnicity and race, and the one I hold, is that they form part of a single family of social identities—a family which, in addition to races and ethnic groups, includes religious (as in Holland), language groups (as in Belgium), and all of which can be included in the most

1. Peter I. Rose, *The Subject Is Race* (New York: Oxford University Press, 1968), pp. 32–33.
2. Joe R. Feagan, *Race and Ethnic Relations,* 2d ed. (Englewood Cliffs: Prentice-Hall, 1984), pp. 5, 7.

general term, ethnic groups, groups defined by descent, real or mythical, and sharing a common history and experience.[3]

Others have opted for a narrow understanding of ethnic groups, one that excludes groups defined primarily in terms of their racial characteristics and limits "ethnic groups" to groups distinguished primarily on the basis of nationality. This narrow use of "ethnic group" derives from the meaning of the Greek word, *ethnos,* originally meaning "nation." It defines an "ethnic group" as a group of persons that is socially distinguished or set apart, by others and/or by itself, primarily on the basis of cultural or nationality characteristics.[4]

This narrow sense of "ethnic groups" does not fall prey to the primitivism of the notion of race as it was used for some time. For this sense of "ethnic group" is not bound to the strictures of physical characteristics and descent in analyzing such groups. Instead, it looks primarily to culture, nationality, and other factors in understanding what were once termed the different "races of mankind." Nevertheless, I use the term *race* and its cognates (instead of "ethnicity" and its cognates) to avoid confusion. I recognize that there may be certain differences, however slight, between ethnic groups and their respective members, and I agree with Ashley Montagu that such differences do not adequately ground a belief in their being different races. But the debate about whether or not "ethnicism" ought to replace "racism" in ordinary usage is beyond the scope of this book.[5] As Anthony Appiah argues, confusion about the sense of "racism" arises out of an inconsistency in its usage.[6] David Goldberg states that "there is considerable historical variation both in the conception of races and the kinds of social expressions we characterize as racist."[7] Perhaps the widespread confusion about this word and the conceptual framework it expresses results at least in part from its neglect by philosophers.

This chapter is devoted to developing a clear and original philosophical understanding of the nature of racism, instances of which ought to

3. Nathan Glazer, "Blacks and Ethnic Groups: The Difference and the Political Difference It Makes," *Social Problems* 18 (1971), p. 447.

4. Feagan, *Race and Ethnic Relations,* p. 9

5. See Ashley Montagu, *Man's Most Dangerous Myth: The Fallacy of Race* (Cleveland: World, 1965); *Race, Science and Humanity* (New York: Van Nostrand Reinhold, 1963). For an etymology of "racism," see Marcus G. Singer, "Some Thoughts on Race and Racism," *Philosophia* 8 (1978): 153–54.

6. Anthony Appiah, "Racisms," in *Anatomy of Racism,* ed. David Theo Goldberg (Minneapolis: University of Minnesota Press, 1990), pp. 3f.

7. David Theo Goldberg, "The Social Formation of Racist Discourse," in Goldberg, ed., *Anatomy of Racism,* p. 295.

be legally prohibited. I use African Americans[8] (in the United States) as the primary, though not exclusive, examples of objects of racism. However, in clarifying the nature of racism, one must become better informed about the function and origin of racism. What *is* racism? Are there different *kinds* of, *motivations* for, *bases* and *degrees* of racism? From where does racism *originate?* Are *all* persons racists? What is the *moral status* of racism?

After I explore some conceptions of racism, I explicate what I refer to as the "cognitive-behavioral theory of racism."[9] I argue that cognitively normal human beings are racists to the extent that they act (discriminatorily) on their ethnically prejudicial beliefs or attitudes that are based on ethnic stereotyping, but that some forms of racism are less morally condemnatory and harmful than others (given contextual considerations). I argue that a racist is one who sometimes engages, intentionally or not, in ethnic discrimination. Although one who commits one racist act is distinct from one who habitually and intentionally engages in racist activity, it is still true that one who commits one racist act is a racist in a meaningful sense.

The Nature of Racism

Some Conceptions of Racism

Philosophers have provided various conceptions of racism.[10] W. E. B. DuBois argues that racism is cultural in the sense that it opposes a race, which itself is culturally defined.[11] Appiah distinguishes between "racialism,"[12] and racism. Racialism is the foundation of various kinds of racisms.

---

8. I use the term *African American* instead of *Black* or *Afro-American* in that it seems to be most descriptive of those whom I mention in my examples. The referent of "African American" is a person who is a member of a family some of whose members trace back to U.S. slavery of Africans.

9. I am sensitive to the problems inherent in the attempt to give a complete analysis of racism which is transhistorical or generic (David Goldberg, *Racist Culture* [London: Blackwell, 1993], pp. 90–91). In fact, at the close of this chapter, I suggest that there may very well be differences in the ways that racism may be understood when we consider, say, anti–African American racism (on the one hand) and anti-Semitic racism (on the other hand).

10. For a helpful discussion of some conceptions of racism, see J. L. A. García, "Current Conceptions of Racism: A Critical Examination of Some Recent Social Philosophy," *Journal of Social Philosophy* 28 (1997): 5–42.

11. W. E. B. DuBois, *The Souls of Black Folk* (New York: Fawcett, 1961), p. 23. One should be mindful of Alain Locke's caution that the concepts of race and culture, though related, are not causally connected. They are, in Leonard Harris's description of Locke's view, "two distinct variables" (Leonard Harris, ed., *The Philosophy of Alain Locke: Harlem Renaissance and Beyond* [Philadelphia: Temple University Press, 1989], chapter 16).

12. Marcus G. Singer points out that "racialism" seems to be the usage predecessor of "racism." See Singer, "Some Thoughts on Race and Racism," pp. 153f.

However, as Marcus Singer argues, one's thinking that there are differences between ethnic groups does not constitute, if it is racism at all, the same sort of thing as one's discriminating against a person because of that person's ethnicity.[13] To use Appiah's terminology, one can be a racialist without being a racist. To be a racialist is to hold to the truth of certain descriptive claims about the perceived differences between ethnic groups. *Racism*, however, involves the mostly invidious moral judgment of someone because she is a member, or is perceived to be a member, of a certain ethnic group.[14] Goldberg recognizes that racism may manifest itself in either personal or institutional ways. He sees a racist as one who explicitly or implicitly ascribes racial characteristics (biological or social) to others and who assumes that these characteristics are different from his own and those he takes to be like him. "The ascriptions," Goldberg writes, "do not merely propose racial differences; they assign racial preferences, and they express desired, intended, or actual inclusions or exclusions, entitlements, or restrictions."[15] What makes someone a racist, he contends, pertains to the content of "the kinds of beliefs they hold."[16] More recently, Lawrence Blum argues that "all the various forms of racism are related to inferiorization or antipathy," and although "personal racism" consists in "racist acts, beliefs, attitudes, and behavior on the part of individual persons," social and institutional racism is defined solely in doxastic terms.[17] Thus the conceptions of racism articulated by Appiah, Goldberg, and Blum (respectively) proffer what might be called "doxastic" conceptions of racism, according to which what is crucial about racism is the content of the racist's belief-system or attitudes.[18]

13. Ibid., p. 156.

14. Appiah, "Racisms," pp. 4–5.

15. Goldberg, "The Social Formation of Racist Discourse," p. 296; Goldberg, *Racist Culture*, p. 98.

16. David Goldberg, "Racism and Rationality," *Philosophy of the Social Sciences* 20 (1990): 319. Although Goldberg does not make ethnic discrimination a necessary component of racism in his formal definition of "racism," he does state that "persons may be judged (more or less) racist, then, not only on the narrow basis of intentions but also where the effects of their actions are (more or less) racially discriminatory or exclusionary" (Goldberg, *Racist Culture*, p. 98). However, this statement does not recognize ethnic discrimination as a necessary feature of racism. In this way, Goldberg's understanding of the nature of racism differs from mine as I articulate it in this chapter.

17. Lawrence Blum, *I'm Not a Racist, but . . .* (Ithaca: Cornell University Press, 2002), p. 9. Although personal racism is characterized by Blum as both doxastic and nondoxastic, he goes on to define inferiorization and antipathy racisms in merely doxastic terms (p. 10).

18. Harry M. Bracken also subscribes to a doxastic definition of "racism" when he writes that racism is "the doctrine which a group may articulate in order to justify its oppression of another group." See Harry M. Bracken, "Philosophy and Racism," *Philosophia* 8 (1978): 241. Doxastic definitions of "first-order discrimination" and "second-order discrimination" are given in Adrian Piper, *Higher-Order Discrimination in Identity, Character, and Morality* (Cambridge: MIT Press, 1990), pp. 285–89.

However, for all of their valuable insights, none of these views of racism explicitly recognizes that there is a nondoxastic element to racism and that there are differences in degrees of severity of racism. Nor does either recognize or affirm the cognitive aspects of racism. In fact, none of them provides even a partial philosophical *analysis* of racism, which, however incomplete, might contribute to conceptual clarity about racism, which is bound to be useful in decisions about the extent to which certain racist actions ought to be legally prohibited. Because of these factors, I offer an analysis of racism as the central core of the cognitive-behavioral theory of racism.

The Cognitive-Behavioral Theory of Racism

I argue for a multifaceted conception of racism, one that requires both that an agent has a certain sort of ethnic prejudice regarding another person (doxastic) *and* that the racist either engages or attempts to engage in ethnic discrimination in relation to the other person (nondoxastic). Racism consists in ethnic prejudice and discrimination. *Ethnic prejudice* (of which an instance amounts to what some refer to as "racist beliefs") is the having of a negative belief about or attitude toward someone because that person belongs (or is perceived to belong) to a certain ethnic group. Ethnic prejudice is a mental state one has about another, usually accompanied by propositional attitudes one has about the other. For instance, one might have a fear (mental state) of African Americans and believe that they are by nature violent persons (propositional attitude). *Ethnic discrimination*, on the other hand, involves one's acting, omitting to act, or attempting to act (as the case may be) toward or against another based on one's ethnic prejudice toward her. It involves one's putting (or trying to put one's) ethnic prejudice into action (or inaction) in such a way that the target of the discrimination is wronged in a way that amounts to a harm and/or an offense.[19] An instance of racist harm can be found in the Jim Crow system in U.S. history, which served to set back the legitimate moral interests of African Americans in particular, thus constituting a harm toward them. Note that this system of racist segregation was hardly offensive to more than a few European American southerners during the time of its functioning, though as time has passed it has fallen into increasing disfavor,

19. According to Joel Feinberg, a harm in the relevant sense is the wrongful setting back of a legitimate interest. See Joel Feinberg, *Harm to Others* (Oxford: Oxford University Press, 1984), p. 36. In the strict or narrow sense, one is offended when one suffers a disliked state attributable to the wrongful conduct of another, where I resent the other for his role in causing me to be in the disliked state (Joel Feinberg, *Offense to Others* [Oxford: Oxford University Press, 1985], p. 2).

even among European Americans in many parts of the South. Thus there can be racist harm without offensiveness. But the case of Jim Crow is also one of racist offense: European American southerners placed African Americans in a humiliated state through the institution of Jim Crow, which whites created and sustained; in return, because of the oppression they experienced under Jim Crow, African Americans resented white southerners. However, there can be racist offense without harm, which I shall refer to as "merely offensive racism." But in referring to it thusly, I do not imply that it is unworthy of serious consideration, morally and/or legally. Take the case of a comedian's use of certain racist epithets (the deservedly famous comedian Richard Pryor often used the terms "nigger" and "honkie" in his routines, to audiences composed largely of African Americans). Although this sort of language is likely to be offensive to others, it does not necessarily count as an offense that harms others. For those who hear it might not count it as an offense to anyone in particular, and/or it might not have actually harmed anyone or any group. Much here depends on the context of the utterances. But the main point here is that merely offensive racism does not amount to a harm. On the other hand, there are "substantial racist offenses." Consider the case where one's ulterior or welfare interests are threatened by being the continual victim of racist hate speech.[20] Critical race theorists have argued forcefully that racist hate speech ought to be outlawed in the United States. If they are correct, then it would seem to be the case that racist hate speech, or at least some of it, falls under this category as that which is both an offense and a harm. And while it is part of the understanding of an offense that the offended party at some point know that she is offended, she need not know at any time that she is harmed by the racism. For victims do not always know they are wronged, yet they can be wronged, even harmed, nonetheless. The unwritten institutional forms of racism that prohibit the hiring or promoting of individuals of certain ethnic backgrounds serve as examples of precisely this sort of racism. Assuming that a legal system would only seek to deal with cases of harms, not mere offenses, then racist harms and substantially racist offenses are the kinds of racism that count as racism for the purposes of this analysis.

Thus racism involves racial prejudice, racial discrimination, harm, and/or offense. At least, this is true of the kind of racism that concerns this analysis, for instance, *the kind of racism that can be dealt with by a viable legal system.* Racism occurs when one *deals with* another person in an adverse or

---

20. For a discussion of racist and sexist hate speech, see J. Angelo Corlett and Robert Francescotti, "Foundations of a Theory of Hate Speech," *Wayne Law Review* forthcoming.

even in a seemingly positive way (perhaps paternalistically or hypocriti-
cally) because that agent perceives that the person belongs to a certain ethnic group.[21] Goldberg identifies exclusion as a fundamental characteristic
of racism.[22] I follow Goldberg on this point, but I maintain that there are
at least two levels in which exclusion manifests itself. The first level is at the
level of ethnic prejudice, where the racist acquires and develops beliefs or
attitudes that are exclusionary of certain ethnic peoples. Another level at
which exclusion becomes real is in discriminatory treatment, where, for example, agents of racism refuse to hire or promote certain people on the
basis of ethnicity. Thus the extent to which exclusion plays a role in racism
is complex. For I might refuse to associate with African Americans because
of my prejudice against them. Furthermore, my understanding of racism
locates some (if not all) racism as originating from human cognitive
processes such as memory and perception. Racism, I argue, occurs when
some person acts, fails to act, or attempts to act in a discriminatory manner toward another person or group of persons and based on the agent's
prejudicial beliefs or attitudes about the targeted person's or group's ethnicity. Not unlike many other activities having moral import, racism manifests itself in active and passive forms, contingent on the extent to which
it is the result of an agent's actions or omissions (actual or attempted).

This construal of racism implies that ethnic prejudice or racist beliefs
are not sufficient for racism proper. But this does *not* mean that such elements of racism are not morally condemnatory. Indeed, epistemically
speaking, one has a duty to eschew error and pursue truth. And one also
has a moral duty to be epistemically responsible (in the dutiful sense). To
the extent that racist beliefs are false representations of self and/or others, one's failure to at least earnestly attempt to rid them from one's belief
system constitutes a failure to live up to one's epistemic and moral duty.[23]
Perhaps it is best to say that I use "racism" to refer to a more robust sense
of this expression, not disallowing that ethnic prejudice and racist beliefs
are essential features of racism. Perhaps they are typically *milder forms* of

---

21. Following Peter Singer, I exclude the notion of arbitrariness from my definition of
"ethnic discrimination." See Peter Singer, "Is Racial Discrimination Arbitrary?" *Philosophia*
8 (1978), pp. 185f. Furthermore, my concept of racism is not inconsistent with the Marxian claim (Goldberg, *Racist Culture*, pp. 1–13, 93), echoed by DuBois in *The Souls of Black
Folk* (xiv), that racism in general is the result (at least in part) of capitalist social structures.
However, I will not delve into this matter, as the sociological or cultural cause(s) of racism
are beyond the purview of this book.

22. Goldberg, *Racist Culture*, chapter 5.

23. For discussions of epistemic responsibility, see J. Angelo Corlett, *Analyzing Social
Knowledge* (Lanham: Rowman and Littlefield, 1996), chapters 5–6; "Epistemic Responsibility," forthcoming.

racism proper. On my view, then, racism proper is a more robust conception than racist beliefs. One reason for my offering this construal of racism is to highlight the fact that there are different degrees of racism, a crucial factor in making moral and legal assessments of racist liability, blame, and censure. Perhaps between racist beliefs and racism proper exist cases of those who do not engage in ethnic discrimination, but who, having racist beliefs, stand ready to act on such beliefs should they have the opportunity.

Kinds, Motivations, and Bases of Racism

What are some of the different *kinds* of racism? There is *individual racism*, where a single person is either the agent or the object of racism. There is also *group racism*, where either the agent or the object of racism is more than one person. There are various species of these kinds of racism: individual-to-individual racism, individual-to-group racism, group-to-individual racism, and group-to-group racism. An example of individual-to-individual racism would be where, say, one member of each of two respective ethnic groups is racist toward the other (but not toward other members of the other person's ethnic group).[24] An instance of individual-to-group racism would be where an individual is racist toward a certain group, whether or not she is a member of the target group. An example of group-to-individual racism would be where a group is racist toward, say, a member (but not other members) of an ethnic group other than its own. An example of group-to-group racism would be where one ethnic group is racist against another ethnic group. But both individual and group racisms can be either institutional or noninstitutional. *Individual institutional racism* occurs when an individual racist acts (fails to act or attempts to act) so as to support some more global institutional structure as, for instance, where a segregationist judge, juror, or legislator supports a segregationist legal system. Or, it may involve a single person's being victimized by a racist system of judges, jurors, or legislators. *Group institutional racism*, on the other hand, takes place when more than one racist within a social structure, such as a racist jury, acts (fails to act or attempts to act) in support of some global institution such as the law. Or, it might turn out that a group of persons is victimized by one or more agents in such a way.[25] Moreover, as Jorge L. A. García writes,

24. Here I assume a case where one is both ethnically prejudiced against the other person as well as ethnically discriminatory toward her. All the while, this racist might, say, be ethnically prejudiced against other members of the other person's ethnic group, while not at all being ethnically discriminatory toward them.

25. For an incisive account of how this kind of racism results from social contract conditions, see Charles Mills, *The Racial Contract* (Ithaca: Cornell University Press, 1997).

To become institutionalized, racism must infect the institution's operations by informing the end it adopts, or the means it employs, or the grounds on which it accepts undesirable side effects (as is normally the case in "environmental racism"), or the assumption on which it works.[26]

There is also *noninstitutional racism* of both the individual and group varieties. *Individual noninstitutional racism* occurs when an agent acts (or omits to act) in a racist way unconnected to any institutional or social structures. Here a private individual might simply be a racist solely out of personal conviction, say, that African Americans are intrinsically evil. In fact, this racist might be against supporting any social structure and may take great personal pride in cultivating and promoting racism out of personal dislike for either African Americans as a group or a particular African American qua African American. Finally, there is *group noninstitutional racism.* Even where culture, government institutions, and the like are not (in principle) in support of racism, there may be racist groups such as the KKK which target individual African Americans and groups of them. In such a case there is no more global social support for such racism, but simply the KKK carrying out its own activities. So there are several kinds of racism concerning individuals and groups each having various species, and each of which admits of degrees of intensity of activation and severity of actual or attempted consequences.[27]

But there are at least two additional kinds of racism. There is *racism between groups* and *racism within groups.* The former is the topic of most studies and discourse on racism. It is where, for example, a group of European Americans targets, in a racist way, an individual or group of African Americans. The racially discriminatory exclusion of African Americans by European Americans from certain sectors of the U.S. workforce serves as an instance of racism between groups. But there also exists racism within groups. This occurs when, for example, certain African Americans experience racism from other African Americans. Sometimes this is based, at least it appears, on the basis of skin color, where certain African Americans of a lighter skin hue (sometimes referred to as "yellows") are racist against African Americans of a darker skin hue. Or, those of darker skin color are racist against those of lighter skin. Moreover, there are cases of darker-skinned African Americans being racist against lighter-skinned ones, the former having internalized a more general racism, which targets *all* African Americans (including *oneself* as an African American).

26. J. L. A. García, "The Heart of Racism," *Journal of Social Philosophy* 27 (1996): 32.

27. For an individualistic account of institutional racism, see García, "The Heart of Racism," pp. 11f.

Each of these kinds of racism may be "driven" (consciously or not) by at least one or more of the following *racist motivations*. Moreover, each racist motivation might be "active" at either the level of ethnic prejudice or at the level of ethnic discrimination, or both. First, it may involve *hatred of others*, where an agent's hatred for the person or group plays a primary motivational role in the racism, and where such hatred is directed at the person in virtue of her ethnicity.[28]

Second, racism may be motivated by a belief about the perceived *inferiority of others*, where the agent presumes the targeted person to be in some significant way inferior to the agent, and this because of the respective ethnic differences between the agent and the target.

Related to inferiority-based racism is *"benevolence"-based racism*, where an agent *appears* to be doing something good for or with a target (at least) because of the target's ethnicity. However, the agent's actions and accompanying prejudice in such a case turn out to be a form of racism. Certain cases of affirmative action come to mind, where some well-intentioned European Americans seek to hire an African American, thinking that they have "done a good deed" (perhaps even thinking that they have "done her a favor") in doing so. This could take the form of either "do-gooders" failing to do the right thing for the right reason, or paternalism (or both). For instance, many European Americans who seek to hire Latinos under the guise of affirmative action programs refuse to hire those Latinos who do not speak Spanish (or a dialect thereof) or "look" Latino, perhaps because they have stereotypes of what we Latinos ought to look like and how we ought to behave and what sorts of things we ought to know. Affirmative action programs are fraught with this problem, partly because European American racists, even with the best intentions, infect the system with their racist beliefs and stereotypes that often lead to racist discrimination.

Third, racism may be motivated by *superiority of others*, where the agent deems her target as being superior to herself because of the differences in ethnicity between the agent and the target. This occurs when a European American, for instance, presumes in her actions or omissions the athletic superiority of most or all African Americans, or the intellectual superiority of most or all Jewish Americans. What is problematic about

---

28. Additionally, the reactive attitude of hatred is inessential to racism. Although hatred accompanies some forms of racism, it need not be present in all forms of it. Racism might very well be motivated by power and greed in some cases, or fear and ignorance in others. Hatred is essential to neither ethnic prejudice nor ethnic discrimination. Although racism may or may not involve hatred, it does seem to entail an agent's intended or unintended (in addition, perhaps the agent's knowingly or unknowingly) disrespecting of her target. The paternalism of several early U.S. slaveholders comes to mind here.

such presumptions is that athleticism is expected from and "reserved"[29] for most or all African Americans,[30] and a certain kind of intelligence (deemed by the racist as a qualitatively better property) is expected of and "reserved" for most or all Jewish Americans. A result of such racism is that African Americans are generally seen as less intelligent than others, regardless of how well many of them do on standardized tests and regardless of how far they progress in higher education.

Racism can also be motivated by *fear* that the racist has of the target. If I harbor sufficiently strong degrees of ethnic prejudice against, say, young African American males such that when I see them approaching me as I walk down the sidewalk I turn and walk so as to avoid them, my avoidance behavior is based at least in part on my discriminatory fear of such youth. Even if statistical evidence suggests that an increasing number of such youth commit violent crimes, my unwillingness to cognitively combat what at least appears to be an instance of the fallacy of composition (in thinking that all young African American males are violent from the supposition that a relative few have committed violent actions) suggests that I have illegitimately discriminated against such persons out of my fear of their committing a violent act against me.[31]

Racism can also be motivated by *power* that the perpetrator seeks to wield over the target. Whether or not racism is always motivated by such power is questionable, however, since it is easy to imagine a case where unintentional racism motivated by ignorance of the target has nothing at all to do with the perpetrator's seeking power over the target. And this holds true even if the gaining of power over targets of racism is construed as sometimes being unintentionally gained.

Although racism can be motivated, jointly or separately, by hatred, perceived inferiority, "benevolence," perceived superiority, fear, and power, it can be based on various factors. Two such factors of racism are ignorance and ideological dogmatism. If I do not take the time and effort to better understand young African American males beyond what the media and certain statistics suggest to me, then my racism toward them is partially

---

29. Inexclusively, of course.

30. An example of this sort of racism is when certain U.S. media announcers state that Venus and Serena Williams have such fine "athleticism," while never commenting on the grace and intelligence that is required to reach the pinnacles of success that each of the Williams sisters has achieved (and at such young ages!). What raises racist suspicions here is the fact that rarely, if ever, do the same announcers say of European American tennis champions that they are (merely) "athletic." Accolades abound about European American tennis champions being "graceful" or "intelligent" or "brilliant."

31. For an account of fear as a motivation for racism, see J. Angelo Corlett, "Racism and Affirmative Action," *The Journal of Social Philosophy* 24 (1993): 163–75.

based on my *ignorance* of them. Any avoidance behavior I would demonstrate toward such young African Americans would be based on my perception of factors other than their simply being young African American
males.

Yet another basis for racism is *ideological dogmatism.* Such dogmatism
can be and often is found in racism against African Americans, even by
those who pretend to support them.[32] A paradigm case of racism based
on ideological dogmatism is the racist ideology prevalent in the early
women's suffrage movement in the United States. When asked what she
thought of the freedom of African Americans, Elizabeth Cady Stanton
replied:

> We do not take the right step for this hour in demanding suffrage for any
> class; as a matter of principle I claim it for all. But in a narrow view of the
> question as a matter falling between classes, when Mr. Downing puts the
> question to me, are you willing to have the colored man enfranchised be-
> fore the woman, I say, no; I would not trust him with all my rights; degraded,
> oppressed himself, he would be more despotic with the governing power
> than even our Saxon rulers are.[33]

Despite Stanton's claim that she supported freedom "for all," her dogmatic
ideology reared its racist head when she refused to support the freedom of
African Americans as long as European American women were not allowed
to have the same rights. But if Angela Davis is correct, "the fact that Black
men might also exhibit sexist attitudes was hardly a sound reason for ar-
resting the progress of the overall struggle for Black Liberation."[34] Stanton's failure to support the freedom of African Americans undogmatically
was based on her attitude toward African Americans as being somehow unworthy of such freedom unless European American women themselves
had their own rights secured. Stanton referred to the freed slaves as "Sam-
bos," doubting their very ability to be just.[35] But on what sort of experience

32. Martin Luther King, Jr., and Malcolm X each expressed dismay at how much more
difficult it was to deal with what they perceived as European American ("northern" or "liberal") racists who were not usually as blatant about their racism as were certain southern
segregationists in the United States. See Martin Luther King, Jr., "Letter from Birmingham
Jail," in James M. Washington, ed., *A Testament of Hope: The Essential Writings and Speeches of
Martin Luther King, Jr.* (San Francisco: Harper Collins, 1986), pp. 286f.; Malcolm X, "America's Gravest Crisis since the Civil War," speech delivered at the University of California at
Berkeley on 11 October 1963, in *Malcolm X: The Last Speeches,* ed. Bruce Perry (New York:
Pathfinder Press, 1989), p. 61.

33. Elizabeth Cady Stanton, Susan B. Anthony, and Matilda Joslyn Gage, *History of
Woman Suffrage,* vol. 2 (New York: Charles Mann Printing Company, 1881), p. 214.

34. Angela Davis, *Women, Race, and Class* (New York: Random House, 1981), p. 85.

35. Stanton, Anthony, and Gage, *History of Woman Suffrage,* pp. 94–95.

did she base her assessment of African American men? They had never
been in a position to oppress women in the United States, yet Stanton had
already formed the belief that African American leadership would be no
fairer or more just than European American men. What, except racist ideology, might begin to account for Stanton's remarks and her rather conditional support of African American liberation? A similar racist attitude
and behavior can be traced to Susan B. Anthony, who is said to believe in
human rights and political equality, yet simultaneously encouraged members of the National American Woman Suffrage Association (of which she
was at the time president) to remain silent about the issue of racism.[36] Thus
it is clear that ideological dogmatism can serve as a basis for racism.

Any combination of these motivations and bases may be present in each
of the kinds of racism and in either or both ethnic prejudice or ethnic discrimination. In a given context a racist's fear might lie at the root of her
ethnic prejudice, while her desire for power might serve as the motivation
for her ethnic discrimination. In other circumstances her ethnic prejudice
might be motivated by hatred of, say, African Americans, while her ethnic
discrimination is motivated by fear and perceived superiority. Furthermore, each of these motivations and bases admit of degrees of intensity
regarding hatred, inferiority, "benevolence," superiority, fear, power, ignorance, or ideological dogmatism that the agent has for or concerning
the target.[37]

The Perpetrators and the Targets of Racism

As I have intimated, racism involves at least one agent or perpetrator and
at least one target or victim of both ethnic prejudice and discrimination.
Racism has fall-out for primary and secondary targets. Primary targets of
racism are the persons directly *intended* (where racism is intentional) by the
racist to experience the ethnic prejudice and discrimination. Secondary
targets of racism are the indirect and *unintended* victims of racism. While
only some African Americans were the primary targets of Eugene "Bull"
Connor's (former police chief of Birmingham, Alabama) segregationism,
there is a significant sense in which each African American was a secondary
target of Connor's racism. For Connor's actions and attitudes sent a message to each African American (and to others as well), namely, that Jim
Crow is and ought to remain institutionalized in the U.S. South.

Doxastically speaking, what is involved in racism are an agent's prejudicial

36. Davis, *Women, Race, and Class,* p. 121.
37. Alternatively, such racism might take on a visceral form, as described by Irving Thalberg. See Irving Thalberg, "Visceral Racism," *Monist* 56 (1972): 43–63. For an informative
alternative taxonomy of forms of racism, see Goldberg, *Racist Culture,* p. 103.

(perceptual or memorial) beliefs, where beliefs are construed as mental states. Nothing about racism necessarily involves the agent's having either an epistemically justified belief or justified true belief about a target's ethnicity. Nor need racism involve an agent's *knowing* something about a target's ethnicity. What is essential to racism (proper) is that an agent have a prejudicial belief about a target's ethnicity, and that an actual or attempted discriminatory act (inaction or attempted action) is involved in relation to that target by the agent. Racism, moreover, need not and usually does not, rear its ugly head each and every time a racist encounters a member of the ethnic group against whom the agent is racist. Just as an evil person is not evil in *all* of her actions, inactions, attempted actions, and thoughts, a racist is not always thinking, acting, not acting, or attempting to act in racist ways.

Racism and Intentionality

Having stated that racism may be either intentional or unintentional, I would now like to clarify what I mean by such a claim. A purely intentional racist intends for the full extent of her racism to be carried-out on his target(s), whereas a purely unintentional racist does not intend to be a racist. Rather his actions somehow end up being racist, that is, having racist results (insulting or otherwise deleterious) and are based on his prejudicial beliefs (ones which he holds sincerely, but are not understood by him to constitute prejudice). An instance of unintentional racism is one of either the paternalist or the "do-gooder" who, say, hires a European American woman with low employment qualifications just subsequent to hiring an African American woman with higher employment qualifications, yet the former is hired at a higher rank and salary than the latter. Even if the intent of those doing the hiring is one of preferential treatment toward women, the result is racist in that two different standards for hire are used: a lower one for the European American woman, and a higher one for the African American woman. A historical example of unintentional racism can be found in U.S. president John F. Kennedy's refusal to send federal troops to the southern states to enforce desegregation, even though in the years subsequent to desegregation legislation numerous African Americans were denied some basic human rights.[38] On a generous interpretation of Kennedy's actions and inactions here, his intent was not racist, but his failure to enforce desegregation laws ended up having significantly racist consequences nonetheless. Racism, then, need not be intentional. For it might be the inability of some well-intentioned folk who do not

---

38. For a telling account of this, see Martin Luther King, Jr., "Letter from Birmingham Jail."

realize that what they are doing is ethnically discriminatory and is based on some prejudicial belief or attitude they have about African Americans,[39] and this despite their efforts (they might insist) to combat the very kind of actions in which they are so clearly engaged.

Furthermore, racism may involve a complex array of mental states, *some* of which are intentional, while others are *un*intentional. A case in point would be where a racist intends to prohibit an African American from being hired at a certain place of employment, though that same racist does not intend to block African American employment per se. The racist here is simply against *his* working with African Americans. Alternatively, the racist might refuse to have an African American employer or supervisor, yet support "separate but equal" employment opportunities for African Americans in other sorts of employment scenarios. Thus the *range of intentionality* concerning his racism is truly damaging, though more limited than the racist who seeks to prohibit *all* African American employment on ethnic grounds.[40]

Just as ethnic prejudice alone does not constitute racism, harmful actions directed at someone do not necessarily constitute racism. For they must be accompanied by an ethnically prejudicial belief or attitude in regards to that person. However, such prejudicial attitudes or beliefs need not be as overt as when Connor explicated his segregationist attitudes while having nonviolent demonstrators (African Americans and their perceived "sympathizers") publicly hosed down and beaten. That Connor's segregationist views contained beliefs that amount to ethnic prejudice is clear. But not all such prejudice need be so overt and crass as that of the European American segregationist.

One thing that becomes increasingly obvious is that by analyzing racism in terms of intentional or unintentional action we cannot simplify racism in terms of who counts as a racist. This view differs from competing analyses of racism, which restrict racism to intentional acts. Not only does racism admit of degrees of kind and motivation, according to my account, but it also admits of intentional or unintentional actions or results of them. Thus the world consists not so much in those who are racists and those who are

---

39. Perhaps, in this case, about the very *worthiness* of African Americans to have their civil rights upheld *equally* to those of European Americans.

40. Here the *harm* of racism may be viewed from different standpoints. A consequentialist might argue that the consequences of racism must be a primary consideration in any moral assessment of racism, and that it follows that a racist act or state of affairs which causes a greater harm is more morally condemnatory than one which causes less harm. A nonconsequentialist, on the other hand, might argue that a racists mental state (hatred, resentment, etc.) is primary in the moral assessment of racism. Be this as it may, my point concerns primarily the range of intentionality regarding racist activities.

not as previous accounts would have it, but rather more realistically and less simplistically, it consists in each of us normal adult cognizers who are more or less racist contingent on both the frequency and extent to which we act, fail to act, or attempt to act on our ethnically prejudicial beliefs.[41] If this line of reasoning is plausible, then each normal adult cognizer, being susceptible to the categorization in which we engage regularly, is to some degree and in some way racist insofar as we act, fail to act, or attempt to act on our ethnic prejudices formed by our incessant categorization. So the issue here is not whether or not one is a racist, but the degree of racism we exhibit, the frequency in which we are racists, and the kinds of racism in which we are engaged. And our admitting this fact about us is the first step in the direction of working singularly and in concert toward the eradication of racism from humankind. To be a racist in a rather mild or minor sense is obviously far better, morally speaking, than being a racist in a strong sense. But refusing to admit that we are racists to some degree is to haughtily insist on one's own simplistic account of the very problem that has plagued the world for far too long. It is to insist against almost all odds that one's human cognitive architecture is fundamentally different, qualitatively speaking, than that of most others, that one is somehow above the very difficulty of racism itself! Such a view disregards the working of human cognition, which is normally geared toward categorization and easily lends itself to negative ethnic stereotypes.[42] We tend mostly to act, omit to act, or attempt to act on the basis of these cognitions. Such a benign view of racism is not only unrealistic, but pernicious. And when it appears in the words of European American leftists, it is reminiscent of what Martin Luther King, Jr., and Malcolm X articulated as one of the main concerns of "white liberals," namely, an incessant hypocrisy that accuses European American rightists (among others, but never European American leftists) of being racists. But if my account of racism is correct, then leftist European Americans are themselves, to one degree or another, active participants in racism. Moreover, they are in some sense more dangerous racists than the rightists, as the rightists are, as King, Jr., and Malcolm often put it, more honest and open about their racism than leftist European Americans have, in general, *ever* been. In dealings with racists, it is often, if not always, better to know what you are up against rather than to face a European American liberal who says one thing but does another. (An assumption

---

41. Contrast, for instance, Blum's claim that "a racist *person* is not merely someone who commits one racist act or acts on a racist motive on a small number of occasions. Motives and attitudes such as bigotry, antipathy, and contempt must be embedded in the person's psychological makeup as traits of character" (Blum, *I'm Not a Racist, but . . .* , pp. 14–15).

42. This point will be articulated below.

here is that trustworthiness of character is important in social life.) If there is any hope of ending racism—or even of minimizing it—all normal adult cognizers must come to terms with the various and sundry ways in which we each actively or passively participate in racism.

Racism and Language

When it comes to attributions of racist language, one must be ever mindful of the use-mention distinction. Some are offended by the *mention* of terms such as "nigger." But the mere mention of a term does not constitute its *use*. When one *uses* "nigger" in a pejorative sense, he or she *believes* the informational content of the expression containing the term and what he or she is saying about a certain person/group. But one's use of the term thusly constitutes more than ethnic prejudice. It constitutes a form of discriminatory action. Moreover, to the extent that it, say, provokes retaliatory violence, it can be prohibited by law.[43]

And so racist language should typically be understood as what I shall refer to as "racist use" of terms such as "nigger." Of course, an ethnically sensitive speaker will clarify her mention or use of such expressions so as to leave no doubt regarding their use or mention. However, much ado has been made over the expression of "nigger," without regard to context, use, or mention of the term. A non–African American's *use* of "nigger" in reference to an African American is typically (but not necessarily) an instance of racist language on the conventional sense of "nigger." But the mention of "nigger" as a way by which to, say, teach persons to *not use* the term, is hardly a case of racist language. Again, racist language is typically racist *use* of language. I say "typically" in that my saying to an African American: "The word 'nigger' applies to you" constitutes an instance of racist language-yet the statement only *mentions* the pejorative term. The use-mention distinction, then enables one to better identify racist language as some instance of language *use*.

Racism and Rationality

Is racism irrational? It is a common belief that prejudice is irrational. However, one *can* be rational in one's prejudice, where "rational" connotes at

---

43. For an excellent discussion of the limitations of free speech, see Joel Feinberg, "Limits to the Free Expression of Opinion," in *Philosophy of Law,* ed. Joel Feinberg and Hyman Gross, 4th ed. (Belmont: Wadsworth, 1991), pp. 295–310. Feinberg points out that speech that provokes retaliatory violence is not protected by the First Amendment (pp. 303f.). If racist language satisfies this condition, then, it ought to be prohibited by law.

least some prima facie *epistemic* evidence or warrant for what one believes prejudicially, or for one's attitude of prejudice. One's belief that one should act in one's own interest, whether or not one's goal is morally justified in a given situation, seems to involve some rationality, at least in a goal or task-oriented way. For example, a U.S. southern slave master's belief that the enslavement of Africans by some European Americans is a good thing, while morally condemnatory and unjustified, was rational in the sense that such enslavement *served the economic needs* of some ruling parties in the United States at that time. Thus while it is correct to emphasize the irrational element in some forms of prejudice, other forms of prejudice are rational (though not necessarily morally justified) in at least a goal- or task-oriented way. Moreover, *racism* can be rational in the sense that the beliefs and actions of the racist are in fact logically coherent with the racist's belief system and life-style. This makes some racism rational as well, since ethnic prejudice (in a generic sense) is necessary for racism.[44] In no way, however, does any degree of racist rationality imply either the reasonableness or moral justification of racism.

Thus my view of racism proper is not merely doxastic, but nondoxastic.[45] For it not only sees the intentional state of the racist and the nature and origin of her prejudicial beliefs or attitudes toward others' ethnicity as crucial to the nature of racism, it holds that actual or attempted discriminatory treatment is a necessary feature of racism. Each manifestation of racism proper will involve some degree of these elements: ethnic prejudice and actual or attempted discrimination. Each of these factors is either intentional or unintentional on the racist's behalf.

Now that the nature of racism is clearer to us, what about its origin(s)? Is racism acquired, or is it something with (or "into") which we are born?

The Cognitive Universality of Ethnic Prejudice

It is important for philosophers to consider the possible applications of cognitive science to moral (and I would add, social and political) philosophy.[46] In the spirit of what I shall call "naturalized ethics," I argue for the

44. For eloquent arguments against the rationality and moral justification of racism, especially ethnic prejudice, see Goldberg, "Racism and Rationality," pp. 317–50.

45. This dualistic understanding of racism is somewhat congruent with, but is not based on, the dualistic view of ethnic prejudice found in Stephen Fuchs and Charles E. Case, "Prejudice as Lifeform," *Sociological Inquiry* 59 (1989): 314. Other dualistic construals of racism include the one found in Kurt Baier, "Merit and Race," *Philosophia* 8 (1978): 122–23. I have in mind here Baier's distinction between "behavioral racism" and "theoretical racism."

46. Alvin I. Goldman, "Ethics and Cognitive Science," *Ethics* 103 (1993): 337–60; *Philo-*

cognitive universality (not the necessity) of the employment of ethnic stereotypes, descriptively speaking. My claim about the universality of ethnic prejudice is based on findings from experimental social cognitive psychology. This provides a cognitive foundation for the cognitive-behavioral theory of racism. I argue that certain aspects of normal cognition provide the opportunity for ethnic (stereotype-based) prejudice, which, when coupled with ethnic discrimination based on such prejudice, often form the basis of racism. I do not argue that each normal cognizer is (e.g., thinks and behaves like) a racist all of the time. Rather, I argue that normal cognizers are (e.g., think and behave like) racists *to some extent* some of the time, making racism universal in the sense that it penetrates the lives of all normal cognizers to some meaningful extent. This claim differs from what most philosophers seem to think about racism, namely, that certain people are racists, while others are not. If my view is correct, then the prevalent philosophical view of racism is facile in that it does not recognize the cognitive complexities of racism.[47]

The Cognitive Origins of Ethnic Prejudice

From where does ethnic prejudice (a necessary feature of racism) originate? Is ethnic prejudice a universal phenomenon? Social psychologists such as Gordon W. Allport have done much to illuminate the origin and nature of prejudice.[48] But since Allport's important work, much has been done in experimental social cognitive psychology to further explain ethnic prejudice as a social and cognitive basis of racism.[49]

As I have argued, racism consists of ethnic prejudice and discrimination. But prejudice is often, though not always,[50] based on stereotypical beliefs or attitudes an agent has about or toward another. *Stereotypes* are attributions

---

sophical Applications of Cognitive Science (Boulder: Westview Press, 1993), chapter 5. Goldman's "naturalized ethics," as I shall refer to it, seems to be motivated by his celebrated naturalized epistemology (process reliabilism) found, among other places, in his *Epistemology and Cognition* (Cambridge: Harvard University Press, 1986). A naturalized *social epistemology* is found in J. Angelo Corlett, "Epistemology, Psychology, and Goldman," *Social Epistemology* 5 (1991): 91–100; "Social Epistemology and Social Cognition," *Social Epistemology* 5 (1991): 135–49; "Goldman and the Foundations of Social Epistemology," *Argumentation* 8 (1994): 145–56; and *Analyzing Social Knowledge* (Lanham: Rowman and Littlefield, 1996).

47. Contrast Jorge L. A. García, who argues that racism is not primarily a matter of cognition. See García, "The Heart of Racism," pp. 12–13.

48. Gordon W. Allport, *The Nature of Prejudice* (New York: Doubleday Anchor Books, 1958).

49. For a review of some of the social psychological experimental research done in South Africa, see John Duckitt, "Locus of Control and Racial Prejudice," *Psychological Reports* 54 (1984): 462.

50. Of course, not all ethnic prejudice results from stereotyping. See Piper, *Higher-Order Discrimination in Identity, Character, and Morality*, pp. 290–93.

of general characteristics to groups.[51] If stereotyping is "racist," then it involves the attribution of certain characteristics to ethnic groups and their members. But there is more to prejudice than stereotyping, and more to stereotyping than attributions. Stereotyping involves social categorization and assimilation. *Social categorization* introduces simplicity and order where there is ambiguity and complexity. As Henri Tajfel states, "The problem of stereotypes is that of the relation between a set of attributes which vary on continuous dimensions and classifications which are discontinuous."[52] In the same vein, Goldberg writes,

> Classification, order, and value are fundamental to the forms of rationality we have inherited. Socially, it is evident that we still labor under the constraints of this rationalized authority; we order our relations with others in its light. . . . The most widespread is that the concepts of *inferiority* and *superiority* implicit in *racial hierarchy* are part of a buried social setting and scientific paradigm.[53]

Social categorization helps bring order to such cognitive complexity in information processing. However, the order and simplicity resulting from such information processing can at times come at too high a price. *To the extent that* racism is based on stereotype-based ethnic prejudice and social categorization obtained via selective attention in memory storage and retrieval, and *to the extent that* the cognitive process of selective attention is a universal one, that is, utilized by all cognizers to some meaningful extent, and *to the extent that* cognizers tend to act (fail to act, or attempt to act, as the case may be) on the basis of their beliefs or attitudes, then racism is universal.

Cognitive *assimilation* is also an aspect of stereotyping. As Tajfel writes,

> In the case of racial attitudes, . . . the learning and assimilation of socially sanctioned value judgments is made even easier through the existence of obvious visual cues which place each relevant individual firmly and instantly in the category to which he belongs. This additional factor of "visibility," combined with the rich linguistic associations of "black" and "white" . . . acts in several directions at once: it not only facilitates the placement of an individual in the appropriate category, but also helps to determine the descriptive

51. Henri Tajfel, "Cognitive Aspects of Prejudice," *Journal of Social Issues* 25 (1969): 81–82. Or, as Hamilton et al. define it, a stereotype is "a cognitive structure containing the perceiver's knowledge and beliefs about a social group and its members." David L. Hamilton et al., "Stereotype-Based Expectancies: Effects on Information-Processing and Social Behavior," *Journal of Social Issues* 46 (1990): 36.
52. Tajfel, "Cognitive Aspects of Prejudice," p. 82.
53. Goldberg, *Racist Culture*, p. 51.

content of the category and a more efficient "filtering" of contradictory information.[54]

Thus social categorization (for example, categorizing people into groups consisting in "us" versus "them") gives shape to intergroup attitudes of prejudice, while assimilation provides the content of such attitudes. But it is an agent's *search for coherence*, cognitively speaking, that helps to explain how and why she tries to cope with changes or introductions of new information about an ethnic group and its members.[55] This search for coherence is not itself either a cause or a source of ethnic prejudice. Rather, it may sometimes become a cognitive means by which ethnic prejudice is "generated."

The Cognitive Universality of Ethnic Prejudice

It is significant to note that the cognitive universality of ethnic prejudice due to stereotyping (based on social categorization via selective attention) does not entail that prejudice is untreatable or beyond one's control to prevent. Simply because ethnic prejudice is cognitive in origin and universal (in varying degrees) does not mean that it is either necessary, native, or unlearned. Indeed, the *processes* of cognition are unlearned. But prejudice, though cognitively based, *is* learned and not native. Moreover, various aspects of cognitive self-monitoring may play a crucial role in minimizing and eventually eliminating prejudicial stereotyping based on ethnicity.[56]

54. Tajfel, "Cognitive Aspects of Prejudice," p. 88.
55. I focus here on the nonaffective aspects of the cognitive origins of ethnic prejudice. However, I do not wish to deny the sometimes central role affect often plays in both ethnic prejudice and discrimination.
56. Hamilton et al., "Stereotype-Based Expectations," p. 53; W. B. Swann, Jr., and R. J. Ely, "A Battle of Wills: Self-Verification Versus Behavioral Confirmation," *Journal of Personality and Social Psychology* 46 (1984): 1287–1302; J. L. Hilton and J. M. Darley, "Constructing Other Persons: A Limit on the Effect," *Journal of Experimental Social Psychology* 21 (1985): 1–18; J. M. Darley et al., "Dispelling Negative Expectancies: The Impact of Interaction Goals and Target Characteristics on the Expectancy Confirmation Process," *Journal of Experimental Social Psychology* 24 (1988): 19–36; S. L. Neuberg, "The Goal of Forming Accurate Impressions during Social Interactions: Attenuating the Impact of Negative Expectancies," *Journal of Personality and Social Psychology* 56 (1989): 374–86; Thomas F. Pettigrew and Joanne Martin, "The Fruits of Critical Discussion: A Reply to Commentators," *Journal of Social Issues* 43 (1987): 151f.; William A. Barnard and Mark S. Benn, "Belief Congruence and Prejudice Reduction in an Interracial Contact Setting," *Journal of Social Psychology* 128 (1988): 125–34; Deborah A. Byrnes and Gary Kiger, "Prejudice-Reduction Simulations: Ethics, Evaluations, and Theory Into Practice," *Simulation and Gaming* 23 (1992): 457–71; Angie Williams and Howard Giles, "Prejudice-Reduction Simulations: Social Cognition, Intergroup Theory, and Ethics," *Simulation and Gaming* 23 (1992): 472–84; and Deborah A. Byrnes and Gary Kiger, "Prejudice-Reduction Simulations: Notes on Their Use and Abuse—A Reply to Williams and Giles," *Simulation and Gaming* 23 (1992): 485–89.

And what is true of prejudice is true of racism, as Russell H. Weigel and Paul W. Howes articulate:

> Since racial prejudice is embedded in a network of beliefs and values that reflect deference to established authority and preoccupation with conventionally accepted standards of conduct, the contemporary racist may be particularly responsive to the forceful invocation of normative standards by persons in authoritative roles. From this perspective, prejudice does not represent an insurmountable obstacle to the types of behavior changes most likely to result in the reduction of prejudice.[57]

Ethnic stereotyping and prejudice result from native processes of human cognitive architecture (such as categorization) applied to the perception of others. They are cognitively universal phenomena among normal cognizers. This means that one is a racist to the extent that one's stereotyping and prejudice eventuate in discriminatory actions (actual or by attempted) that are ethnically based. Whether it is information acquisition and elaboration, or information seeking and belief testing, there are a variety of ways in which stereotypes affect the ways in which agents consider others, ethnically speaking. Consider what Hamilton et al. have to say here:

> The perceiver's attention to the available information is necessarily selective. Properties both of the perceiver (e.g., momentary goals, generalized beliefs, current mood states) and of the information (e.g., importance for immediate goals, salience, self-relevance) can affect what the perceiver attends to. The information thus initially acquired then becomes the basis for several processes by which perceivers expand and elaborate their understanding of the meaning of persons and events. Thus, perceivers interpret the meaning of a target person's behaviors; they make inferences about people's abilities, motives, and personality attributes; they make causal attributions about why certain events occurred; and they react affectively to the persons and events they observe. All of these processes are subject to the influence of stereotype-based expectancies. These processes are of crucial importance in social perception because it is the information *as elaborated* in these ways that becomes represented in memory and hence available to guide the perceiver's subsequent judgments and behaviors.
>
> As a consequence of the influence of stereotypes on these processes, the perceiver's mental representation of the available information can differ in significant ways from the actual information on which that representation is based. In many cases these discrepancies are of little import, . . . In other

---

57. Russell H. Weigel and Paul W. Howes, "Conceptions of Racial Prejudice: Symbolic Racism Reconsidered," *Journal of Social Issues* 41 (1985): 135.

cases, however, the effects of stereotypes on these processes can result in more serious misconceptions and biases that may have undesirable consequences and ramifications.[58]

This does not mean that all persons are "predisposed" to engage in ethnic prejudice. Instead, it is that normally cognitive persons sometimes are ethnically prejudiced to the extent that they do not monitor their cognitive processes, which can and do sometimes become the origin of ethnic prejudice. This lack of self-monitoring may be caused, wholly or in part, by socialization.

Stereotyping forms part of the basis of ethnic prejudice, which, when coupled with ethnic discrimination, is a crucial element of racism. We utilize our cognitive processes of selective attention and social categorization constantly. When we consider persons, we often process information about them in light of their respective ethnicities. As a matter of learned cognition, then, we typically form stereotypes of persons based in part on the fact that they belong to a certain ethnic group. These ethnic stereotypes form ethnically prejudicial beliefs. If we tend to behave, roughly speaking, according to our beliefs, then we are ethnically discriminatory to the extent that we hold ethnically prejudicial beliefs and have ethnically prejudicial attitudes. Therefore, it is reasonable to infer the universality (not the necessity) of racism from its bases and prevalence in human cognition. Again, this is not to say that each person is a racist all of the time. Rather, each cognitively normal person is a racist sometimes and to some extent. Just as "the question is not *whether* stereotypes influence judgments of individuals, but rather *when* such effects are manifested,"[59] the question of who is a racist is not *whether* we are racists, but the *extent* to which we are.

One should not draw the inference that, since everyone is (e.g., thinks and behaves like) a racist sometimes and to some extent, that racism is unimportant, or that anti–African American racism, say, is somehow either not so bad after all or that it is on par with anti–European American racism, generally speaking. Just as instances of racism manifest themselves with different motives and bases, and in different kinds, the extent of the badness of various cases of racism also differs. For not all instantiations of racism are equal in their badness or the extent to which they eventuate in racist harms or offenses. What we need is an excursion into the moral status of racism to better understand that there exist different levels and degrees of racism, with some forms of racism being worse or more morally culpable than others.

58. Hamilton et al., "Stereotype-Based Expectancies," p. 37.
59. Ibid., p. 43.

The Moral Status of Racism

What is the *moral status* of racism? Most everyone agrees that racism is a bad thing. However, it is important to understand *why* racism is morally wrong. A consequentialist would argue that racism is wrong because it brings about a balance of economic, social, political, and/or moral evil over good in the world. If the consequentialist is a utilitarian of sorts, she would argue that racism is to be rejected because it does not maximize overall satisfaction in society. A deontologist, on the other hand, would argue that, the results of racism aside, racism is to be rejected in that it does not treat humans as ends in themselves, but rather as mere means to the end of, say, power and greed. Moreover, racism disrespects the dignity of humans qua humans, regardless of their respective ethnicities. It fails to treat persons as having intrinsic value and dignity apart from their ethnicities. Of course, there seems to be nothing logically inconsistent in ones arguing that racism is morally wrong for all of the above (consequentialist, utilitarian, and deontological) reasons.[60]

Thus there are various reasons why one might argue that racism is morally problematic. But if racism is a learned result of human cognitive architecture, then it might seem that one cannot be legitimately blamed for engaging in it, especially if racism is unintentional and beyond one's control.

However, ethnic stereotyping, though universal and highly prevalent, is *not* a *necessary* part of human cognition. Cognizers can and some often do monitor themselves so as to reduce or minimize the extent to which they utilize stereotypes. Susan T. Fiske states that

> the issue of intent really concerns whether stereotyping is to some degree controllable. When sufficiently motivated, can perceivers form relatively individuated impressions? Our own research suggests that interpersonal

---

60. Perhaps the weakest of the reasons why racism is morally wrong are those given by the consequentialist. For her argument against the moral viability of racism is contingent on the claim that racism results in evil for society. But what if, as in the U.S. southern states prior to emancipation, it can be shown that a certain social excellence can be realized by way of even the most ruthless form of racism, i.e., slavery? Recall that many supporters of the Old South argued precisely that slavery is the key element to the South's success and stability. Surely, it might be argued, such slavery and the racism which served as its foundation brought a degree of economic, social, and political power and stability to the South— even for the slaves who might well have otherwise had a worse-off life, all thing considered, as free people. Would this not defeat, or at least render dubious, the consequentialist objection to racism? Considerations such as this lead many to reject racism on deontological grounds. For on such grounds, no such example of social benefit from racism can justify the disrespect for humanity that it entails.

outcome dependency can motivate people to individuate under circumstances in which they would normally form category-based impressions. . . . When "it's worth it," people can stop themselves from stereotyping. Hence, if stereotyping is controllable, then it hardly seems accurate to characterize it as unintentional.[61]

Thus agents can cognize without the use of ethnic stereotypes. Furthermore, there is a significant extent to which racists, each of us, are morally responsible (liable) for our lack of self-monitoring in this area. Racism, then, is in part a result of one's lack of self-monitoring, which is related in some way to one's epistemic and moral negligence, that is, one's failure to look diligently after one's belief system and attitudes and make sure that both the beliefs and attitudes one has and the ways in which one acquires them are morally justified (nonracist).

Racism and Responsibility

Generally speaking, the racist is both epistemically and morally responsible (liable). Moreover, she is epistemically responsible (in a duty sense) for diligently monitoring herself in regards to the beliefs and attitudes that might shape her own moral character when it comes to minimizing her use of ethnic stereotypes that might support ethnic prejudice. She is morally responsible (in a duty sense), not only for self-monitoring of epistemic matters concerning ethnic judgments, but also for not discriminating against others based on their ethnicity. Just as a moral agent is morally responsible (liable) for what she omits to do as well as for what she does, so can racial attitudes (prejudice) take the form of one's omitting to, say, consider the genuine value of ethnically out-group members. Such actions and omissions, when racist in nature, are among those for which an agent is morally responsible (liable). As Howard McGary contends, "people are often blind to their own biases and . . . it takes concerted intellectual and moral effort to recognize and eliminate them."[62]

But one's moral duty to minimize one's own ethnic prejudice extends beyond one's cognitive self-monitoring to the monitoring of others' ethnic prejudice. This is a point made by Du Bois who argues that racism cannot

---

61. Susan T. Fiske, "On the Road: Comment on the Cognitive Stereotyping Literature in Pettigrew and Martin," *Journal of Social Issues* 43 (1987): 115.

62. Howard McGary, "Philosophy and Diversity: The Inclusion of African and African American Materials," *American Philosophical Association Newsletter on Feminism and Philosophy* 92 (1993): 53.

be eliminated or minimized by simply monitoring people's straightforwardly and ethnically prejudicial beliefs. Instead, persons must also be
made conscious of those beliefs they hold that are prima facie morally "innocent" or nonculpable, yet actually amounting to ethnic prejudice.[63]

Lower-Order and Higher-Order
Ethnic Prejudice and Racism

Racism is based on either a lower- or higher-order form of ethnic prejudice. Often this takes the form of having a prejudicial belief. But such beliefs may be of either the lower- or high-order variety, cognitively speaking.
Lower-order ethnic prejudice consists in one's sincerely assenting to a claim
such as:

(a) All African Americans are less intelligent than European Americans,

where "less intelligent" carries with it the notion of inferiority and has some
normative or prescriptive import. One who believes this claim is not necessarily a racist in that one must, according to the cognitive-behavioral theory of racism, also engage or attempt to engage in ethnic discrimination
in light of that prejudicial belief.[64] Simply acquiring an ethnically prejudicial belief is one thing; discriminating on the basis of it is quite another.
However, when such prejudice is accompanied by ethnic discrimination,
then there is *lower-order racism.*

But there is also *higher-order ethnic prejudice.* This occurs when an agent is
in some significant way conscious of the fact that one, say, believes (a). At
this level, one of a number of responses is open to the agent. First, one
might try as one may to resist the temptation to further, foster, or nurture
such prejudice. Moreover, one might take positive steps to eradicate it from
one's belief-system. This is part of what is meant by cognitive self-monitoring. I refer to this sort of prejudice, when it leads to racism, as *higher-order
unwilling racism.* Second, one might remain conscious of one's prejudice,
yet either through negligence do nothing to minimize it or actually defend
it as being justified. This higher-order form of ethnic prejudice requires
the agent to provide some sort of reasoning in favor of her belief(s). When
such prejudice underlies racism, I call it *higher-order willing racism.*

63. Ibid., p. 52.
64. This does not imply, however, that such ethnic prejudice is not morally condemnatory, or that it ought never to be restricted by law.

Thus there are various "orders" or "levels" of ethnic prejudice that in many cases lead to racism. However, racism is even more complex than this categorization of it might suggest. For one may be a racist against one ethnic group, yet not a racist against another. That is, one may direct one's racism against African Americans, yet not against Asian Americans. Or, one might be a racist against Asian Americans, but not against African Americans. Furthermore, the degree to which one is a racist against more than one group may vary as one, say, exhibits strong racism against African Americans and weak racism against Latino Americans. These complexities regarding racism hold true whether one is a lower- or higher-order racist.

Moreover, these "orders" of racism exist in the context of one or more of the "kinds" of racism discussed earlier. One may be a lower-order racist in the context of, say, one's being either an individual-to-individual or an individual-to-group institutional racist, an individual-to-individual or an individual-to-group noninstitutional racist. Or, a group might be engaged in group-to-individual or group-to-group institutional or noninstitutional racism. Furthermore, one might be a higher-order unwilling racist in the context of one's being an individual institutional racist, an individual noninstitutional racist, or a group might be engaged in either institutional or noninstitutional racism. Likewise, one may be a higher-order willing racist while one is at the same time an individual-to-individual or individual-to-group institutional racist, or an individual-to-individual or individual-to-group noninstitutional racist, or a group might be engaged in either group-to-individual or group-to-group institutional or noninstitutional racism. To make racism even more complex, each of these forms of racism may be motivated by and/or based on hatred, perceived inferiority, "benevolence," perceived superiority, fear, power, ignorance, and/or ideological dogmatism. To be sure, the varieties of kinds of racism provide the contexts in which the various orders of racism (and their respective motivations and bases) function.

Additionally, it is possible to categorize these orders of ethnic prejudice on a scale according to their severity. Higher-order unwilling racism seems to be the least severe in the sense that the agent involved is both conscious of her prejudice and unwilling to engage in it again. As an unwilling racist, she constantly struggles against the social and cognitive factors that "drive" her toward racism.

More severe than the higher-order unwilling racist is the lower-order racist. This is a dangerous person for a number of reasons. First, this racist has little or no clue *that* she is a racist. She who does not know she is a racist surely cannot hope to eradicate it from the lives of others (not to mention herself!). Since the lower-order racist is not aware of her racism, she is unaware as to *why* or *how* she is a racist. This racist might *deny* that she is a racist, which makes her much worst-off than the higher-order unwilling racist. If becoming an authentic person is to, among other things, know or understand oneself, the higher-order unwilling racist (unlike the lower-order racist) is at least able to do just that. The lower-order racist fails to recognize that it is *not* better to remain in ignorance or denial regarding her racism. Just as the unexamined life is not worth living, neither is the life of the lower-order racist worth living to the extent that her life is unexamined for the presence of ethnic prejudice and discrimination.

United States history is replete with higher-order willing racists: former Alabama governor George Wallace, former Georgia governor Lester Maddox, "Bull" Connor, and others like them. Unlike the higher-order unwilling racist, this racist welcomes and affirms his racism—he even revels in it! Unlike the lower-order racist who might very well strive to change his ways and thoughts on being educated about his own racism, the higher-order willing racist—even when confronted with his own racism—seems unconcerned with the possibility of his eradicating racism from his life.

How are these different types of racists to be assessed, morally speaking? To the extent that racism is morally wrong, and assuming that all other things about a racist state of affairs are equal between cases, a higher-order unwilling racist should be seen as being less morally responsible (liable) for harm resulting from her racism than a lower-order racist. This is because of the internal struggle a higher-order unwilling racist puts herself through in continually battling against the cognitive forces that tend to influence her to become the agent of ethnic prejudice and discrimination. Also, there is an authentic sense in which the higher-order unwilling racist is unhappy and resentful about her being a racist. The lower-order racist, on the other hand, experiences nothing of the inner turmoil of the higher-order unwilling racist. She cannot even strive to eliminate from her own life that for which she thinks she is not morally responsible (liable).

However, a lower-order racist is less morally responsible (liable) for racist harms than the higher-order willing racist. This is because the lower-order racist does not cherish and defend her racism, as does the higher-order willing racist. The lower-order racist's ignorance about her own racist condition seems to serve as somewhat of a mitigating factor in our moral assessment of her. But it is not an excusing one. For as long as a cognizer to some extent acts freely (and acts knowingly, intentionally, and is at fault), she is justifiably held morally responsible (to some meaningful extent, blameworthy) for her racism. It seems that with the higher-order agent or cognizer, the fewer mitigating conditions of moral liability obtain. In any case, there seem to be degrees of moral liability concerning racism.

A racist harm is one that results from a racist act, omission, or attempt. A racist act is one that is performed out of ethnic prejudice and discrimination, and a racist omission is one that "results from" ethnic prejudice and discrimination. Moral liability assessments for racist harms ought to take into consideration (at least) the degree of the racist's intention, the severity of the consequences[65] of her actions, and the degree of that agent's freedom of action and the agent's knowledge in reference to the racism in question. The racist's malice toward the target might play a role in such liability assessments, though not all forms of racism involve hatred.

Racism, Color-Consciousness, and Color-Blindness

African Americans who instill in themselves a sense of positive African, black, or African American pride along with personal and social constructiveness can hardly be said to be racists. It is only if such pride turns to

65. The consequences of racism vary greatly. On the one hand, "racism has put black self-respect and self-esteem under siege" (Bernard Boxill, *Blacks and Social Justice* [Totowa: Rowman and Littlefield, 1984], p. 188) so much that, in some cases, African American former slaves have been said to forgive their former masters for the atrocities of slavery (Howard McGary and Bill Lawson, *Between Slavery and Freedom* [Bloomington: Indiana University Press, 1992], chapter 6). For some persons, this attitude of forgiveness bears the telltale signs of ex-slaves who have lost their self-esteem and self-respect. For others, it follows from the tenets of "true Christianity." Still others might argue that there are cases of "authentic" forgiveness that are the product of genuinely self-creative attitudes having nothing to do with a lack of self-respect *or* "true Christianity." On the other hand, there is racism, which (by and despite itself) seems to have unnoticeable or immeasurable effects on its victims. So the results of racism fall somewhere on a scale from worst to minimal, depending on the particular circumstances of each case.

Also see McGary and Lawson for an illuminating account of the various ways in which African Americans were affected by slavery in the United States. Of course, it would be mistaken to think that such adverse effects on African slaves no longer manifest themselves in significant ways. The following are a few incisive accounts of some of what African slaves endured, and how subsequent generations of African Americans were adversely affected by the racism of American slavery: Mortimer J. Adler, ed., *The Negro in American History*, 3 vols. (New York: Encyclopedia Britannica Educational Corporation, 1969); Stanley W. Campbell, *The Slave Catchers: Enforcement of the Fugitive Slave Law, 1850–1860* (New York: Norton, 1970); Stanley M. Elkins, *Slavery*, 2d ed. (Chicago: University of Chicago Press, 1968); John Hope Franklin, *From Slavery to Freedom: A History of Negro Americans*, 3d ed. (New York: Alfred A. Knopf, 1987); Oscar Handlin, *Race and Nationality in American Life* (New York: Doubleday, 1957); August Meier and Elliott Rudwick, eds., *The Making of Black America: Essays in Negro Life and History*, vol. 1, *The Origins of Black Americans* (New York: Atheneum, 1969); Alphonso Pinkney, *Black Americans* (Englewood Cliffs: Prentice-Hall, 1969); Benjamin Quarles, *The Negro in the Making of America* (New York: Collier, 1964); and Richard C. Wade, *Slavery in the Cities: The South, 1820–1960* (Oxford: Oxford University Press, 1964).

attitudes and actions *against* members of other ethnic groups that makes racist the focus on one's own ethnic group's welfare. Related to the notion of ethnic pride is the issue of whether or not color-consciousness is racist. Bernard Boxill defines a "color-conscious policy" as one "designed to treat people differently because of their race."[66] It follows that color-consciousness, according to Boxill, is the treating of people differently because of their ethnicity. On this construal, color-consciousness is racist, that is, if "differently" entails "adversely." For it involves, it seems, both ethnic prejudice and ethnic discrimination. Boxill correctly argues that color-conscious policies are not always wrong because they are color-conscious, but when they are wrong, they are wrong for other reasons.[67]

However, there are different ways to be color-conscious, on the one hand, or color-blind, on the other hand. I define "color-consciousness" as "an agent's taking into account one's own or another's ethnicity." "Color-blindness," as I define it, is "an agent's *not* taking into account one's own or another's ethnicity."

I argue that color-consciousness is neither a necessary nor a sufficient condition of racism. What constitutes racism has been discussed above, and an attitude of color-consciousness was omitted from the analysis. The reason for this is that one can be color-conscious without being a racist. An example of color-consciousness that is not racist is the African American who takes great pride in her ethnicity, but does not engage in ethnic discrimination (recall that both ethnic prejudice and discrimination are necessary and sufficient for racism). This suggests that color-consciousness is not sufficient for one's being a racist.

On the other hand, color-blindness *is* racist *to the extent that* the ignoring of ethnicity contributes to the ethnic prejudice and discrimination of persons. When color-blindness contributes either to an agent's demeaning her own ethnicity, or to her not taking seriously the ethnicity of others, then it can contribute to that agent's either being ethnically prejudiced or to her being a racist. For instance, policies that seek to disallow African Americans from forming and participating in special groups or organizations (e.g., black student unions, black business associations, etc.) to promote African American interests, tend to, often in the name of color-blindness, not take sufficiently seriously the special needs of African Americans. To deny, in the name of color-blindness, the need for such groups and organizations is to minimize the special needs of African Americans to better secure themselves (by way of, for instance, in-group socialization) in the increasingly

---

66. Boxill, *Blacks and Social Justice,* p. 10.
67. Ibid., p. 11.

racist culture of the United States. It is to deny them their moral right to social self-defense against the ever-present forces of racist evil against them.
In a real sense, color-consciousness may and often does lead many African
Americans to take pride in their rich heritage. And the same might be said
of other ethnic groups. Moreover, such pride need not and usually does
not involve racism against other persons and groups. Indeed, the forming
of such social groups and organizations is a means by which African Americans work within the system to effect positive social, political, and economic change. In some cases, it is a means by which an oppressed people
copes with its being the continual targets of significant forms of racism.
Thus it is false to claim that color-blindness cannot be racist. It follows that
color-consciousness is *not* a necessary condition of racism, assuming that
one cannot be both color-conscious and color-blind at the same time, in
the same respect, and concerning the same target(s) of racism.

The cognitive-behavioral theory of racism differs from Appiah's and
Blum's respective views of racism in at least one important respect. Their
conceptions of racism lack a nondoxastic element, which my view em-
braces. I argue, unlike Appiah, that racism must involve both ethnic prejudice and discrimination. Moreover, the assigning of ethnic preferences
that Goldberg and Blum (and to some extent, Appiah) see as crucial to
racism is captured in my concept of ethnic prejudice. This helps to explain
that Appiah's, Goldberg's, and Blum's respective concepts of racism, as
well as my view of ethnic *prejudice,* are doxastic.

Furthermore, the cognitive-behavioral theory of racism is naturalized in
the sense that it draws from and utilizes certain evidence from cognitive social science in order to in turn draw some normative inferences about the
nature, scope, and origin of racism. It is the only philosophical view that
holds to the universality of racism without resorting to some unfalsifiable
or existentialist notion of the universality of racism. It also does not, as
some tend to do, conflate racism with ethnic prejudice, or ethnic prejudice
with discrimination.

After defining "racism" as involving both prejudice and discrimination
that leads to harm and/or substantial racist offense, I argued for a conception of racism as a cognitively based universal phenomenon, the adverse
aspects of which can and should be minimized through self-monitoring.
There are various kinds of racism, but not all of its manifestations are
equally condemnatory, morally speaking. In any case, the main goal of this
chapter was to provide the conceptual foundations of an plausible understanding of the nature of racism that would be especially useful in legal
contexts.

There remain other queries about racism, which need philosophical exploration: for example, if racist language *does* constitute a form of ethnic discrimination, should it be prohibited by law as a limitation of free speech? How does the "color-consciousness" versus "color-blindness" issue[68] relate to racism (beyond what has been said about it herein)? Are there any significant differences between anti–African American racism, and say, anti-Semitism? Are there other differences between the ways in which racism manifests itself when it involves ethnic groups other than African Americans as targets? If so, might this affect the definition of "racism"? Perhaps most important, how might racism be *un*learned?[69] These and other questions deserve our most serious philosophical attention.

68. These concepts are discussed in Richard Wasserstrom, "Preferential Treatment, Color-Blindness, and the Evils of Racism and Racial Discrimination," American Philosophical Association (Pacific Division) Presidential Address, *American Philosophical Association Proceedings and Addresses* 61 (1987): 27–42.

69. For an informative discussion of various attempts to solve or minimize racism, see the discussion of separatism and integrationism in Howard McGary, "Racial Integration and Racial Separatism: Conceptual Clarifications," in *Philosophy Born of Struggle,* ed. Leonard Harris (Dubuque, Iowa: Kendall/Hunt, 1983), pp. 199–211.

5

Surviving Evil in the United States:
African and Native Americans

Having dispensed with the concept of race, replacing it with a viable notion of ethnicity for purposes of positive public policy administration, the interpretation of medical research data accuracy, self-esteem, and ethnic group solidarity, and having developed a conception of racism that is both doxastic and nondoxastic, it is important to focus attention on some of the worst racist harms in human history: the United States' racist evils against Native and African Americans, respectively. In so doing, the conceptions of ethnicity and racism developed in the preceding chapters will be tested insofar as their viability within a reasonably just legal system is concerned. What is the extent of the racist evils that the U.S. government has inflicted on Native and African Americans, and how, if at all, ought such human rights violations to be remedied? In this context, "Native American" and "African American" refer respectively to the descendants of those groups, the members of which were actually harmed by the U.S. government.

It has recently been argued that what best explains the disparate degrees of survival or "success"[1] between Jewish and African Americans *as distinct classes of persons* and despite their experiencing the evils of holocaust and slavery (respectively) is that Jewish Americans possess both autonomy and a narrative while African Americans have no narrative and lacked autonomy under slavery.[2] I will challenge the factual claim that "Blacks have

---

1. For purposes of this chapter, I take "success" to be primarily, but not exclusively, material and economic.

2. Laurence Thomas, *Vessels of Evil* (Philadelphia: Temple University Press, 1993), pp. 169–205; "American Slavery and the Holocaust: Their Ideologies Compared," *Public Affairs Quarterly* 5 (1991): 191–210. Group autonomy, it is stipulated, is "a characteristic of

languished since American Slavery."[3] Moreover, I seek to neutralize the conceptual claim about the nature and function of narratives. Then I will argue that, though African Americans did not have autonomy under slavery, they *did create a narrative* (or narratives) for themselves, contrary to the factual claim that they had (and have) no narrative (or that their African narratives were completely stripped from them by slavery). Furthermore, I will challenge the conceptual claim that "it is not possible for a people who have been profoundly oppressed to flourish as a group in a relentlessly hostile society—at least not in the absence of an independent narrative."[4] Following this I will argue that what better describes the differences in successes between Jewish and African Americans is that the former group came to the United States and was recognized as being humans to whom (at least, for the most part) the contents of the Constitution, Bill of Rights, and Declaration of Independence applied, while members of the latter group were not perceived as being humans in this sense *from the time of their "arrival"* to the "New World" as Africans. Furthermore, African Americans had whatever autonomy and narratives they enjoyed in Africa largely stripped from them by slavery, unlike Jewish Americans many of whom arrived in the United States on their own free will (in the sense, that is, that they had reasonably acceptable options at that time other than settling in the United States) and with many or all of their rights and privileges protected by the U.S. government. As a result of being enslaved in the United States, African Americans were less likely to be able to assimilate into U.S. society, which systematically oppressed them. Finally, I will compare the relative successes of African Americans to those of Native Americans and

---

a group that is regarded by others as being the foremost interpreters of its historical-cultural traditions, it being understood that the aim of others is not to show that those traditions should be jettisoned by the group of adherents" (Thomas, *Vessels of Evil*, p. 182), while a narrative is said to define values and positive goals, fix points of historical significance, and specify ennobling rituals for group members, and to define a people's conception of the good (Thomas, *Vessels of Evil*, pp. 197–98).

3. Thomas, *Vessels of Evil*, p. 169. In the preface (x), Thomas states that "Jews as a people have flourished more than Blacks as a people." This statement has a different informational content than his claim that Jewish Americans have flourished while African Americans have languished. The two statements are logically distinct. One statement (x) makes a comparative judgment about the successes of Jewish Americans versus those of African Americans, while the other (p. 169) also claims that African Americans have languished since their slavery in the United States. Although Thomas himself is unclear about this matter, the first statement might be true, while the second one is false. For surely Jewish Americans can have out-flourished African Americans in the United States in the face of African American flourishing in the United States. It is this conceptual confusion which leads me to make the point I make about African American flourishing in the United States, contrary to Thomas' assertion of their languishing.

4. Thomas, *Vessels of Evil*, p. 190.

attempt to explain, to some meaningful extent, why *African Americans* have *flourished* while *Native Americans* have *languished* in U.S. society. I will consider this last point in light of their respective baseline experiences of oppressive racism at the hands of the U.S. government, among others, as well as in consideration of their respective economic and political starting points.

The claim that African Americans languished subsequent to slavery is ambiguous in that it fails to specify precisely what is meant by "success," "flourish," or their cognates in the context of comparisons between African Americans and Jewish Americans. There are at least two ways by which to attempt to judge the relative "successes" ("flourishings" or the lack thereof, "languishings") of Jewish Americans on the one hand, and of African Americans, on the other. One way is to judge the respective current degrees of success of these ethnic groups merely in light of the kinds, levels, and durations of racist oppression each group has experienced. However, this method of judgment fails to account for significant differences in racist oppression that determine, in large measure, a group's economic and political starting point in a society, a factor that is crucial for an accurate account of a group's fuller range of experiences. There is, though, a more promising way to judge the relative successes of these groups in U.S. society. It is to consider, in addition to the baseline experiences of racist oppression each group has suffered, their variant economic and political starting points in U.S. society. Since Jewish or African American success is relative to a baseline standard, it is argued that the standard used ought to be one that recognizes the rather significant disparities between the economic and political starting points of these respective ethnic groups as well as the differences between the levels, kinds, and durations of racist oppression each group has experienced. When *this* is taken into consideration, it is no longer clear that Jewish Americans have flourished while African Americans have languished. For it might be argued that, relative to their respective starting points in the United States (including the full range of anti-Semitism for Jewish Americans, slavery and the full range of anti-African American racism for African Americans), African Americans have indeed outperformed Jewish Americans at least in certain respects. But even if this specific claim turns out to be false, it is plausible to argue that African Americans as a group have *not* languished, but have instead done remarkably well in light of their daunting circumstances of racist oppression in the United States.

It appears that as a group Jewish Americans have done quite well in areas such as (but not limited to) business, higher-education, politics, law, and medicine. But whatever successes many Jewish Americans have made in these areas seems to be matched in comparison to the contributions of many African Americans to U.S. politics (for instance, the abolitionist movement, SNCC, SCLC, NAACP, the Black Panther party, and other accomplishments), athletics of numerous kinds, music, and entertainment. If it is true that some Jewish Americans owned and operated aspects of the music and entertainment industries, for example, it is also true that the greatest talents of that industry lay with the performers, rather than with the often highly exploitative business persons, many of whom reaped *most* of the profits from the toil of actors, musicians, and other artists and entertainers, many of whom, as it turns out, were African Americans.[5] Moreover, how could African American successes like these be legitimately construed as "languishing," especially in light of the significant contributions and continual progress of African Americans in business, education, medicine, and law and often in the face of obstacles that Jewish Americans have never known? For while Jewish Americans as a group experienced *generations* of harsh forms of racism (anti-Semitic quota policies, for example) in the United States, African Americans as a group for *centuries* continually experienced evils of racist oppression.[6] One would think that whatever successes have been achieved by African Americans under such circumstances are hardly less than spectacular indeed! So it appears that the statement that African Americans have "languished" since slavery is misleading, if not false. For it does not seem to take into account the variant economic and political starting points of Jewish Americans, on the one hand, and of African Americans, on the other. Nor does it take into account the variant levels, kinds, and durations of racist oppression each of these groups has experienced in U.S. society. When these factors are considered, it is not clear that as a group African Americans are languishing (though it is obvious that many African Americans are languishing, and understandably so given their historic roots in slavery and other gross forms of anti-African American racist oppression).

But let us assume, for the sake of argument, that African Americans *are* languishing according to some objective standard of what counts as

5. This exploitation of many African Americans by many Jewish Americans would appear to explain, moreover, certain tensions between African Americans and Jewish Americans, at least on a minimally Marxist analysis of capitalist exploitation. *This,* more than African American envy over either Jewish American economic success or there being Jewish American autonomy (Thomas, *Vessels of Evil,* p. 186), explains why many African Americans are distrustful of many Jewish Americans. Let us never forget the role that social and economic *class* plays in the systematic racist oppression of a people.

6. This claim is in no way meant to deny that Jewish Americans and African Americans experience racism today. They most certainly do. This chapter, however, seeks to focus on the evils that each of these ethnic groups has experienced in the past.

languishing. The reason, it is argued, why African Americans languish is because they lack a narrative. But precisely what *is* a narrative? It is said that a narrative

> defines values and positive goals and fixes points of historical significance and ennobling rituals that cannot be readily appropriated. . . . narratives of a people define their conception of the good, while providing both signifi-cant historical reference points that anchor various values and ennobling rituals. . . . Narratives need not be true as such but are a kind of folklore of value that serves as a point of reference. . . . they connect the past with the future, even the ones that have shameful aspects to them.[7]

Moreover, it is argued that "a group that conceives itself simply in terms of negative goals—that is, of harms to be avoided. . . . is a group without a narrative."[8] Indeed, a narrative, in most cases, defines the self-identity of a people to whom the narrative applies. It defines goods that are irreducible to individual gain. Although a narrative can be distorted or can change,[9] "only a people with a narrative can flourish in a hostile society, because only a people with a narrative can engage in affirming cooperation. A people with a narrative identify both with one another and with shared positive goals. Moreover, they take enormous delight in having a hand in the real-ization of these goals."[10] I will refer to this as the "narrow" conception of a narrative.

But this notion of a narrative, though it appears to be descriptive of the Jewish (and certain other) narratives, is overly narrow if it is taken to be the sole notion of the nature and function of a narrative. For there are other kinds of narratives, according to which there exist no "ennobling rit-uals," but which satisfy other features essential to what a narrative is and does. Nor must such narratives involve a religious element. To deny this would be to imply that ennobling rituals (usually derived from religious teachings) are necessary for narratives. But this would appear to constitute a self-serving or question-begging analysis of a narrative insofar as, say, Jew-ish Americans are concerned, one which includes as narratives only those promoting ennobling rituals (based on religious teachings). Yet for this narrow construal of the nature and function of a narrative, we would need supporting argument. (It would imply, implausibly, that atheists who also believe that rituals are superstitious and foolish are unable to have a nar-rative!) What is needed is a more refined notion of a narrative's nature and

7. Thomas, *Vessels of Evil*, p. 156.
8. Ibid., p. 197.
9. Ibid., p. 198.
10. Ibid., p. 199.

function, one that makes conceptual space for narrowly construed ones that have a religious foundation that is unique to a particular ethnic group and that may promote ennobling rituals (such as with Judaism), but one that also makes conceptual room for narratives more broadly construed yet having the same basic positive effects for the group that created the narrative. These latter kinds of narratives might include those without religious bases or rituals of any type.

Furthermore, given the content of the narrow conception of the nature and function of a narrative, it is important to ask, among other things, whether or not a narrative "belongs to," waits for, is "bestowed upon"[11] members of an ethnic group such as Jewish Americans or African Americans. This kind of language seems to suggest, without careful qualification, that a narrative is something over the content of which a people have little or no say. According to such language, it appears as if the narrative is provided for the group by an out-group member, or by some supernatural entity.

On the contrary, a narrative can and often does take on a rather different form. Narratives, I argue, are *created* by peoples in order to make sense of themselves and the world. This is true of all narratives, whether Jewish or not. Narratives may contain historical fact and fiction, the usual stuff out of which myths are constructed.[12] But whatever else narratives are or do, they are created by a people. There is no reason, it seems, to think that the content of a narrative is not constructed wholly by members of the group to whom the narrative applies. This is an important point. For it serves as the basis of a critique of the claim that African Americans have no narrative:

> blacks born into Slavery were bereft of any experiences that could anchor the narratives of Africa.[13]
>
> Absolutely telling against the idea that black religious tradition is informed by an African narrative is the unmistakably Christian nature of the black religious tradition in the United States, for Africa is utterly irrelevant to the Christian narrative.[14]

These statements seem to assume that an African American narrative needed to be (historically speaking) grounded in an African one and that African Americans lack a narrative even to this day.[15] It is one thing to argue

11. See Ibid., pp. 202–3, for the use of such phrases to describe the relationship between a people and its narrative.

12. Joseph Campbell, *The Hero with a Thousand Faces* (Princeton: Princeton University Press, 1949); *The Masks of God*, vols. 1–4 (New York: Viking Press, 1968).

13. Thomas, *Vessels of Evil*, p. 155.

14. Ibid., p. 158.

15. Ibid., p. 202.

this line, adding that today's "blacks can create a narrative for themselves."[16] However, as I shall argue, it is quite another thing to argue that African Americans *had created their own narratives*, woven together into a single one, which like other narratives (at least many of them) evolve over time and in light of a people's experiences. If narratives are indeed created by a people, then would it not make sense to think that, at least in many cases, that narrative would evolve as its people do? And if a people (many Africans) were enslaved and largely stripped of their cultures and such that it would be impossible, let us suppose, for them to create a narrative anchored in African narratives, would it follow that these people did not create a narrative nonetheless? Did not African Americans create out of their oppressive experiences as slaves and as former slaves, a kind of narrative that is based on positive goals and a conception of the good and that seems to identify African Americans as a distinct ethnic group? And even if it did include, to some extent or another, Christian influences, would that suffice to disqualify it as a narrative? Would it suffice to disqualify it as being their own (independent) narrative? If so, then what would be the non-question-begging or nonarbitrary argument in favor of answering these questions negatively? It has been argued that the creation of this kind of an African American narrative is certainly possible.[17] But if this is true, then why would not one also think that, given the evolving nature of a narrative (at least some of them), African Americans were since their enslavement as Africans creating (and re-creating) their own narratives, ones that (not unlike parts of the Jewish American narratives) include accounts of their liberating themselves from the hands of their oppressors?

Did African Americans have a narrative? Do they have a narrative today? Again, it is said that, although Africans themselves had and have narratives, those Africans taken into slavery were acculturated such that they had no narrative. Even today, it is argued, African Americans have no narrative. But are these claims true? Although one must be sensitive to the possibility of a single African American narrative,[18] one must understand that African Americans are a rather complex ethnic group (as are Jewish Americans), and that they created out of U.S. slavery various narratives, which, woven together sometimes (but not always) with either Christianity or Islamic faith, constitute what one might refer to as the "African American experience." (So as not to overly complicate this discussion, I shall write as if there is one such narrative). Like Jewish Americans, not all of whom are

16. Ibid., p. 203.
17. Ibid.
18. Ibid.

robustly religious (nonetheless, such persons often do follow certain Jewish rites such as Bris, Bar/Bat Mitzvah, and Jewish burial rites) but many of whom respect the Jewish faith, not all African Americans are religious, though many respect religious African Americans. The fact is that U.S. slavery serves to remind future African Americans that they can as a people endure and succeed under the most horrible circumstances of evil perpetrated against them. The study of U.S. history is itself a testament of faith and stupendous successes of a group of peoples (Africans of various countries) who were brutally alienated from their respective traditions, yet who, relative to their experienced racist oppression and starting points in U.S. society, eventually survived and have thrived rather well, especially considering their adverse experiences.

And it is precisely some of the details of this rich African American history that (in the minds and hearts of many African Americans) has and does serve as the basis of an African American narrative. Whether it is the awe-inspiring story of Harriet Tubman and her role in the underground railroad; Frederick Douglass's spirited abolitionism; Sojourner Truth's striving for equal rights and her moral indictment and exposure of the U.S. woman's suffrage movement as profoundly racist;[19] W. E. B. DuBois's contributions to human knowledge; James Baldwin's enlightening and spirited writings; or Jackie Robinson's monumental role in U.S. sports; Muhammad Ali's, Venus and Serena Williams' inspiration of millions of African Americans (and millions of others!) toward new heights of self-esteem and confidence; or whether it was the soulful singing or playing of various African American musical performers in recent years; or the political activism of Malcolm X, Martin Luther King, Jr., or Angela Davis, just to name a select few, African Americans (indeed, *all* U.S. citizens!) have good reason to be proud of a story that can be told of African Americans who are in the process of completing their own liberation. One cannot help but be inspired by the narrative that can be told and is indeed repeated in churches and in other contexts throughout the United States. And it is a narrative that is essentially and uniquely that of the African American. This is simply the beginning of an ongoing story of people who were brutally enslaved, suffering unimaginable racist oppression, including murders, rapes, alienation from families and cultures, but people who are in the process of liberating themselves toward complete freedom. That whatever sacred texts (mainly Christian or Muslim) are part of this or some version of African American narrative were not brought to the Americas

19. Angela Davis, *Women, Race, and Class* (New York: Random House, 1981), chapters 3–4.

by enslaved Africans hardly discounts these narratives as being uniquely African American. For what many African Americans take to be most sacred is how certain religious texts "speak" to *their own* liberation as African Americans and to their flourishing both in the here and now and in the hereafter. One example of this is that some Christian scriptures used by many to support African slavery in the United States were reinterpreted by many African Americans to articulate their own liberation from racist oppression and rules by which to live. Thus what was used to rationalize on religious grounds a primarily economic and racist motivation for enslaving Africans in the United States was and is used to articulate an account of why U.S. slavery was morally wrong.

One might argue that it is a narrative that is not essentially the African Americans' because it is by and large based on Christianity. After all, the African American consciousness has been highly influenced (to say the least) by the varieties of Christianity that were "taught" to African slaves in the United States as a means of acculturating the slaves into "civilization." Thus any African American narrative that includes an essentially Christian element is one that is "foreign" to African Americans. It follows, this concern states, that a Christian-based African American narrative is not one that belongs to African Americans, in other words, *it is not their own*. For it is imposed on them by an out-group source.

In reply to this concern, it is argued, as it was previously, that the claim that a Christian-based African American narrative cannot (is not?) one that *belongs to* African Americans is in need of independent argumentative support. This is especially true given the nearly universal nature and appeal of Christianity, when plausibly construed, and the fact that millions of African Americans (not all of whom can, qua Christians, plausibly be seen as being engaged in self-deception or self-hatred-based acculturation) find Christianity liberating and fulfilling. Thus it is plausible to hold that African Americans *did* create their own (perhaps Christian-based) narrative, and, like all narratives, it is an evolving one, one that grew to include secular elements such as the ones noted above. Thus it is false to claim that the reason why many African Americans are "languishing" is because African Americans lack a narrative of their own.[20]

20. Indeed, it is plausible to argue that African slaves in America, especially in the United States, had in large part "adopted" a *particular Christian liberation theology* as part of *their own* narrative, replete with ennobling rituals of baptism, marriage, etc., and the promotion of positive group goals and the like. And such a narrative provides a means by which to identify African Americans and to assist them in self-identification as African Americans, namely, by holding that those who are African Americans are those who have familial ties to both U.S. slavery and Africa. It articulates a conception of the good, namely, that found in the Christian scriptures, properly interpreted. And this is the kind of narrative that can

Moreover, the above sketch of an African American narrative is, as a matter of fact, one that *has* been *created by* millions of African Americans throughout history and especially in recent years. (Interestingly enough, it makes no reference to Christianity or distinctly Christian principles.) If the groups that have narratives create them themselves instead of narratives being created by out-group members *for* in-group members or instead of narratives being "bestowed" on them, then lacking some plausible argument to the contrary, should we not think that African Americans *have had and do have* a narrative (namely, the one that many of them have created), contrary to what has been argued? As long as narratives are created and evolve, then there is nothing that would make it absurd for such an African American narrative to not only exist, but to have already been in existence, created by and for African Americans.

Furthermore, it is plausible to devise an African American narrative (one that most African Americans throughout recent U.S. history have internalized qua African Americans) and to also see it as evolving, in recent years, into a narrative in terms of Kwanzaa: an increasingly celebrated African American "holiday" among those of African decent. Kwanzaa involves ennobling rituals (nonreligious) and promotes positive group goals based on a conception of the good, thus satisfying the criterion for a narrative on the narrow account of narratives. That such an African American narrative does or does not satisfy the condition of being religiously based or promoting ennobling rituals (conditions of a narrative on the narrow conception) hardly counts against its being an authentic and unique narrative on a broader conception of the nature and function of a narrative. Thus if one wants an example of an extant African American narrative that satisfies the narrow conception's conditions of a narrative, one only need to look as far as the growing numbers of African Americans (and those of African decent worldwide) who celebrate Kwanzaa.

Briefly, Kwanzaa is a seven-day celebration of African culture and is one of the fastest growing holidays in the United States. Celebrated from 26 December through 1 January, Kwanzaa is rooted in African harvest festivals and derives its name from the Kiswahili phrase "matunda ya kwanzaa," which denotes the first fruits of the harvest. Holiday rituals, including the lighting of candles, reciting prayers, singing songs, and gift-giving, all

---

and *has* served as a primary source of inspiration for African American flourishing in education, as well as in many other areas of U.S. social life. For an account of African American liberation theology from a Christian perspective, see James H. Cone, *Black Theology and Black Power* (New York: Seabury, 1969); *A Black Theology of Liberation* (Philadelphia: Lippencott, 1970); *For My People: Black Theology and the Black Church* (Maryknoll: Orbis, 1984); *God of the Oppressed* (Maryknoll: Orbis, 1997); and *Risks of Faith* (Boston: Beacon, 1999).

demonstrate the spirit of Kwanzaa: unity. Kwanzaa was founded in 1966 by Maulana Karenga with the primary aim of assisting African Americans in identifying with and nurturing their African heritages and to unify African American families and communities. Kiswahili, an East African language, was selected as the language of Kwanzaa in that it is not associated with any particular tribe of Africa and it is spoken almost universally throughout Africa. Like the African harvest festivals on which it is founded, Kwanzaa celebrates life and creation, commemorates the past, and promotes basic principles, both moral and spiritual. These seven principles ("Nguzo Saba") are *unity* ("umoja"), self-determination ("kujichaglia"), collective work and responsibility ("ujima"), cooperative economics ("ujama"), purpose ("nia"), creativity ("kuumba"), and faith ("imani"). Kwanzaa is not associated with any religious or political movement. Although it is a relatively new holiday, it is commemorated throughout the world by millions of people of African decent. An estimated 10 million African Americans celebrate Kwanzaa each year.[21]

Are African Americans as a group "languishing"? African Americans have been in so many ways quite successful in the face of anti-African American racism. That there are many African Americans who have not done well is unfortunate and their respective plights ought to be addressed. But this fact is understandable given the degree of evils experienced by their forebears (and in many instances, by themselves). It is no surprise that Jewish Americans have far fewer of their own in poverty (in the United States) than there are African Americans in poverty. The former were not enslaved in the United States. Nor were Jewish families torn asunder as African American ones were, and for so many generations. Nor were Jewish American women raped as slave masters and many others raped African slaves and even African American women. Nor were Jewish Americans fully denied various voting, educational, due process rights as have African Americans. For anti-Semitism in the United States has never even roughly resembled the depths and duration of the evils experienced by African Americans. To suggest otherwise would be to engage in dishonesty, delusion, or disrespect toward African Americans and what they have experienced.

Let us "never forget" that it is one thing to, for example, have quotas instituted to limit the numbers of Jewish Americans serving in higher-level offices and professions in the United States because many people in U.S. society deemed Jewish Americans as being evil or anti-Christian, but it is

---

21. Maulana Karenga, *Kwanzaa: A Celebration of Family, Community and Culture* (Los Angeles: San Kore Press, 1998).

quite another thing altogether for African Americans to *not be allowed to even train themselves to become qualified to have such quotas instituted against them because they were not seen by U.S. society as being fully human!* Let's become clear about one thing: anti-Semitism in the United States was never as qualitatively or quantitatively harsh as the cumulative evils experienced by African Americans. Moreover, many Jewish Americans who came to the United States were those who survived the Jewish holocaust in Nazi Germany. But in coming to the United States, such Jewish Americans *no longer lived under the government and with the people which and who oppressed them!* Jewish Americans had a relatively new beginning in the United States,[22] while African Americans (though there was talk by a few who wanted to and did go back to Africa after slavery) remained with the evil empire under which they were slaves, and under which they are at best moderately respected even today. With this in mind, is it any wonder that some African Americans do not succeed in the same ways and to the same extent as Jewish Americans? Or, is it nothing short of remarkable that *so many and increasing numbers of African Americans have succeeded in the United States in light of their most disadvantaged initial position compared to the starting point of, say, Jewish Americans?* The strategy seems to have been to compare two groups that have experienced vastly different things in different countries and with different political structures and to ask why one group "flourishes" while the other "languishes." But is this so interesting a question given that they have such widely differing experiences and in vastly different contexts? Would anyone seriously wonder why African Americans (given their circumstances of centuries of slavery) have not performed as well as Jewish Americans in certain ways in U.S. society?

To the extent that a group's circumstantial ability to successfully assimilate provides its members opportunities to flourish in a society, it is understandable why Jewish Americans succeeded *in certain ways more than* African Americans in the United States. Even if one supposes for the sake of argument that African Americans had no narrative, it would still suffice to explain why they have not succeeded in the United States as well as Jewish Americans for one to argue that the status of one's entrance into a society largely determines ones opportunities within it for business, politics, and other forms of socialization. Jewish Americans were perceived by most in the United States as being humans, despite the harshness of anti-Semitism that Jewish Americans experienced in the United States. However,

---

22. I say "relatively" because Jewish Americans did experience (and today still do experience) an array of anti-Semitic attitudes and behaviors that Latinos, Asians, and certain other ethnic groups similarly experienced, speaking generally.

Africans were viewed by most everyone in the "New World" and the United States as being chattel. And African Americans have inherited the racist legacy that fuels such a view. For the theory (that African Americans have languished and are languishing due to their lack of a narrative) to succeed, it must be shown that my proposed (partial) explanation (namely, that African Americans have never enjoyed the relative *autonomy* Jewish Americans have experienced in the United States) of the comparative variances of success between Jewish and African Americans is implausible as a major explanation. This claim posits that African slaves and for some time ex-slaves and their offspring were systematically deprived of authentic citizenship in U.S. society. Without the inheritance of full citizenship, African Americans enjoyed few, if any, rights. Whatever moral and legal rights they did have were disrespected, often in unspeakable ways and even by the U.S. government. (Governments, many believe, are supposed to *protect* the rights of their citizens). In light of this long history of maltreatment of African Americans and their ancestors in the United States, it is plausible to argue that they as a group had no real ability or opportunity to fully assimilate into U.S. society as most other ethnic groups have done (e.g., *at the rate of success* that most other ethnic groups have). *This*, more than their alleged lack of a narrative, explains why in certain ways African Americans have not succeeded in some ways that Jewish Americans have succeeded. The fact is that the race to succeed had long begun for Jewish Americans before African Americans were allowed into the stadium to compete as persons to whom the U.S. Constitution, Bill of Rights, and Declaration of Independence fully applied.

So even if one accepts as true what is said about African Americans languishing since slavery and their lacking a narrative, the claim that the reason why African Americans languished is because of their lack of a narrative is problematic. Consider the case of Schmews, who are just like Jewish Americans except that Schmews, unlike Jewish Americans, were sold into slavery just like many Africans were sold into slavery centuries ago and shipped to the United States. But the slavery of Schmews, unlike African slaves in the United States, did not entail the complete estrangement of the Schmewish people from anything Jewish. The slavery of the Schmews left them with their narrative and with autonomy. For Schmews were seen as foremost interpreters of their own experience, and slave masters never tried to alienate Schmews from their tradition. In fact, the savvy slave masters knew that Schmews would be better slaves if they retained their tradition.[23] For in retaining their traditions, Schmews would be happier slaves,

---

23. This understanding of group autonomy is found in Thomas, *Vessels of Evil*, p. 182.

content with the status quo. However, it entailed that they were not protected by U.S. rules of law and such, and they were brutalized and largely unprotected by U.S. law, as were the African slaves. Under such conditions, it is reasonable to think that the Schmews would *not* flourish well in the United States. For the effects of centuries of slavery would surely prohibit rapidity in growth and flourishing within U.S. society, yet they would have both autonomy (in the relevant sense) and a narrative. In fact, let us suppose any attempt at progress within the Schmewish communities would be met with certain violence against Schmews, which would both destroy all tries at success and go unpunished by the government.

What the example of the Schmews suggests is that having both autonomy and a narrative are insufficient for flourishing under conditions of evil.[24] But what the example also suggests is that more than a group's having both autonomy and a narrative is necessary for surviving evil, namely, *that a group of oppressed people has the genuine sociopolitical and economic opportunity to flourish according to the rules of the game as established by the dominant group(s) in the regime.* Would Schmews, unlike African Americans, possess the genuine opportunity to flourish in U.S. society after being enslaved in it? It is unlikely that Schmews would succeed at all under such circumstances. If Jewish Americans flourish in the United States better than African Americans, it is because, among other things, Jewish Americans have not shared anything like the same experience as African Americans *in the United States.* Schmews, on the other hand, would likely fare no better than African Americans, even though, *un*like African slaves in the United States, they possessed both autonomy and a narrative. For Schmews are not likely to be able to survive (much less "*flourish*") any better than African slaves if U.S. laws and institutions work against them in any manner akin to the ways in which they worked against Africa slaves and African Americans. In light of these considerations, it is unsurprising that Jewish Americans, some of whom survived the Jewish holocaust, thrive in the United States, whereas African Americans have not done as well in certain ways. Thus a group's being autonomous and having a narrative is insufficient for its flourishing.

Furthermore, a group's having a narrative is not even necessary for its flourishing under racist oppression. Consider the case of African Americans. Let us assume that they as a group have no narrative, but that they enjoy a significant degree of freedom in the United States. So African Americans as a group (an ethnic group) have freedom but no narrative in

---

24. Of course, Thomas does not deny this point. However, this point is left unclear by his discussion.

a context of anti-African American racism.[25] But let us also suppose that another century passes under such conditions but with no African American narrative. Is it not plausible to think that the successes already registered by African Americans would serve as inspiration for further progress? Would it not be plausible to argue that African American successes would *increase* significantly as more and more African Americans attend good universities and flourish as a result, and this despite the anti-African American racist oppression? It is not that African American crime or poverty would be expected or imagined to be eliminated. Rather, it is that another century of successes and flourishing would be reasonably expected. Yet there is no African American narrative! Of course, the notion of success here is largely an economic or material one. It alone would not necessarily imply the successes of the development of group esteem or self-esteem of its members, which are deeper indicators of qualitative ethnic group flourishing. However, with ever-increasing strides in African American education would likely follow significant increases in their group esteem and the self-esteem of many African Americans as individuals. Thus a group's having a narrative in the narrow sense is not a necessary condition of that group's flourishing under racist oppression.

Now it might be argued that all that the example just given shows is that individual African Americans can flourish quite apart from the group of African Americans flourishing. But what this line of criticism misses is that often times one individual African American's success serves as another's inspiration (part of another's overall narrative?) to flourish, just as with others in society. The fact is that the African Americans in the example have no narrative, but have freedom (where such freedom is accompanied by their genuine opportunities for social progress perhaps backed by a system of rights and duties, among other things, to protect the freedoms of African Americans as well as others), yet have furthered the already impressive extent to which many African Americans have flourished. Thus it is by no means obvious that African Americans have languished since slavery, or that they are without a narrative in some meaningful sense. But even if they had languished and had nothing even resembling a narrative, perhaps the most important reason for whatever African American problems in succeeding there are is that *African Americans, unlike Jewish Americans who came to the United States as free persons starting life "anew," remain in the society which enslaved them and continues to force varieties of racism on them.* Such a fact helps to explain why Jewish Americans as a group have succeeded in some ways that African Americans (as a group) have not. How much more would

25. This, in fact, is a claim the truth of which Thomas does not deny.

one be unsurprised at this comparative result should African Americans have, as a group, a morally justified distrust of the society which enslaved them? How easy it is to understand why it is so difficult for African Americans to succeed as a group when one considers how their understandably distrustful attitude toward U.S. society can and does stand in the way of African Americans succeeding in that society! It is not that a narrative is not *helpful* in some circumstances of racist oppression to build and sustain group identity and esteem for purposes of group solidarity and the group's coping with the damaging effects of the oppression. Rather, the point is that such a narrative is not a necessary condition of a group's flourishing under circumstances of racist oppression.

Consider also the fact that the two groups are stereotyped in significantly variant ways. While in the context of higher-education Jewish Americans are stereotyped by most as being intelligent, African Americans are deemed unintelligent. In the end, the comparative successes of African Americans and Jewish Americans is something of a bad one in that it seeks to compare the relative successes of two groups from vastly different cultures and circumstances. This in no way seeks to minimize the historical or current U.S. racist attitudes against Jewish Americans. However, honesty requires a recognition of the differential levels, kinds, and degrees of harshness of anti-African American racism versus anti-Semitism in the United States Furthermore, the effects of these respective racisms would be expected to differ, it would appear, given the fact that a significantly greater percentage of Jewish Americans have always been in a much better-off position in the United States than have most African Americans. Rather than their lacking a narrative, whatever degree to which African Americans "languish" is due mostly to the harshness of their historic oppression (as well as the degree to which anti-African American racism persists) in U.S. society.

A significantly more interesting comparison of relative "flourishing" between groups is one that considers groups within a society and experiencing oppressive racism from the same source(s), rather than one which looks at groups from different societies experiencing such racism from different sources. Consider, then, the cases of Native Americans and African Americans in the United States. Here we have a much more interesting comparison and contrast of groups, one of which has not "flourished" in U.S. society, while the other has made tremendous strides within it. One only need visit several Native American "reserves" today to find that so many Native Americans live in conditions of poverty that few African Americans have ever seen. Not only is the level of rampant poverty much greater among Native Americans that it is among African Americans, but the levels and kinds of flourishing experienced by Native Americans hardly matches those experienced by African Americans, and this seems to be true despite the obvious factual differences that Native Americans were marked for holocaust in the name of "manifest destiny," while African Americans were not. This might explain the disparity of progress by these respective ethnic groups. More specifically, why is it that African Americans have flourished so well (especially) given the harshest conditions of slavery and past and present anti-African American racism, but Native Americans as groups have not? Is it because Native Americans have no narrative? Is it that Native Americans' lack autonomy? Or is it something quite different?

Native (North) Americans (the Diné, the Zuni, the Crees, the Cherokee, and other tribal groups) possess respective narratives (including rituals, customs, and rites) and autonomy (they were seen as autonomous in the sense that they were seen by European invaders and later by U.S. citizens as being the foremost interpreters of their own historical-cultural traditions), yet in no way do they come close to mirroring the much higher degrees of successes in U.S. society that African Americans exhibit. It has been noted that the perception by most invaders that Native Americans were backward and heathens helped explain why invaders found it so easy to rationalize the evils they perpetrated against Native American nations.[26] But what might explain, at least for the most part, why Native Americans as groups have languished while African Americans (as a group) have flourished (by comparison to Native Americans as a conglomerate of groups) in U.S. society? One major reason for this is that Native Americans posed a much greater threat to manifest destiny than did African Americans. African Americans were by and large acculturated into the myth of manifest destiny and European culture (religion and values) while most Native Americans were not successfully acculturated in this way. (Several attempts were made by the U.S. government and churches to succeed along these lines, for instance, the former's attempt to acculturate Native American children by forcing them into Indian boarding "schools.") President Abraham Lincoln's decision to free African American slaves did not pose a substantial challenge to the status quo of manifest destiny and the invasion of Native American lands because these former slaves did not oppose these ideals and actions. Europeans could eliminate the forces that held down African Americans in the form of slavery and without serious threat to the invasion of North America.

26. James P. Sterba, "Understanding Evil: American Slavery, the Holocaust and the Conquest of the American Indians," *Ethics* 106 (1996): 424–48.

But it appears that the Native American holocaust could not, except by sacrificing much (if not all) of manifest destiny, be turned back or diminished. This provides a powerful (though incomplete) explanation as to why Native Americans (as groups) have not flourished (though they have often, in the face of even current U.S. governmental pressures to violate their rights, succeeded in keeping alive their respective cultures, at least to some meaningful extent) as well as African Americans (as a group) have. For the former have never experienced consistent peace with the European invaders, while the latter not only gained their own freedom from slavery, but were in some measure used by the U.S. armed forces (witness the "Buffalo Soldiers") to, among other things, further conquer Native Americans. In short, while African Americans used their freedom from slavery to assimilate into the European invader's culture, Native Americans could not, except by opting out of their own cultures, do the same as African Americans subsequent to slavery. The freedom from slavery of African Americans posed no serious threat to the morally unjust acquisitions and transfers of Native American lands.

However, the very existence and viability of strong Native American populations posed a direct threat and challenge to manifest destiny. The policy of manifest destiny and the ability of the U.S. military to execute it serve as crucial underlying explanations of why African Americans were permitted to survive at a rate unmatched by Native Americans. What is *not* true is that Native Americans had no narrative, or that they had no autonomy in the relevant sense. What is crucial is that African Americans, who were once perceived by most other U.S. citizens as being subhuman, were later on viewed by a growing number of Americans as at least being superior to the "savages"[27] who stood in the way of manifest destiny. African American freedom from slavery did not pose a major threat to manifest destiny as did the respect for the moral rights of Native Americans to *their own lands, that is, cumulatively, North America.* Basically, Native Americans did not have the opportunity to succeed in U.S. society without giving up what was most crucial to them (their lands and cultures), and what was in place long before the evil forces that invaded them were even born, whereas African Americans had more of a willingness to assimilate into U.S. society. The institution of slavery in the United States had deprogrammed, and then reprogrammed, most enslaved Africans to believe that assimilation was acceptable under the circumstances in which they found themselves as

27. That Native Americans were deemed "savages" by most European invaders and, later on, by most U.S. citizens and their governments, is logically consistent with their seeing Native Americans as being sufficiently autonomous folk with whom to make (and break!) treaties.

African Americans. Native Americans, on the other hand, found themselves fighting for the very existence of all that was meaningful to them. To
assimilate meant to resign themselves to what had virtually annihilated
them. In the minds and hearts of most Native Americans, it would be a
rather severe form of self-hatred and resignation of self-empowerment to
the invaders. So whereas both African Americans and Native Americans
each had little or no opportunity to succeed in U.S. society, the former possessed a certain (albeit often reluctant) willingness to assimilate into U.S.
society, while the latter saw no reason to give up all that was meaningful to
themselves (*their* narratives, *their* lands, *their* cultures).

So even *if* Native Americans *had* an opportunity to succeed in U.S. society, they, *un*like African Americans, had (and still have) good reason to be
unwilling to assimilate largely because of their desire for cultural self-
preservation (where Native American cultural preservation is tied to their
inhabiting the lands of the Americas that they once inhabited but no
longer inhabit due to the European invasion of the Americas). After all,
Native American nations were in North America several centuries prior to
the European invasion, and such native peoples had already established
traditions, including narratives. Why *should* such folk assimilate into the *invader's* society? This unwillingness to assimilate into U.S. society is justified
in that it is unreasonable to expect or require, morally speaking, that oppressed persons seek to live with their oppressors. It is easy to understand
why there might be a significant degree of unwillingness of many Native
Americans to assimilate into the society, which perpetrated (and still per-
petrates) evil against them. Moreover, it is easy to see how the reluctance
to assimilate into U.S. society by such Native Americans would make it difficult for them to "flourish" in U.S. society. *This*, perhaps more than anything else (and certainly instead of a group's having or not having a
narrative), explains why in certain ways African Americans as a group have
out-"flourished" Native Americans in U.S. society.

In sum, the narrow conception of a narrative is dubious in that it appears
to be question-begging, rendering problematic the claim that African
Americans have languished since slavery because they lack a narrative. But
even if these claims were true, and even if it were true that their lacking a
narrative is crucial for their languishing, there is still a more crucial consideration as to why African Americans as a group have not flourished in
the ways that Jewish Americans have flourished. It is because African Americans have been denied the opportunities to flourish that are afforded
in some significantly greater measure to Jewish Americans and most others in the United States. The analysis of why Jewish Americans flourished
more than African Americans (e.g., because the former both had and have

autonomy and a narrative, while the latter do not) does not work for the comparison of Native Americans and African Americans. For Native Americans have "languished" even though they had profoundly rich narratives and autonomy sufficient for others to recognize them as the foremost interpreters of their own historical-cultural traditions. Finally, Native Americans' lack of "flourishing" compared to African American "flourishing" is best (though not fully) explained in terms of both the holocaust instituted against the Native Americans by European invaders and the U.S. government seeking to fulfill the goal of manifest destiny. Also important is a fundamental unwillingness of several Native Americans to assimilate into a society that had oppressed and still does oppress them in extreme ways, whereas African Americans as a group have been more willing (in the face of a wide range of social pressures) to assimilate.

While it seems at least prima facie plausible to argue that a narrow kind of narrative enabled Jews as a people to cope reasonably well with the horrors of the Jewish holocaust, it is doubtful that: (1) African Americans are languishing, especially given their starting point in the "New World" and in U.S. society; (2) African Americans lacked a narrative of their own, one which enabled them to flourish to some meaningful extent in the face of a most horrendous racist oppression; (3) that even had African Americans lacked a narrative (according to the narrow conception of the nature of a narrative), that this is why they languish today. For the kinds, levels, and degrees of racist oppression against Africans and African Americans provides at least a prima facie and significant causal explanation of whatever African American languishing does exist. Even if African Americans had a narrative in a narrow sense, it is not obvious that they would be in a better position as a people to flourish under conditions of racist oppression where significant freedom is lacking for African Americans. It is reasonable to believe that a just and fair system of fairly enforced rights[28] and duties, among other things, would go much further toward the flourishing of African Americans under such circumstances. African Americans must have, above all else, fair and equal opportunities to flourish, and it is *this* fact more than whether or not African Americans possess a narrative or autonomy, that explains the current "success" status of African Americans. A group's flourishing is contingent, among other things yet quite significantly, on the group's having fair opportunities for thriving within the society in which it lives. Rights, if they mean anything at all, must be *respected*.

28. Joel Feinberg, "The Nature and Value of Rights," in *Rights, Justice, and the Bounds of Liberty,* ed. Joel Feinberg (Princeton: Princeton University Press, 1980); *Freedom and Fulfillment* (Princeton: Princeton University Press, 1992), chapters 8–10.

And it is a respect for rights that provides an opportunity for justice, fairness, and flourishing in society.

It is clear that a fair-minded study of U.S. history demonstrates that the United States has violated many basic human rights of Native and African Americans (as well, of course, as enslaved Africans). The question to which I shall eventually turn is whether or not the harms experienced by Native and African Americans (and enslaved Africans) at the hands of the U.S. government are compensable, normatively speaking. Are reparations to Native and African Americans by the U.S. government morally required? Does the balance of reason favor the claim that Native and African Americans ought to be compensated via reparations by the U.S. government? If so, then Native and African Americans have moral rights to such reparations, corresponding to moral duties the U.S. government has to pay them. And if this is true, then what form(s) ought such reparations take?

Prior to delving into questions of reparations to Native and African Americans, however, it is important to answer queries regarding public policy administration to Latinos in particular, and to ethnic groups more generally. Do Latinos deserve reparations or some other form of compensation for racist harms experienced in U.S. society? More generally, how ought justice to ethnic groups be construed along these lines?

6

Affirmative Action for Latinos?

Thus far I have argued that, owing to conceptual problems, the concept of race ought to be replaced with a viable concept of ethnicity. Using the concept of Latino identity as a test case for the concept of ethnic identity, I articulated and defended the genealogical conception of Latino identity, a notion that is intended to be generalized to other ethnic groups and their classifications of their respective members. Then I set forth and defended a cognitive-behavioral theory of racism, one that explains a complex array of kinds, motivations, and bases of racism that demonstrate that racism is far more complex than previous philosophical conceptions of it admit. And in chapter 5, I discussed some of the differences between the respective experiences of racist oppression of Jewish persons under the Nazi regime in Germany, and of African and Native Americans in the United States. As examples of some of the worst evils in human history, many would argue that these human rights violations require rectification. Chapters 8 and 9 are devoted to philosophical discussions of arguments in favor of reparations to Native and African Americans, respectively, along with discussions of numerous objections to such arguments. But prior to an examination of those important matters, it is helpful to explore some of the issues related to nonreparative means of public policy administration aimed at addressing racist harms. The example in this (and the next) chapter will be Latinos and whether or not we ought to be one of the groups targeted for preferential treatment in the United States in light of racist harms against us in the United States over the past several generations.

After decades in which U.S. citizens have lived with affirmative action programs, there is increasing doubt among many as to the justifiability of the very policies on which such programs are based. As philosophers continue the discussion of the moral status of affirmative action programs,[1] arguments lead rather naturally to questions of ethnic group membership. Several would argue that if affirmative action programs are morally justified, then public policy ought to be enacted so that such programs are instituted and sustained in viable and fair ways. However, in order for affirmative action programs to be instituted with a minimum of unfair play, it is imperative that they function according to a sound and workable notion of ethnic group membership concerning the groups targeted for affirmative action. Latinos constitute one such group. And so it is crucial that affirmative action programs operate according to a plausible and workable idea of Latino identity. In chapters 2 and 3, I sought to provide a viable conception of Latino identity (and more generally, of ethnic identity). Thus there is a vital conceptual connection between Latino identity and affirmative action.[2]

Certainly one position to argue about Latino identity and affirmative action is that not only is there no fixed (essentialist) conception of Latino identity that reaches across time and circumstance, universally, but that even if there were such a view of Latino identity, affirmative action policies ought not extend to Latinos for reasons of either equal opportunity or reparations. Jorge J. E. Gracia discusses the concept of Hispanic/Latino identity[3] and argues that affirmative action is *not* due Latinos for reasons

1. Some important philosophical discussions of affirmative action include: William T. Blackstone and Robert D. Heslep, eds., *Social Justice and Preferential Treatment* (Athens: University of Georgia Press, 1977); Bernard Boxill, *Blacks and Social Justice* (Totowa: Rowman and Littlefield, 1984); Marshall Cohen, Thomas Nagel, and Thomas Scanlan, eds., *Equality and Preferential Treatment* (Princeton: Princeton University Press, 1977); Robert K. Fullinwider, *The Reverse Discrimination Controversy* (Totowa: Rowman and Littlefield, 1980); Alan H. Goldman, *Justice and Reverse Discrimination* (Princeton: Princeton University Press, 1979); Kent Greenawalt, *Discrimination and Reverse Discrimination* (New York: Alfred A. Knopf, 1983); Barry R. Gross, ed., *Reverse Discrimination* (Buffalo, N.Y.: Prometheus Books, 1977); Thomas E. Hill, Jr., "The Message of Affirmative Action," *Social Philosophy & Policy* 8 (1991): 108–29; Howard McGary, *Race and Social Justice* (London: Blackwell, 1999); Thomas Nagel, "Equal Treatment and Compensatory Discrimination," *Philosophy and Public Affairs* 2 (1973): 348–63; Richard Wasserstrom, "Preferential Treatment," in *Philosophy and Social Issues,* ed. Richard Wasserstrom (Notre Dame: University of Notre Dame Press, 1980).

2. This connection is recognized in Richard Delgado and Vicky Palacios, "Mexican Americans as a Legally Cognizable Class," in *The Latino: A Condition,* ed. Richard Delgado and Jean Stefancic (New York: New York University Press, 1998), pp. 284–90, where it is deemed important for legal and public policy purposes to define legally "Mexican American" and "Chicano."

3. In Jorge J. E. Gracia, "Affirmative Action for Hispanics: Yes and No," in *Hispanics/ Latinos in the United States: Ethnicity, Race, and Rights,* ed. Jorge J. E. Gracia and Pablo De-Greiff (London: Routledge, 2000), pp. 201–21. Gracia's view of "Hispanic identity" is more fully articulated in Jorge J. E. Gracia, *Hispanic/Latino Identity* (London: Blackwell, 2000).

of equal opportunity or reparations because Latinos have not been treated in the harsh ways in which African Americans and women have been treated in U.S. society. Instead, affirmative action for Latinos is justified on forward-looking grounds that it is vital for Latinos to be able to participate in the life of the United States. Another position would be that there *is* an analysis of Latino identity and that Latinos *should* qualify for programs of affirmative action for reasons of, say, past injustices against them. Indeed, there are other such views about Latino identity and affirmative action. But I shall confine myself to a discussion of these particular viewpoints within the context of the U.S. legal system. I shall argue that if affirmative action itself is morally justified, then Latinos *are* deserving of affirmative action for backward-looking reasons.

Even if it could be shown that there is a way by which to identify Latinos for public policy purposes, Gracia argues, Latinos hardly qualify as plausible candidates for such policy administration, at least for reasons of reparations. While African Americans and women have been treated very badly and deserve reparations, he argues, Latinos have not and do not:

> Affirmative action for Hispanics considered as a whole, and understood to aim at equal opportunity and reparation, is not justified. The reason is that, although some Hispanics have suffered unequal treatment, and they are harmed by such treatment, not all, or even a majority of us have, and for those who have, it is very difficult to demonstrate that they have done so because they are Hispanics.[4]

In contrast with African Americans and women, the argument based on reparation does not seem to work for Hispanics for three reasons: (1) not all, or even most, Hispanics have suffered discrimination; (2) the degree of discrimination and abuse some have suffered never reached the levels suffered by African Americans or women; and (3) it is difficult to prove that the reason some Hispanics have suffered discrimination and abuse is because they are Hispanics. Hispanics have not been subjected to the kinds of abuse to which African Americans and women have been subjected. Hispanics have never been slaves; we were not brought into this country against our will to work for others and be subservient to their whims; we were not deprived of our culture, language, religion, freedom, basic human rights, education, or dignity; and, unlike women, we have not as a whole played a secondary role in society. Under these conditions, repara-

---

4. Gracia, "Affirmative Action for Hispanics: Yes and No," p. 208.

tion does not seem justified. There is nothing, or not much, that must be given back to Hispanics as a group because it was taken away from us. And there is no harm to us as a group that cries out for repair.[5]

Is affirmative action justified for reasons of reparative justice? If so, is such affirmative action to *Latinos* justified? It is helpful to clarify the nature of reparations, especially in light of Gracia's implication that affirmative action can be a kind of reparation.

However, whether or not affirmative action is justified for Latinos for backward-looking reasons, it is a category mistake to construe affirmative action as a means of reparations. For as indicated by the definitions of "reparations" and "affirmative action" (in *Black's Law Dictionary*), reparations are a matter of a group's being compensated for harms experienced unjustly, and reparations are *un*earned. However, affirmative action programs typically involve hiring or promoting someone to perform a task or fill a position for which she will perform and *earn* compensation. Furthermore, affirmative action, unlike reparations, need not be grounded in backward-looking reasons. Thus it is misleading to construe affirmative action programs as forms of reparations. When affirmative action is construed in terms of backward-looking considerations (for reparative aims), it is a category mistake.

Nonetheless, even though affirmative action is not in fact a legitimate mode of reparations, it might be seen as being justified for other reasons, for instance, as a means of achieving *distributive* justice.[6] The basic idea here is that Latinos should be beneficiaries of affirmative action programs because this would allow Latinos a more equal opportunity in education and employment. Such affirmative action is not based on backward-looking reparative considerations, but rather on present realities of anti-Latino racism and the significant inequalities they produce in U.S. society.

Gracia's statement of the various reasons in favor of affirmative action is rather insightful. However, one might take issue with him on the issue of whether or not Latinos are, on average and as a class, deserving of affirmative action and on what grounds.

Gracia implies that Latinos do *not* deserve reparations in the form of affirmative action because "not all, or even most, Hispanics have suffered discrimination." Of course, this is an empirical claim, and it is crucial that it enjoy sufficient support by way of empirical evidence if we are to accept it as being true. Surely the majority of us Latinos (as well as numerous

5. Ibid., p. 209.

6. Gracia makes room for this reason for affirmative action. Other philosophers have sought to ground affirmative action in matters of distributive justice. See, e.g., Nagel, "Equal Treatment and Compensatory Discrimination."

others) *believe* that we as a people, or cluster of peoples, have experienced and continue to experience significant ethnic discrimination here in the United States. Perhaps this serves as prima facie evidence of anti-Latino discrimination. If so, then we need reasons why most of us are indeed *not* discriminated against in order to defeat the considered judgments of those millions of us who believe that we *are* in some significant measure treated poorly. Nonetheless, this prima facie evidence of in-group members' widespread perception of anti-Latino racism in the United States is insufficient to defeat the claim that Latinos as a whole have been and are discriminated against so as to warrant their being recipients of affirmative action programs based on reparative justice considerations.

But if the experimental social cognitive psychology of racism (as discussed in chapter 4) is reasonably accurate, then racism is much more widespread than most people think it is. Indeed, ethnic prejudice is virtually universal in scope, and discrimination is much more universal in practice than most understand it to be. As argued in chapter 4, there are a variety of kinds, motivations, and bases of racism, and racism need not be limited to specific ethnic groups. Moreover, a target of racism need not know or believe she is a victim of racism in order to be its victim. The nature and functions of racism make it inductively plausible to believe that most, if not all, Latinos *have* suffered some significant form of ethnic discrimination in the United States, whether or not they are conscious of the discrimination.

Gracia argues that it is "very difficult to demonstrate" that most of us Latinos are discriminated against "*because*" we are Latinos. In reply to this point, it might be argued that whether or not Latinos *deserve* either affirmative action or reparations is not contingent on the difficulty of *proving* that we have been discriminated against *because* we are Latinos. Rather, it is contingent on nothing other than whether we *have in fact* been discriminated against because we are Latinos. For they can indeed deserve what a court of law finds itself unable to award in damages, given certain rules of evidence and due process. Yet this would hardly demonstrate that Latinos do not *deserve* such benefits or awards.

But even if it is a condition of Latinos deserving affirmative action or reparations that it be *shown* that Latinos are discriminated against *because* they are Latinos, then, it might be argued, this criterion might count against *any* ethnic group's receiving affirmative action benefits. For it is often, if not always, just as difficult (especially in a court of law) to show that, for example, African Americans are discriminated against *because* they are African Americans. Yet would we deny that at least most African Americans have been (and continue to be) targets and victims of racism?

Nonetheless, the history of Latinos in the United States is transparent on the matter of anti-Latino discrimination, whether it concerns the discriminatory practices against us in the U.S. military; the social relations that lead to the 1940s zoot suit riots in Los Angeles, California; and current and longstanding negative attitudes of European Americans toward us, especially concerning "border issues." Whether in the form of ethnocentric-based anti-Latino cultural imperialism or institutional or noninstitutional racism, evidence that we are discriminated against *because* we have been and are Latinos is plain. Anti-Latino racism is in principle no more difficult to demonstrate than it is to show that certain other ethnic groups have been discriminated against *because* of what they are, ethnically speaking. And this fact holds despite the unforgivable levels and kinds of harms committed against Native and African Americans, respectively, in and by the U.S. government and numerous of its citizens, making racism against these groups even more easily identifiable than that of anti-Latino racism. Thus not only have a majority of Latinos been discriminated against, we have been discriminated against *because* we are Latinos. Throughout the history of the United States, anti-Latino attitudes have often given rise to anti-Latino discrimination based on such attitudes.

Furthermore, simply because Latinos have not been treated as harshly as Native and African Americans have been treated in no way means that Latinos are not deserving of affirmative action for backward-looking reasons. For there are degrees of racist harm inflicted on us Latinos (as with other ethnic groups) and corresponding degrees of affirmative action that might be awarded by legislative policy. For instance, while a court might award, upon due consideration of the facts of each case, Native and African Americans rather substantial amounts of reparations[7] and forms of affirmative action, it might award to Latinos considerably lesser forms of affirmative action. Latinos most certainly *have* been treated unjustly in U.S. society when it comes to basic human rights, including educational rights and rights to human dignity.[8]

Even if it is true that Latinos have been and are discriminated against because we are Latinos, is it true that "the degree of discrimination and abuse some have suffered never reached the levels suffered by African Americans or women"? It is obvious that in the United States African Americans have

---

7. For a philosophical discussion of this problem, see J. Angelo Corlett, *Responsibility and Punishment* (Dordrecht: Kluwer Academic Publishers, 2001), chapter 9. Also see chapters 8–9 of this book.

8. Rudolf Acuña, *Occupied America,* 3d ed. (New York: Harper Collins, 1988); T. Almaguer, "Historical Notes on Chicano Oppression," *Aztlan* (1974); James Diego Vigil, *From Indians to Chicanos* (Prospect Heights: Waveland Press, 1980), pp. 173–84.

suffered significantly more than Latinos. But is it true that anti-Latino discrimination has "never" reached the levels of discrimination against *women?*

Gracia intimates that Latinos (presumably, on average and as a group) have not been treated as poorly as women (on average and as a group) in the United States. In reply to this position, it might be argued that although *women (and men) of color*[9] have been treated rather poorly in the United States, even by American women such as Susan B. Anthony and Louisa May Alcott,[10] it is false to claim or imply that American women were, on average and as a group, treated more poorly than Latinos. If women have played a secondary role in U.S. society, then Latinos have played an even *more* secondary role. For European American women in the United States were, and remain, among our more ardent oppressors! Many such women (as a class) were, and remain, members of a ruling class of European Americans that serves as an incessant source of racism.[11] It seems naive for one to think that such racism among European Americans would not extend in significant measure to us Latinos. Basic everyday practices confirm this point. It is true that many European American women were and are raped and otherwise abused by men. But then again, so were and are many Latinas! It is true that many European American women do not receive a fair wage for their labor, but this is even truer of Latinos (especially Latinas!) as a group! It is true that in general European American women are disrespected in U.S. society, *though in some ways they are placed on pedestals when it comes to standards of physical beauty.* But the dominant society has never thought that *brown* is beautiful, unless, of course, the brown person in question has various European American physical features that make her "acceptable" to European American eyes. Although European American women suffer from psychological issues regarding their physical selves, this is typically based on the shapes of their bodies. But Latinas suffer this and even more. For they suffer not only the issues regarding their being judged according to the physical shapes of their bodies, but they suffer also from perceptions of themselves and others regarding the *color* of their bodies (as well as various morphological characteristics Latinos typically have in contrast to most European Americans)! This is a kind and degree of discrimination that European American women have not experienced in U.S. society. In fact, this latter kind of suffering is experienced

9. Mary Romero, *Maid in the U.S.A.* (London: Routledge, 1992).

10. Angela Y. Davis, *Women, Race, and Class* (New York: Random House, 1981), chapters 3–4, 7, and 9.

11. bell hooks, *Ain't I a Woman: Black Women in Feminism* (Boston: South End Press, 1981); *Talking Back: Thinking Feminist, Thinking Black* (Boston: South End Press, 1989); *Yearning: Race, Gender, and Cultural Politics* (Boston: South End Press, 1990).

by Latinos as well. It goes without saying that perception of skin color is one way in which we as cognizers tend to categorize one another, and sometimes for racist purposes. European American women hardly suffered from sexism to the extent that we Latinos suffered the harms of racism and sexism. To suggest otherwise would do violence to a reading of U.S. history.

Moreover, and for the most part, European American women participated in a system of racial segregation in the United States that prohibited Latinos from living in "white only" neighborhoods, thereby effecting school segregation, which in turn meant that Latino children were not accorded an equal opportunity in education. In light of this, the claim that the discrimination and abuse *some* Latinos have suffered "never" reached the levels experienced by women becomes a profoundly surprising assertion. For if the right to vote in a relatively democratic society counts as a significant possession, we must bear in mind that European American women were guaranteed by the Nineteenth Amendment to the U.S. Constitution (1920) the right to vote. Yet it was almost half a century later that Latinos and other people of color in the U.S. were actually permitted to vote, subsequent to generations of harshly imposed segregation laws and mores throughout the land. Thus European American women enjoyed a significant democratic right to vote much more than did Latinos. European American women could in principle and often in reality attend any school they could afford to attend far sooner than Latinos could, whereas segregation and racist mores kept Latinos out of European American schools until (even) *after* the passage of the Civil Rights Act. The fact that relatively few European American women stood up for Latino rights is significant evidence that European American women as a whole were content, like the rather bad Samaritans they were, to sit alongside their European American male counterparts in even some of the higher seats of power that effected anti-Latino discrimination. Not only, then, is it false to claim or imply that the degree of discrimination and abuse some of us Latinos have suffered "never" reached the levels suffered by women, but European American women themselves were perpetrators of much of the anti-Latino racism!

Thus the argument for Latino affirmative action because of historic injustices toward them is significantly stronger than some would admit. For anti-Latino racism in the United States was and is sufficiently significant and harmful to Latinos that backward-looking reasons would ground claims to affirmative action for Latinos based on (not only distributive justice, but) corrective justice.

After reviewing some of the defining features of Latinohood, I discussed the moral status of affirmative action programs for Latinos residing in the

United States. Not only do we have a workable notion of Latinohood for purposes of public policy, but there is good reason to think that Latinos deserve affirmative action based on backward-looking reasons.

Now let us consider how what has been argued about Latinos might be generalized to other ethnic groups. What is the nature of ethnicity, and how might public policies such as affirmative action programs be administered in a fair manner so as to delimit or even eliminate arbitrariness in the categorization of persons into ethnic groups?

7

Ethnic Identity and Public Policy

Must the same stereotypes and categories that underlie racism serve as the grounds by which we enact public policies, say, concerning affirmative action? If so, is this a good thing? If not, then how ought we to categorize ourselves, if at all, in order to avoid racist categorizations? And how might programs of affirmative action be justified if implementation of them requires (in order to avoid moral arbitrariness in ethnic classification) proper classification of persons into ethnic groups? Assumed throughout this chapter is the idea that such governmental policies are either morally justified or required, or both. Of course, this assumption requires special defense if it turns out that ethnic categorization is overly problematic.

Having in the previous chapter discussed the plausibility of affirmative action programs for Latinos in light of the genealogical conception of Latino identity, I shall now extend my previous analysis to cases of affirmative action concerning certain ethnic groups more generally. Assuming that affirmative action is itself morally justified (whether or not various existing such programs falling under this category are justified) or even required, what might the genealogical conception of Latino identity imply about who ought to qualify as a member of this or that ethnic group? And what sort of analysis of ethnic group membership is needed in order to best ensure against (or minimize) moral arbitrariness in the implementation of such public policies?

Ethnic Identity and Ethnic Complexity

Most concur that there is one human race, if, that is, it makes sense to speak of a race at all. However, as mentioned in chapter 3, much confusion has arisen in discussions of the concept of race partly because such discussions often simultaneously and perhaps unwittingly proceed along two lines. There are discussions of the *metaphysics of race*[1] wherein racial realists affirm the existence of more than one human race (traditionally, Negroid, Causasoid, and Mongoloid "races"),[2] while racial antirealists deny this division. But the concept of the plurality of races also proceeds along ethical lines where moral evaluations of the employment of racial categories are prevalent. In discussions of the *ethics of race*, racial realists argue not only that races exist, but that we ought to recognize the differences between races. Racial antirealists, on the other hand, argue that the concept of race is groundless and ought to be abandoned in favor of some other way by which to make sense of ourselves in the world, because the concept of races has all too often led many people to engage in rampant racial discrimination against others, often with horrendously evil results. Without the concept of races, those proponents argue, we stand a significantly better chance of ridding the world of racism.[3]

In chapter 1, I argued that the concept of race as identifying different categories of humans recognizable by way of morphological and other genetically transmitted traits such as skin color is problematic.[4] But even if such primitive race theories are problematic, it may nonetheless be helpful to identify humans as belonging to various groups, say, for reasons of public policy administration (See chapters 2–3, 6).[5] This is vital to a just society, or one seeking to become just, because it is the primary function of the state to do justice to and for individuals. And insofar as individuals belong to ethnic groups in a pluralistic society, the state's duty, among other things, is to protect the rights of such groups, and this includes the right to be properly compensated for, say, racist harms against members of the wronged groups, "as long as we realize that we are talking about historical oppressions based on what race was falsely thought to be."[6] I shall argue that, though metaphysical conceptions of race are problematic, both the history of racism and

1. Charles Mills, *Blackness Visible* (Ithaca: Cornell University Press, 1998), chapter 3.

2. What Naomi Zack refers to as the "Old Paradigm of Race" would fit this description, and philosophers such as Immanuel Kant and David Hume would be among its proponents [Naomi Zack, "Philosophy and Racial Paradigms," *Journal of Value Inquiry* 33 (1999): 299–308].

3. Naomi Zack, *Race and Mixed Race* (Philadelphia: Temple University Press, 1993); Naomi Zack, ed., *Race/Sex* (London: Routledge, 1996), chapter 2; Naomi Zack, *Thinking About Race* (Belmont, Calif.: Wadsworth, 1998), chapters 1–3.

4. Anthony Appiah and Amy Gutmann, *Color Conscious* (Princeton: Princeton University Press, 1996), p. 32; Zack, *Race and Mixed Race; Thinking About Race.*

5. See Zack, "Philosophy and Racial Paradigms," p. 307: "Logically, the implementation of equal protection under the law depends on prior identification based on race."

6. Ibid., p. 314.

retributive justice taken seriously demand that humans be categorized, not as natural kinds, but in terms of (largely) socially defined ethnic groups based (somewhat) essentially on genealogical factors. As Naomi Zack argues,

> Given the lack of evidence for biological race and the racisms that have been perpetrated using biological race as an excuse, care should be taken with liberatory identities so that they do not continue to reproduce false deterministic taxonomies of biological race. One way in which this can be done is through a reconfiguration of race as ethnicity, because ethnicity is known to be cultural. Another way is to reconstruct race as family heredity only, because human families do transmit biological traits and much of the false taxonomy of race has supervened on existent human genealogy.[7]

In chapters 2 and 3, I articulated and defended an analysis of Latino identity that is congruent with the idea that, though there is one human "race," there are various ethnicities. Furthermore, ethnicity admits of degrees, and mixed ethnicity is more the rule in human experience rather than the exception to the rule. Thus I concur with Zack that construing humans in terms of ethnic groups to which each of us belongs is more fruitful than accepting the problematic notion of races. Moreover, I agree with her that a genealogical conception of ethnicity is crucial for a proper understanding of sameness within and difference between groups.

The Importance of Ethnic Identification

But I would reason even further than Zack does in this direction. Although Zack argues that respect for the Fourteenth Amendment to the United States Constitution implies that there is some plausible manner by which to categorize people into groups deserving of equal protection, she mostly refers to affirmative action and other kinds of programs of distributive justice along these lines.

However much I might concur with Zack's points just mentioned, I would add that corrective and compensatory justice sometimes require the plausible identification/classification of ethnic group membership. More specifically, without a genealogical conception of ethnicity grounding our conceptions of identity, governments and courts would appear to have no means by which to accurately and fairly award damages to those who have been victimized by racist aggression or discrimination. For there would seem to be no viable basis on which to base the awarding of damages in

7. Ibid., p. 314.

that we would not have a nonarbitrary way of doing so. Thus while I am a racial antirealist concerning the metaphysics of race, I am a racial realist regarding the ethics of race, so long as it is understood that the concept of races is supplanted by one of ethnicities. That there is only one race and that the notion of races ought to be replaced with the categories of ethnicities is consistent with the following claim: "That race *should* be irrelevant is certainly an attractive ideal, but when it has *not* been irrelevant, it is absurd to proceed as if it had been."[8] This perspective on race and ethnicity casts doubt on the plausibility of "color-blind" conceptions of them. For if color-blind views are taken seriously, then we ought not to see one another in terms of race or ethnicity, but in terms of the "humanness of the other." However admirable the spirit of this position on ethnicity, it does little to enable governments to carry out justice in cases of racist oppression and discrimination. For it provides governments no way by which to identify members of those wronged by racism for the primary purpose of awarding to them damages *via* compensatory justice.

Those who have raised problems for conceptions of races have generally argued that there seems to be no set of necessary and sufficient conditions, or no essence, to those who would qualify as falling under racial categories. Although it is clear that humans fall under one race, it is not obvious that all, say, Causasoids share this or that trait in common, or that all Negroids or Mongoloids do. Of course, this also means that members of various "racial groups" do *not* have distinctive traits.[9] Genetically speaking, this claim is supported by the recent breakthrough in human genome research. As a metaphysical position, this critique of "primitive race theories"[10] seems rather plausible. But it fails to provide a rationale or grounding for the implementation of policies that would target members of certain ethnic groups in light of previous or current wrongs done to them. This difficulty was apparent in the nineteenth century, when several European Americans attempted to marry into Native American nations in order to receive the meager subsidies given, not altogether consistently, by the U.S. government to Native Americans. One policy that was adopted in many cases was to assign the status of Native Americans to those who were at least one-eighth Native American, a proportion that was decided solely on genealogical considerations. She who was not at least one-eighth Native

8. Mills, *Blackness Visible*, p. 41.

9. See chapter 2 of this book; Appiah and Gutmann, *Color Conscious;* Mills, *Blackness Visible;* and Zack, "Philosophy and Racial Paradigms." Even though primitive race theories are implausible, it is helpful to understand them insofar as we are interested in grasping the bases of racism.

10. See chapter 1 of this book for the introduction of this term.

American did not qualify for such programs. So a genealogical conception of ethnicity can in a reasonably successful manner ground U.S. public policy in the interest of justice.[11]

But the typical critiques of primitive race theories end up leaving no rational manner by which to identify us as members of this or that (or more than one) ethnic group for purposes of public policy administration. Having inadequate rational grounds according to which policies might be enacted serves the interests of capriciousness and arbitrariness. Justice requires that we search for legitimate ways to base such means of combating current racism and correcting past racist harms. Adequate and nonracist ethnic categorization, then, is important because it enables governments and courts to effect compensatory justice to the victims of racism. That governments and individuals have used racial categorizations in the past to oppress or otherwise harm members of various ethnic groups in no way dictates that ethnic categorization must or ought to be used in such vicious ways now, or in the future. It simply does not logically follow that past abuses of racial classification will necessarily lead to such misuses of ethnic identities today.

Furthermore, ethnic identity is important because it enables us to relate to and connect with others who are like ourselves in both experience and circumstance. Of "cultural groups" (including ethnic groups), Michael Walzer writes: "Individuals are stronger, more confident, more savvy, when they are participants in a common life, when they are responsible to and for other people. . . . For it is only in the context of associational activity that individuals learn to deliberate, argue, make decisions, and take responsibility."[12] Many of us Latinos, for instance, find it comforting to see and befriend others like ourselves (but not only those like ourselves, of course), especially in light of the long-standing and pervasive forms of racism against us—even by many self-proclaiming do-gooder-type European Americans! Indeed, ethnicity can become, if it does not devolve into racism, a source of positive ethnic pride. This is especially the case to the extent that one can embrace in positive ways both one's own ethnic identities and those of others. This approach, I argue, will tend to promote the unity of humans while recognizing and respecting the general differences between us—culturally, morphologically, and linguistically. While the

11. Assumed here, of course, is that those who are one-eighth Native American merit justice in this sense. Moreover, by "one-eighth" is meant that, given their family tree, they are one-eighth of this or that ethnicity. In this case, the ethnicity is that of Native American, otherwise known as being a member of an indigenous nation of the Americas: Diné, Cherokee, Zuni, etc.

12. Michael Walzer, *On Toleration* (New Haven: Yale University Press, 1997), p. 104.

previous reason for the development of a viable conception of ethnicity concerns matters of compensatory justice for racist harms, this argument assumes that considerations of distributive justice, if they are legitimate, urge us to articulate a viable understanding of the nature of ethnic groups. This would include an analysis of the conditions under which it would be correct to say that a person belongs to this and/or that ethnic group. The analysis of ethnicity that follows is an extension of my genealogical conception of Latino identity articulated and defended in chapters 2 and 3.

A Genealogical Analysis of Ethnicity

John Rawls recently argues in favor of a "realistic utopia"[13] in which nations are modeled roughly along the lines of a reasonably just democratic regime that he spent the bulk of his philosophical career articulating and defending.[14] The promotion of self-respect and respect for others is important in a Rawlsian society, and there is good reason to suppose that he means to include respect for ethnic groups here. This is at least consistent with Rawls's concern for inclusiveness of such groups (religious, ethnic, political, and other groups) in a well-ordered society.[15] In light of Rawls's view, and in light of the claim that the cultivation of democracy must go hand in hand with the construction of ethnic identities, I proffer the following *ethical analysis of ethnic identity: A person belongs to an ethnic group to the extent that she has a significant genealogical tie to that group.* Important factors of ethnicity also include her respect for and command of some particular language (or dialects thereof) of her ethnic group; her bearing names that are commonly given to those in her ethnic group; her respect for and participation in the culture of her ethnic group; self-realization and identification of her membership in the group; recognition of her membership in the ethnic group by other in-group members, and recognition by out-group members of the ethnic group that she is a member of the ethnic group. Although these secondary characteristics are important for determining, *for purposes of public policy administration,* the degree to which one is a member of his or her ethnic group(s), *what is necessary and sufficient for ethnic group membership is the extent to which he or she is genealogically tied to that group.*

13. John Rawls, *The Law of Peoples* (Cambridge: Harvard University Press, 1999).

14. John Rawls, *A Theory of Justice* (Cambridge: Harvard University Press, 1971); *Political Liberalism* (New York: Columbia University Press, 1993); *Collected Papers,* Samuel Freeman, ed. (Cambridge: Harvard University Press, 1999); *The Law of Peoples; Justice as Fairness: A Restatement* (Cambridge: Harvard University Press, 2001).

15. Rawls, *Political Liberalism.*

Assumed here is the fact of mixed ethnicity (what some refer to as "mixed race"); most, if not all, persons belong to more than one ethnic group. Thus my ethnicity is really a matter of my belonging to a plurality of ethnic groups, even though I might say, for purposes of polling or census information, that I am, for instance, (predominantly) a Latino.[16] Here I might realize and respect the fact that I am also, say, to some degrees, a Native American and/or a European American of some sort or another. But for various reasons, not the least of which is ease of discourse, I might simply declare or affirm that I am a Latino because that is what I am predominantly: genealogically, and perhaps, as the case may be, in some of the other (secondary) ways mentioned. This implies that *ethnicity is a matter of complexity of kinds and of degree.* Thus if my genealogy is such that I am one-half Latino, one-fourth Native American, and one-fourth African American, then I am predominantly a Latino, though I am also a Native American and an African American. Self-respect and respect for others would suggest that I respect each aspect of my overall ethnicity and the overall ethnicities of others. But even though public policy considerations require that genealogy play the fundamental role of defining our ethnicity, ethnicity in a metaphysical sense involves more than genealogy, or something quite different altogether. Concerning the ethics of ethnicity, however, the extent to which I respect and have a command of the languages and dialects of my ethnic group(s) will determine the *depth* of which I am a member of my ethnic group(s). Moreover, the extent to which my names reflect customary names of those in my ethnic group(s) will in some way reflect the extent of my membership in the group(s). And similar things might be said of my respect for and participation in the culture of my ethnic group(s).

But as argued in chapter 2, Latino identity (and I now wish to argue that more generally, ethnic identity) involves more than the aforementioned traits of genealogy, language competence, possession of names germane to my ethnic group(s), and participation in the culture. It involves self-identification as a member of the group(s), in-group identification of me as a member of the group(s), and out-group identification of me as a member of the group(s). But again, *for purposes of public policy administration, genealogy alone is necessary and sufficient for ethnic identity.* These conditions of self, in-group, and out-group identification, like the others (other than genealogy), are not ones that make one a member of this or that ethnic group(s). They do, however, determine the *extent* to which one is a member of the group(s), metaphysically speaking.

16. This assumes, among other things, that one is asked to choose, in self-identification, only one ethnic group for membership status.

To review briefly some points made in chapters 2–3 concerning the genealogical conception of Latino identity, what I shall call the "genealogical conception of ethnic identity" holds that the proposed conditions other than genealogy are neither necessary nor sufficient for ethnic identity when it comes to public policy considerations. The same reasoning that demonstrates that one's having a command of some Latino language or dialect is neither necessary nor sufficient for Latino identity can be generalized to show that one's having a command of the language(s) or dialect(s) of an ethnic group is neither necessary nor sufficient for membership in that group. The same reasoning that demonstrates that one's having a name traditionally given to members of some Latino group is neither necessary nor sufficient for Latino identity can be generalized to show that one's having some name traditionally given to members of an ethnic group is neither necessary nor sufficient for membership in that group. Moreover, the same argumentation marshaled to show that good faith participation in a Latino culture is neither necessary nor sufficient for Latino identity can be garnered to demonstrate that cultural participation is neither necessary nor sufficient for ethnic identity more generally. The same can be argued for ethnic self-identification, in-group recognition of ethnic identities, and out-group recognition of the same.

It is important to note that this analysis of the nature of ethnic group membership need not and should not "racialize" the nature of ethnicity, making ethnic categories much like traditionally racial ones: natural kinds or racial essences. Rather, ethnic group membership is significantly a matter of social construction. This is a metaphysical fact about race and ethnicity. However, this metaphysical fact must not serve as a barrier to our using carefully the socially constructed ethnic categories in attempting to correct ethnic injustice or racist harms. Thus there is no conceptual inconsistency in my being a racial antirealist concerning the metaphysics of race and my being a racial realist regarding the ethics of race, so long as it is understood that primitive race theories are supplanted by a viable conception of ethnicities. Again, *only ethnic genealogical ties are necessary and sufficient for ethnic group membership insofar as public policy administration is concerned.* The other conditions are relevant and important for determining the level or depth or extent to which one is a member of this or that ethnic group beyond considerations of public policy.

For those who would argue that knowledge of or respect for languages or dialects of ones ethnic group(s), the having of names traditionally associated with names of members of the ethnic group(s) to which one belongs, participation in and respect for the cultural aspects of ones ethnic group(s), self-identification with ones ethnic group(s), in-group ethnic identification, and/or out-group ethnic identification ought to be included in a public policy-based analysis of ethnicity, it bears noting that there are various difficulties facing such a view. First, how much knowledge and use of the languages or dialects used by members of one's ethnic group(s) is necessary and/or sufficient for group membership? Is a reading competence sufficient? Or is fluency in speaking also requisite? And what of those who would argue that certain ways of pronouncing, say, Spanish are more genuine than others? Second, how many and exactly what sorts of names are necessary and/or sufficient? Are names such as "Juan" more acceptable than those of "Chucho"? Third, how participatory in a Latino culture and how much respect for it is necessary and/or sufficient? Need I as a Latino respect cock fighting or bull fighting in order to be a "real" Latino? Must I prefer certain foods? If so, how much must I prefer them? And which ones ought I to prefer? Fourth, if I immerse myself in, say, Latino culture yet have no genealogical tie to it, what exactly counts as necessary and/or sufficient for Latinohood? Listening to what kinds of music and for what length of time? Speaking with a Latino accent? How much Latin foods must I eat and enjoy in order to become a Latino under such a view? Indeed, this view seems to make ethnicity more of an exercise in ethnic stereotyping in adopting whatever identity one is drawn to in the moment or from year to year than a matter of pride in one's heritage. Fifth, how many in-group members' acceptance are necessary and/or sufficient to make one a member of the group, and to what extent ought the acceptance to accrue? What counts as acceptance, exactly, in such circumstances? Finally, to what extent do out-group members have to identify one as being a member of a particular ethnic group in order for ethnic group membership to obtain?[17] What exactly counts as ethnic identification in such cases? How long does such out-group identification need to occur? As we can begin to see, then, the six conditions mentioned here can hardly serve as being necessary and/or sufficient for ethnicity, especially when it comes to considerations of public policy.

Ethically speaking, what is both necessary and sufficient for ethnic identity is the degree to which I have a genealogical tie to a particular group. Additionally, the features of language, culture, surname, in-group, out-group, and self-ethnic identification might each serve as secondary but important means by which to further determine the degrees to which I

17. It bears noting that many well-intentioned but racist European American leftists do not consider a person to belong to a particular ethnic group if that person does not speak the language(s) or dialect(s) of that group, and/or appear physically to be a member of the group, etc. Current affirmative action hiring is often predicated on such leftist racist stereotyping in the name of honoring and promoting "diversity."

belong to this or that ethnic group, for purposes *other than* those of public policy administration. I assume that most, if not all, persons are of mixed ethnicity, and that purity along these lines is unlikely, if not a myth. Again, that ethnicities are not fully traceable to their origins, though indeed a problem for the metaphysics of race, is not as much of a problem for the ethics of ethnicity. For what is needed for purposes of public policy administration is the ability to trace with reasonable accuracy a few generations or so of the genealogical history of existing ethnic groups targeted for affirmative action or reparations.

Ethnic Identity and Public Policy Administration

What implications might this new conception of ethnicity have for public policy administration? It implies that we must begin to construe ethnic identity in more complex terms than even the U.S. Census Bureau has begun to, and in more than one way. First, we must begin to understand that each of us belongs to more than one ethnic group, and that it is a mistake of sometimes racist proportions to identify oneself or another solely as a member of a particular group. Several people engage in a kind of "racial pride" wherein their focus on their own ethnicity blinds them to certain objective realities.[18] We ought to respect our own complex ethnicities, and this is likely to lead to a greater respect for the widening array of ethnicities worldwide. For if I know that I am, say, a Latino (of a particular "mix"), an African American (of a particular "mix"), and an Asian (of a particular "mix"), then I am more likely to respect these clusters of ethnic groups if I respect them *as my own*. Of course, I ought not to simply respect them as my own. For this might preclude a good reason to respect ethnicities to which I do not belong. But it is one step in the direction of mutual respect between ethnic groups.

Second, we must begin to see that it is an error to lump together several groups into one set of "disadvantaged" or "minority" ones just as it is an

18. Although numerous examples exist, one which stands out in a particularly conspicuous manner is the claim (or assumption) of the originality of "the Holocaust," where this event is said to refer exclusively to the European Jewish experience of oppression in Nazi Germany (A. Margalit and G. Motzkin, "The Uniqueness of the Holocaust," *Philosophy & Public Affairs* 25 [1996]: 65–83). What makes the article an example of blind racist "pride" or focus is that it is arguable that the *American* Holocaust of *Native Americans* satisfies each of the criteria of alleged uniqueness of the Nazi Holocaust, yet the authors in no way even mention the American Holocaust of Native Americans! The very fact that the authors refer to the Nazi holocaust of certain Jews as "the Holocaust" seems to reveal a rather ignorant kind of racist "pride" masquerading as philosophical analysis and scholarship.

error to not recognize other groups subsumed under the categories we often use in shorthand: Asians, Latinos, African Americans, and others. For the experiences of each group are different, whether racist or sexist (or both), and the extent to which members of each group have experienced harm from racism and sexism varies widely. Moreover, each of these groups has been victimized in the United States—not only by the ruling majority ethnic classes—but by members of other "disadvantaged" or "minority" groups. Once again, and generally speaking, European American women have served as a constant source of racist harm to folk of color, and Jewish people have often engaged in racism against certain people of color, and we Latinos have often been a source of racism against African Americans in particular, and this is only an abbreviated listing. This is unsurprising when one considers the universality of racism, as discussed in chapter 4.

Each of these factors seems to suggest that any public policy of compensatory or distributive justice ought to become and remain sensitive to variant levels and kinds of programs and benefits of affirmative action, each targeting a different ethnic group that has, on average, experienced significant harm due to racism and/or sexism. For example, Native and African Americans are deserving of significantly and greater kinds and degrees of compensatory justice than any other groups in U.S. history based on the racist oppression against them continually (even today!) by the U.S. government and its citizenry,[19] as a fair-minded reading of U.S. history reveals. That same reading of U.S. history is likely to clarify that certain other ethnic groups have experienced greater racist and/or sexist discrimination than certain others. Although European American women have for generations been prohibited from full participation in U.S. society, their complicity in the racism against people of color condemns them as racist oppressors (to some meaningful extent). And it would be an unjust public policy indeed that would award European American women anything akin to what it awards to, say, Latinos and certain other ethnic groups of color. It would be even more unjust for public policies to award compensation to Latinos or European American women in anything akin to what such policies award to Native and African Americans.

U.S. affirmative action policies and programs were developed for the most part by many well-intentioned European Americans, and by some well-meaning people of color. But by not seeing the complexities of ethnicity,

---

19. Bernard Boxill, *Blacks and Social Justice* (Totowa, N.J.: Rowman & Littlefield, 1984); J. Angelo Corlett, *Responsibility and Punishment* (Dordrecht: Kluwer, 2001), chapter 9; Howard McGary, *Race and Social Justice* (London: Blackwell, 1999).

racism, and sexism, such policies lacked the specificity necessary to guide programs of affirmative action in ways that would be immune from charges of unfairness. Such specificity would include a working principle that would ground affirmative action benefits on what members of racially oppressed groups *deserved* in light of the *amount* of racist harms experienced in U.S. society, all things considered. And a fair-minded study of U.S. history reveals that European American women deserved far fewer benefits from affirmative action programs than did at least a few ethnic groups in U.S. society. So even those programs that were designed to level the playing field of opportunities in U.S. society against racial discrimination had the effect of improving the plight of European American women undeservedly over various folk of color. The fact that European American women rarely, if ever, challenged such programs along the lines mentioned here condemns them (in general) on moral grounds of egoistic self-interest. But that is quite congruent with what some of the leaders of the women's suffrage movement held all along. Recall from chapter 4 that it was Elizabeth Cady Stanton who, in her 26 December 1865 letter to the *New York Standard*, wrote: "It becomes a serious question whether we had better stand aside and see 'Sambo' walk into the kingdom first. . . . In fact, it is better to be the slave of an educated white man, than of a degraded, ignorant black one."[20] What European American women knew about being slaves is highly dubious, and for a European American woman to speak of herself as even possibly being a slave to another in the face of African American slavery is perhaps a form of racist insensitivity or insult (or perhaps even massive ignorance beyond comprehension). But what is clear here is that even the leadership of the European American women's movement in the United States was thoroughly racist (though significantly less racist than, say, the typical member of the KKK) and can hardly be reasonably counted among those who are *oppressed* in ways any where akin to the ways in which many folk of color have been racially oppressed. And if the (relatively enlightened) leadership of the European American suffrage movement was racist, then one can only imagine what the rank-and-file supporters were like.[21] It is an open question precisely how racist the contemporary women's movements are in the United States. But the consistent lack of great numbers of people of color in their ranks tends to suggest that some degree of the long-standing European American feminist racism

20. Angela Y. Davis, *Women, Race and Class* (New York: Random House, 1981), p. 70.

21. This assumes that the leadership is somewhat more enlightened than typical rank and file members. Of course, it is important to bear in mind that racism admits of degrees, and that there are European American women who are significantly less racist than others, all things considered.

is still entrenched amongst many European American feminists—even some of those who purport to support means of justice for racist harms.

If there are to be policies and programs of affirmative action, they must reflect the histories and complexities of ethnicity and racism in a particular society such as the United States. Only then will there be any reasonable hope that concerns of justice will be addressed fairly, providing Native and African Americans with highest kinds and degrees of *compensation such as reparations and perhaps affirmative action programs,* on the one hand, and European American women with significantly lower kinds and degrees of *affirmative action benefits,* on the other. To do otherwise, as we have been doing for decades, is to not take seriously the facts of history and the complexities of ethnicity and racism in U.S. society. It is also inconsistent in that such policies and programs seek to benefit folk because of their ethnicities, yet each of the target groups is treated by the programs in "color blind" ways. Consistency (in terms of proportional harms suffered and rectified) requires that public policies and programs targeting groups victimized by racism (color consciousness) retain color consciousness in the implementation of such programs.

However, public policy must not permit the influx of recent *immigrants* of color to adversely effect the genuine purpose of affirmative action programs. If the aim of such programs is to counterbalance the racist and sexist discrimination in U.S. society, then only those groups that have been significantly harmed by such racism and sexism ought to qualify as targets of such public policy. Thus it is improper to lump together African and Native Americans, say, with recent immigrant Haitians or East Indians or the like for purposes of reparative justice, as the former groups (and several like them) were not a part of the systemic racist oppression in the United States. Ignoring this fact of history concerning ethnic relations in the United States does harm to those ethnic groups deserving of reparations and/or affirmative action programs because it depletes the resources allocated to such compensation and programs by the public policies, thereby cheating those most deserving of the benefits of the programs. In short, it violates principles of desert and proportionality concerning corrective justice, whether by reparations or affirmative action programs.

My analysis of ethnic identity better enables public policymakers to devise programs that target more precisely those ethnic groups most deserving of affirmative action programs. It would be a policy that sets up differential affirmative action opportunity programs. *Only reparative justice via compensation can in some significant measure begin to correct the wrongs done to Native and African Americans by the U.S. government.* As I have argued in the previous chapter, reparations and affirmative action are two totally separate matters. The latter is not a legitimate replacement of the former, as many seem to believe. However, such a policy by its very nature and magnitude cannot begin to address or serve as adequate compensation for wrongs done to, say, Native or African Americans, as an adequate policy of reparations can. Reparations are awarded, when they are awarded, to groups based on the extent of the harms suffered by a particular group at the hands of, say, the state. So there are degrees of reparations, based on a complex array of factors: harms suffered, the *mens rea* of perpetrators, and so forth. But to the extent that affirmative action programs are justified as means toward achieving justice in the face of past and current racist discrimination in U.S. society, such programs must begin to differentiate between the kinds and levels of benefits awarded to various groups: Native Americans, African Americans, Latinos, Asian Americans, and others.

If affirmative action programs are going to evade charges of morally arbitrary implementation, they not only require an analysis of the nature of ethnic group membership, but they also need to be sensitive to the varying degrees and levels of racist discrimination that have been and are experienced, on average, by members of various groups. One of our guiding principles here ought to be Aristotle's claim that like cases ought to be treated alike (and conversely, dissimilar cases ought to be treated dissimilarly). Once again, a fair-minded reading of U.S. history shows us that Native[22] and African Americans have by far experienced and continue to experience the worst sorts of racist oppression. Subsequent to or simultaneous with reparative compensation, affirmative action programs ought to reflect this in the kinds and amounts of benefits awarded to members of these groups. Perhaps Latino and Asian groups, or certain subgroups of each, ought to be construed as the next most deserving of affirmative action programs. Again, a fair-minded reading of U.S. history is essential here. Whatever the case, neither of these ethnic groups has any rightful claim to affirmative action benefits that would even remotely match the claims of Native or African Americans. After these ethnic groups are awarded their due amounts and kinds of affirmative action benefits, then perhaps European American women (women of color would presumably have already been included in one of the preceding groups) would deserve and ought to receive some amount of affirmative action. After all, in the midst of their complicity in the racist evil that oppressed Native and African Americans for generations, European American women were prohibited from voting and lacked certain other employment and educational opportunities.

---

22. Included in the ethnic category of Native Americans are Native Hawaiians as well as the dozens of Native American nations on the continent, now known as the U.S. mainland.

Of course, all of this and much more was withheld, and much more violently, from Native and African Americans, as any fair-minded study of history will point out. And the same can be said, but to a significantly lesser
extent, regarding Latino and Asian Americans. So European American
women would be deserving of perhaps the lowest levels and kinds of affirmative action compared to the other groups mentioned. Of course, certain other ethnic groups need to be placed on the list of qualifiers of those
that are deserving of affirmative action benefits based on the harms they
have experienced in the U.S. And a fair-minded study of U.S. history must
become and remain the government's guide in making these determinations insofar as the administration of public policy is concerned.

This might mean that, for instance, qualified European American
women might be hired by way of affirmative action provisions *only subsequent* to the hiring of qualified Native Americans, African Americans, Latinos, Asian Americans, and other seriously wronged groups according to
their respective harms, considered proportionally. And where there is no
qualified person from such groups, then there is to be a moratorium on
hiring for European Americans unless it can be shown that there is simply
an inadequate supply of targeted group members (because of lack of interest, say) in a particular field of employment or career area. Although
this is a radical proposal, it is far better than the status quo that continues
to benefit the least deserving groups targeted by affirmative action programs far greater than it benefits much more deserving groups, based on
kinds and duration of harms experienced by such groups. While this proposal might not be as well implemented in some areas that seem to be perceived least desirable by folk of color, generally speaking, there seems to
be no such supply problem for the suggested demand in the vastly more
popular (and lucrative!) areas of business, law, and medicine, to name a
few. Thus while my suggested differentialist policy of affirmative action in
hiring might not work well in some areas of comparatively low interest (currently, and in some cases, historically) of folk of color, it seems to be a step
in the right direction in attempting to turn the tide of a grossly unjust situation.

More specifically, my differentialist strategy of affirmative action in hiring would, until the noted problem is adequately resolved, treat European
American women as it would treat European American men (with the
proviso that should the noted problem be resolved, European American
women would be reinstated as justified beneficiaries of affirmative action
hiring). Moreover, based on the duration, degrees and kinds of racist/sex-
ist oppression experienced by Native Americans in U.S. society over the
centuries, Native American women would enjoy the category of most
highly ranked in this program because they have not only experienced the

evils of racist oppression as did Native American men, but the evils of sexism also. Native American men would constitute the second most highly ranked group targeted for affirmative action programs of hiring. African American women would rank third, and African American men fourth for similar reasons of racism and sexism experienced by the former, and racism experienced by the latter. Furthermore, as noted earlier, this proposed program in no way serves as a substitute for the reparations that might be deserved by each of these groups, as explored in the following chapters. Long after these groups on the differentialist list would rank certain other ethnic groups, perhaps Latinos, Asian Americans of various groups, and some others. And in each case, as with Native and African Americans, the groups are to be categorized dualistically by gender because of the ranked group targeted for affirmative action programs of hiring. In every case, a fair reading of U.S. history is crucial to our understanding of which groups deserve what level(s) of affirmative action benefits.

Because of the substantial amounts of reparative compensation and affirmative action benefits, it might be advisable to make the membership in ethnic groups at least 25 percent of one's genealogy. Perhaps a figure of 33 percent to 50 percent is preferable for public policy purposes. But I see no clear way of arbitrating disputes along these lines. Perhaps the pool of funding for such programs ought to dictate, to some degree, the "affordable" percentages of what the government can pay in affirmative action programs. But the concern with such a suggestion is that a racist government would then use its "inability" to pay as an excuse to overly tighten restrictions on ethnic group membership.

The point here is not to suggest that the calculation of public policy programs designed to better the lots of various ethnic groups amounts to an exact science. Surely it does not.[23] However, governments not only require some rational and reasonable method by which to identify members of ethnic groups so that they can identify those who deserve benefits, but they need to nonarbitrarily award such benefits so that those whose ancestors actually assisted in the racist oppression of various ethnic groups, for example, European American women, do not end up benefiting more than other groups that deserve more compensation by well-intentioned but wrongheaded public policy. This follows from the moral/legal principle that a person ought not to benefit from her own wrongdoing.[24] An historical and

23. For to a large extent, determinations of ethnic genealogy are grounded in self-identification, which is not altogether reliable. Yet this difficulty seems to plague alternative theories of ethnic/racial identity also. Thus it serves as no uniquely decisive objection to my analysis.

24. This principle can be found in the early writings of Ronald Dworkin, for example, Ronald Dworkin, *Taking Rights Seriously* (Cambridge: Harvard University Press, 1978).

harm-based approach to public policy would, in cases of affirmative action programs, refine our thinking about who we are so that we construe ourselves as complex ethnic identities, thereby increasing the odds that we would respect ethnic groups to which we do not see ourselves as belonging currently, but it would award benefits to those most deserving of them, according to a principle of proportional racist (i.e., ethnicist) harm.

The time has arrived when we must cast aside the mantle of self-serving support of the well-intended programs of affirmative action that have to some extent, admittedly, improved socioeconomic power for some people of color in the United States. But much more could and should have been accomplished along these lines had it not been for policies and programs that unwarrantedly assisted European American women when it could have instead assisted many more deserving people of color. This is a qualitative and a quantitative claim. For if not for programs of affirmative action assisting European American women, those same benefits could and should have been used to provide much more deserved benefits for greater numbers of Native and African Americans, and in more profound and lasting ways.

Objections and Replies

It might be objected that the last statement, if taken seriously, would lead public policy about affirmative action programs to ignore the plights of European American women altogether in favor of their focusing on people of color or those more generally deserving of affirmative action. But this would be true only if we assume, as I do, that there is a limited pool of funding for such programs. And if there is, then the rational thing to do is to devise programs, consistent with Rawls's fair equality of opportunities principle,[25] for the most disadvantaged and deserving relative to racist and other forms of injustice. And it is difficult to imagine how anyone but Native and African Americans can make that claim in the United States. Certainly European American women, with their history of complicit racist oppression against people of color, are *not* in a moral position to claim any right to affirmative action, unless, that is, there is such a large pool of funding for such programs that there is funding left over, after all of the more deserving folk of color have received due support, for them.[26] So it is not

25. Rawls, *A Theory of Justice.* For a collection of critical reflections on Rawls's theory of justice, see J. Angelo Corlett, ed., *Equality and Liberty* (London: Macmillan, 1990).

26. And *subsequent* to *adequate reparations* to victims of racist oppression: Native and African Americans.

that European American women deserve nothing for their being discriminated against and for so long. It is that their claims to affirmative action benefits hardly "weigh in" heavily compared to the claims of various people of color based on the history of harms against them.

Affirmative action need not become otiose in U.S. society. As they stand, the policies supporting and defining affirmative action programs are vague and too imprecise to be continued. But I have provided a starting point for rethinking how affirmative action programs can and should be reworked so that both ethnic group membership is understood more clearly (for public policy purposes) and affirmative action benefits are awarded far less arbitrarily than they are currently awarded. This revision of affirmative action programs requires numerically large political groups such as European American women to support, in a non-self-serving way, a system that is far more just and fair than the programs currently implemented nationwide. It requires, in short, that European American women step aside and permit justice and fairness to run their proper courses in terms of their targeting in greater ways people of color. Where funding for such programs is always going to run short of what is needed, priorities must be established that target the most deserving. This requires, in turn, that European American women support what is *not* in their self-serving interests. It requires something that many European American feminists have advocated, but have inconsistently lived, for years: reasonable ethnic (racial) justice and fairness in a nonideal world. It is time for European American women to do much more of walking the challenging walk, rather than merely talking the cheap talk, of justice.

It might also be objected that my analysis of ethnic identity for purposes of public policy administration might well lead numerous individuals to not marry outside of their ethnic groups. For to do so would very well eventuate in offspring no longer receiving benefits of certain public policy programs. A Latino family might discourage its offspring from marrying non-Latinos so that those offspring would in the future not jeopardize their opportunity to receive affirmative action benefits. To marry outside the group might well threaten such opportunities, it might be believed. This kind of attitude might lead to or foster existing racist attitudes toward members of other ethnic groups. Thus, it might be argued, my analysis of ethnic identity unwittingly promotes the possibility of racist attitudes based on the fear of members of certain ethnic groups that their numbers (according to the analysis) might dwindle, and so will the opportunities for their children, and their children's children.

To ignore this concern would be a mistake, especially since the attitude in question is already alive and forceful in the minds and hearts of many in U.S. society. But if public policy administration is not to be further corrupted by arbitrariness in ethnic identification, we ought to nonetheless utilize the analysis to identify ourselves, as it seems to be the most useful way to do so. The answer to the concern at hand ought not to be addressed by discarding a rather reasonable method of ethnic categorization. Instead, we must make ardent efforts at combating racism through educative measures. After all, it is not necessarily racist for a group to not want its members to marry members of other ethnic groups (certain Jewish, Roman Catholic, and other families, on the one hand, and KKK families, on the other hand, have done this for generations), though it is often motivated by some form of intentional or unintentional racism. But when, for instance, an ethnic group is striving for ethnic preservation without wanting deleterious consequences for other ethnic groups, then there seems to be nothing particularly racist about an internal attitude of members of the group not "intermarrying" with out-group members. Whatever the cause or motivation of the attitude against intermarriage, it ought not to be viewed as being necessarily racist. Nor ought it to be prohibited. Instead, it ought to be respected as an ethnic group's right[27] to protect itself from dissolution through intermarriage should the members of the group intentionally and voluntarily choose such a life form.

Another objection concerns the very genealogically based analysis of ethnic identity I have articulated and defended. It regards the claim that pure socialization is insufficient for ethnicity. Suppose a European American couple with no Latino genealogical heritage moves from Germany to la Ciudad de Mexico and conceives a child there, remains there to raise their daughter for her entire childhood. In fact, the family remains there permanently, as they have adapted to the culture and language quite well. Even if the parents in this case are European Americans (as no amount of socialization in Mexico can "convert" them into Latinos), is it not the case that the daughter is a Latina? She speaks the language, respects it and the culture as if it were her very own. In fact, she knows no other culture but the Mexican one. Is there not a real sense in which the Mexican culture and ethnicity is *her own*?

In reply to this case, it might be argued that for public policy purposes, the young woman is not and never has been a Latina. For her genealogical heritage is European American, not Latino. And for public policy considerations, this much ought to be the case, quite clearly. For purposes of public policy administration, there is not an interesting or appreciable dif-

27. For an analysis of collective rights, see J. Angelo Corlett, "The Problem of Collective Moral Rights," *Canadian Journal of Law and Jurisprudence* 7 (1994): 237–59.

ference between the young European American woman, on the one hand, and a European American woman who at a later date in her life learns and appreciates Latino culture, and even teaches and promotes the culture and language to others, on the other hand.

But, the objection continues, might not the genealogical conception of ethnicity run into trouble when, say, Latinos and their histories are considered? The fact is that Brazilians, Argentinians, and certain others have histories such that their ancestors came from Portugal, Spain, Italy, and other such European countries. Precisely when did *they* (the immigrants to Latin America) become Latinos? Is the answer that they were always Latinos? If so, then what made *them* Latinos from the outset, historically speaking?

The answer to this set of important and probing questions is that they seem to conflate the metaphysical questions of ethnicity with those of the ethical ones. The metaphysics of ethnicity seems to be fraught with uncertainty, to be sure. Indeed, chapter 1 has articulated some such problems with primitive race theories. However, the ethics of ethnicity can and ought to invoke the appeal to public policy administration, not to simply evade the problems raised in the query, but to focus our concern where it truly needs to be focused in order to address critical matters of racism in U.S. society. In light of this, the problem of the "true" original Latinos is not one that has to be answered, except by the metaphysics of ethnicity. The ethics of ethnicity need only impose concerns of public policy administration in order to argue plausibly that the daughter of the European Americans is also a European American woman, and that she ought not to be categorized as a Latina. This genealogical reply has the virtue of not categorizing a person as a Latina who shares no morphological features of Latinas obtained from genealogy, generally speaking, that would lead many European American women themselves, for instance, to see her as a Latina and to form racist attitudes toward her because of those features. To deny the plausibility of my analysis of ethnic identity would be to court the very same disasters that accompanied Native Americans in their receipt of meager U.S. government subsidies that were defrauded by some European Americans "becoming" Native Americans by marriage.

Another objection to my analysis of ethnic identity and public policy is that some ethnic groups, such as Latinos, might be defined so broadly that some of its subgroups are more deserving of benefits from public policy administration than others, due to facts of history. For example, it might turn out that some Latinos as a group actually persecuted other Latino groups, both prior to their immigration to the United States, and even thereafter. And this is a difficulty that has the potential of pervad-

ing each and every ethnic group. Should public policies aimed at level-
ing the playing field in U.S. society reward those within such groups who
have actually discriminated against or oppressed others within their ethnic group?

The reply to this important query is negative, as public policy might be
articulated and administered in such a way that it is sensitive to such injustices. The grounds for such administrative policy sensitivity would be the
legal one (already noted, above) that no person should be allowed to profit
from her own wrongdoing. And this principle might apply, for practical
purposes, to individuals within an ethnic group who have wronged significantly other members of that group, or to entire ethnic groups themselves
who have oppressed others. In no way ought a Native American, an African
American, a Latino, an Asian American, or a member of any other ethnic
group be permitted to benefit substantially from public policy administration when she herself has victimized others in severe ways. This is one important reason why, as we saw, European American women barely qualify,
if they qualify at all, for affirmative action benefits, normatively speaking.

Yet another objection to my analysis of the ethics of ethnicity is that in
the end, it assumes that categories of ethnicity are real. But if they are real,
how does my view of ethnicity differ from the primitive race theories I have
argued against in previous chapters? The only main difference between
primitive race theories and my analysis of ethnicity seems to be that the latter admits of several more categories than the former.

In reply to this concern, it must be pointed out that my analysis admits,
indeed, insists, that all humans belong equally to one human "race" or family. This is both a metaphysical and ethical claim. This is a claim to which
Immanuel Kant and David Hume do not subscribe, as each makes claims
of racial superiority of "Caucasoids" over "Negroids."[28] Moreover, my moderate conception of ethnic identity admits not only to the social construction of ethnic groups as being real and evolutionary over time, making
ethnicity unfixed, however genealogically based it is. This is yet another
way in which my analysis differs from primitive race theories. Thus while I
believe that ethnic groups are real, they are socially constructed categories
based, historically, on genealogy. But they are neither fixed metaphysical
essences, nor natural kinds as primitive race theories suggest.

Finally, it might be objected that my conception of compensatory justice
to groups is strongly contingent on there being a plausible conception of
desert. Yet it might be argued that the concept of moral desert is prob-

---

28. Robert Bernasconi and Tommy Lott, eds., *The Idea of Race* (Indianapolis: Hackett,
2001).

lematic. Several leading contemporary philosophers have argued that the concept of desert is unfounded, and for a variety of reasons.[29] Thus, the objection goes, to the extent that the concept of desert is itself problematic, so is my argument in that it is contingent on the plausibility of some notion of desert.

In reply to this concern, it must be pointed out that it is not at all obvious, except, perhaps, to those who have already concurred pretheoretically with some leading political liberals, that the notion of desert is incoherent. For the arguments against the plausibility of the concept of desert seem to, in the end, presume without argument that voluntariness and responsibility fail to obtain in society. Perhaps they argue thusly and in part because of the pervasiveness of moral luck and its tendency to serve as a voluntariness-reducing factor, vitiating against moral and legal liability responsibility, and the concept of desert on which such responsibility is based. However, that certain groups suffered racist harms (and in some measures continue to do so) at the hands of others is a fact of history. Moreover, this historical fact demonstrates insufficient evidence that oppressors acted involuntarily, unintentionally, and unknowingly and are not responsible for what they did in committing the atrocities they did against members of certain other groups. Although the concept of desert might not be properly applicable to each and every circumstance of human injustice/justice, it hardly follows that it applies legitimately to none. Furthermore, it would stretch the bounds of credulity to even insinuate that at least many of the evils experienced by, say, Native Americans were not performed knowingly, intentionally, and voluntarily by the U.S. government for the express purpose of "manifest destiny." So it seems that there is some legitimate application of a workable notion of desert[30] here to matters of public policy, contrary to the stated objection.

In sum, I have argued in favor of a complex ethical analysis of ethnic identity, which is important to determine for public policy purposes. Ethnic genealogical heritages are what are both necessary and sufficient for the ethics of ethnicity. Metaphysically speaking, the extent to which one

29. Robert Goodin, "Negating Positive Desert Claims," *Political Theory* 13 (1985): 575–98; Amy Gutmann, *Liberal Equality* (Cambridge: Cambridge University Press, 1980); Thomas Nagel, *Mortal Questions* (Cambridge: Cambridge University Press, 1979); Rawls, *A Theory of Justice;* Richard Wasserstrom, "Racism and Sexism," in *Today's Moral Problems,* ed. Richard Wasserstrom (New York: Macmillan, 1985), 1–29.

30. The exact nature of the plausible notion of desert is beyond the scope of this chapter, though some incisive discussions of desert are found in Corlett, *Responsibility and Punishment,* chapter 5, and "Making *More* Sense of Retributivism: Desert as Responsibility and Proportionality," *Philosophy* (forthcoming); Louis Pojman and Owen McLeod, eds., *What Do We Deserve?* (Oxford: Oxford University Press, 1999).

belongs to this or that ethnic group is the extent to which she respects and knows the particular language(s) or dialects of the groups, respects and participates in their respective cultures, has a name that is traditionally associated with members of the group(s), is recognized as a members of the group(s) by in group members, self-identifies as a member of the group(s), and is recognized as a member of the group(s) by out-group members. The purpose of this analysis is positive only, for the administration of public policy in a nonarbitrary way. This needs to be done in a largely historical manner, where a fair-minded study of U.S. history would inform us as to the kinds and levels of reparative compensation and other public policy measures that members of each ethnic group ought to receive. Any attempt to misuse such categorizations for racist aims ought to be combated in the arena of education, and when appropriate, in the criminal and tort contexts.

Thus the genealogical conception of ethnic identity is both genealogical and historical. This genealogical-historical analysis of ethnic identity and public policy holds that persons and governments ought to construe ethnic groups genealogically (as described herein) and the extent of their deserved public policy benefits are to be understood historically. With this analysis of ethnicity in place, it is now time to consider the plausibility of arguments in favor of reparations to Native and African Americans by the U.S. government for historic racist oppression against these groups.

8

Reparations to Native Americans?

North American history is replete with accounts of atrocities being inflict-ed by members of one group on members of another. Some such exam-ples include the seizure by the French, the British, the Spanish, the Dutch governments (and later by the United States and Canadian governments, respectively) of millions of acres of land inhabited by Native (North) Amer-icans; the genocide (or attempt therein) of various Native American na-tions[1] by the U.S. military at the order of, among others, former U.S. president Andrew Jackson; the enslavement of several Native Americans in the United States, and other acts of oppression.[2] These and other significant

1. Similar points might well apply to Native Americans in Central and South America. Indeed, Native Americans in (former) island nations of the Americas, for example, the Hawai'ian islands were victimized (accompanied in the end by threat of military force) by unjust takings by the United States and others. See Michael Dougherty, *To Steal a Kingdom: Probing Hawai'ian History* (Waimanalo: Island Style Press, 1992). That Hawai'ian culture was significantly affected by the intrusion of Europeans is noted in Martha Beckwith, *Hawai'ian Mythology* (Honolulu: University of Hawai'i Press, 1976).

2. William L. Anderson, ed., *Cherokee Removal* (Athens: University of Georgia Press, 1991); Garrick Bailey and Roberta Glenn Bailey, *A History of the Navajos* (Santa Fe: School of American Research Press, 1986); Robert Berkhofer, Jr., *Salvation and the Savage* (New York: Atheneum, 1965); Dee Brown, *Bury My Heart at Wounded Knee* (New York: Henry Holt, 1970); Angie Debo, *A History of the Indians of the United States* (Norman: University of Okla-homa Press, 1970); *And Still the Waters Run* (Norman: University of Oklahoma Press, 1989); John Ehle, *Trail of Tears* (New York: Anchor Books, 1988); Grant Foreman, *Indian Removal* (Norman: University of Oklahoma Press, 1932); Michael D. Green, *The Politics of Indian Re-moval* (Lincoln: University of Nebraska Press, 1982); Robert V. Remini, *The Legacy of Andrew Jackson* (Baton Rouge: Louisiana State University Press, 1988); David E. Stannard, *American Holocaust: The Conquest of the New World* (Oxford: Oxford University Press, 1992); Ian K. Steele, *Warpaths* (Oxford: Oxford University Press, 1994); Clifford E. Trafzer, *The Kit Carson*

harms have found little justice in the form of reparations. This chapter seeks to clarify the nature of reparations and analyzes philosophically objections to policies of reparations to historically and seriously wronged groups with the primary focus being on the Native American experiences in the United States.[3]

It is an embarrassing fact that major Western political philosophies by and large ignore (or, at best, give short shrift to) the claims of Native Americans[4] to property.[5] And given the importance of the concept of private property rights in historic and contemporary Western political philosophy,[6] it is vital to delve into problems which, among other things, question

---

Campaign (Norman: University of Oklahoma Press, 1982); Peter H. Wood, Gregory A. Waselkov, and M. Thomas Hatley, eds., *Powhatan's Mantle* (Lincoln: University of Nebraska Press, 1989); Grace Steele Woodward, *The Cherokees* (Norman: University of Oklahoma Press, 1963).

3. Other philosophers who have written on reparations, but concerning the African American experience, include Bernard Boxill, "The Morality of Reparations," *Social Theory and Practice* 2 (1972): 113–22; J. L. Cowan, "Inverse Discrimination," *Analysis* 33 (1972): 10–12; Alan H. Goldman, "Reparations to Individuals or Groups?" *Analysis* 35 (1975): 168–70; Howard McGary, *Race and Social Justice* (London: Blackwell, 1999); James W. Nickel, "Discrimination and Morally Relevant Characteristics," *Analysis* 32 (1972): 113–14; "Should Reparations Be Made to Individuals or to Groups?" *Analysis* 34 (1974): 154–60; Rodney C. Roberts, "The Morality of a Moral Statute of Limitations on Injustice," *Journal of Ethics* 7 (2003): 115–38; "Why Have the Injustices Perpetrated Against Blacks in America Not Been Rectified?" *Journal of Social Philosophy* 32 (2001): 357–73; Roger A. Shiner, "Individuals, Groups, and Inverse Discrimination," *Analysis* 33 (1973): 185–87; Philip Silvestri, "The Justification of Inverse Discrimination," *Analysis* 34 (1973): 31; Paul W. Taylor, "Reverse Discrimination and Compensatory Justice," *Analysis* 33 (1973): 177–82. The main philosophical works that focus on reparations to Native Americans include J. Angelo Corlett, "Reparations to Native Americans?" in *War Crimes and Collective Wrongdoing*, ed. Aleksandar Jokic (London: Blackwell, 2000): 236–69; David Lyons, "The New Indian Claims and Original Rights to Land," *Social Theory and Practice* 6 (1977): 249–72. Other philosophers have written on the problem of reparations to Aboriginals in Australia. See John Bigelow, Robert Pargetter, and Robert Young, "Land, Well-Being and Compensation," *Australasian Journal of Philosophy* 68 (1990): 330–46; Robert Goodin, "Waitangi Tales," *Australasian Journal of Philosophy* 78 (2000): 309–33; Roy W. Perrett, "Indigenous Language Rights and Political Theory: The Case of TE REO MAŌRI," *Australasian Journal of Philosophy* 78 (2000): 405–17; Robert Sparrow, "History and Collective Responsibility," *Australasian Journal of Philosophy* 78 (2000): 346–59; Janna Thompson, "Historical Injustice and Reparation: Justifying Claims of Descendants," *Ethics* 112 (2001): 114–35; "Historical Obligations," *Australasian Journal of Philosophy* 78 (2000): 334–45; "Land Rights and Aboriginal Sovereignty," *Australasian Journal of Philosophy* 68 (1990): 313–29.

4. I assume that Native Americans are indigenous peoples to North America, and that even if they are not so indigenous, that they acquired the lands on which they resided in North America in ways that did not violate the principle of morally just acquisitions and transfers, discussed below.

5. James Tully, "Aboriginal Property and Western Theory: Recovering a Middle Ground," *Social Philosophy & Policy* 11 (1994): 153.

6. Jules L. Coleman, "Corrective Justice and Property Rights," *Social Philosophy and Policy* 11 (1994): 124–38; Gary Lawson, "Proving Ownership," *Social Philosophy and Policy* 11

who ought to be seen as having the overriding moral claim or right to, say, the lands on which entire countries and their respective citizens reside, such as with the United States. For the moral legitimacy of a country, it is assumed, is contingent on at least the extent to which that country acquires justly the land on which it and its citizens reside. The problem of reparations to Native Americans raises queries concerning the fundamental moral legitimacy of the United States. For it challenges the moral basis of putative U.S. rights to lands which, it is assumed, are necessary for its economic and political survival.

What *are* reparations? And are reparations to Native Americans by the U.S. government morally required? This chapter seeks to answer these and related questions as they concern the Native American lives and lands lost to the United States by means of crimes committed against various Native American nations by the U.S. government and its military.

Reparations, according to *Black's Law Dictionary,* involve "payment for an injury; redress for a wrong done." They are payments "made by one country to another for damages done during war." Reparations involve restitution, which is the "act of restoring . . . anything to its rightful owner; the act of making good or giving equivalent for any loss, damage or injury;[7] and indemnification. . . . A person who has been unjustly enriched at the expense of another is required to make restitution to the other."[8] Those receiving reparations are typically groups, though there seems to be no moral or logical preclusion to individuals receiving them. Often the evils perpetrated are such that there is no "just" or genuinely sufficient manner by which to rectify matters between the wrongdoer (or her descendants) and the party wronged (or her descendants). *Reparative compensation* is the main form of reparations. It seeks to rectify severe wrongs of the distant past by providing the wronged parties or their descendants a sum of money

---

(1994): 139–52; A. John Simmons, "Makers' Rights," *Journal of Ethics* 2 (1998): 197–218; "Original Acquisition Justifications of Private Property," *Social Philosophy & Policy* 11 (1994): 63–84. It is assumed herein that the concept of property rights is itself an important part of a plausible political philosophy.

7. "Reparation 'sets things straight' or 'gives satisfaction' . . . for redress of injury." Joel Feinberg, *Doing and Deserving* (Princeton: Princeton University Press, 1970), pp. 74–75.

8. Note that nothing in this conception of reparations requires that the reparations be "paid" or rendered by the perpetrators of wrongdoing only. (Compare the conception of reparations set forth in D. N. MacCormick, "The Obligation of Reparations," *Proceedings of the Aristotelian Society* 78 [1977–78]: 175). Contrast this notion of reparations with one articulated by Bernard Boxill: "Part of what is involved in rectifying an injustice is an acknowledgement on the part of the transgressor that what he is doing is required of him because of his prior error." Bernard Boxill, "The Morality of Reparations," in Barry R. Gross, ed., *Reverse Discrimination* (New York: Prometheus, 1977), p. 274.

(often collected by general tax revenues),[9] property, and other tangible goods that might be (roughly) proportional to the harms experienced by them. *Reparative punishment,* if it is ever morally justified, should be reserved for those who are themselves guilty of intentionally not paying substantial compensatory reparations. Moreover, reparative compensation/punishment must, I argue, always conform to the principle of proportional compensation and/or punishment: *Compensation and/or punishment for significant wrongdoing is always to be meted out in (albeit rough) proportion to the wrongdoing(s) committed.*

Although reparations are for the most part a compensatory matter, they share much in common with some of the "expressive functions" of punishment articulated by Joel Feinberg.[10] Feinberg describes four expressive functions of punishment as "hard treatment." Punishment involves "authoritative disavowal" of a society of a criminal act. It says publicly that the criminal had no right to act as she did, that she did not truly represent society's best aims and aspirations in committing the criminal deed. Punishment also involves a society's "symbolic nonacquiescence" or its speaking in the name of the people (when it is a democratic society) against the criminal's wrongful deed. Punishment involves "vindication of the law" as a society goes on record by way of its statutes to reinforce the genuine standards of law. Finally, punishment "absolves the innocent" of blame for what a criminal does. Reparations, I argue, share with punishment these expressive features. Like punishment, reparations disavow the wrong(s) committed and charges that the wrongdoers had no right to perform such evil(s). Reparations, like punishment, say publicly that wrongdoings do not represent society's highest aims and aspirations. In democratic regimes, reparations speak in the name of the people against the wrongdoings in question, and they uphold the genuine standards of law in the face of past failures of the legal system to carry out true justice. In addition, reparations alienate a reasonably just society from its corrupt past, absolving society of its historic evils. These are some of the specific expressive functions of reparations.[11] Some of these expressive functions of reparations are articulated by Feinberg when he states that "reparation can express sympathy, benevolence, and concern, but, in addition, it is always the

---

9. Sanford Levinson, "Responsibility for Crimes of War," *Philosophy and Public Affairs* 2 (1973): 250.

10. Feinberg, *Doing and Deserving,* chapter 5.

11. That reparations also recognize the personhood of victims is argued in Mari Matsuda, "Looking to the Bottom: Critical Legal Studies and Reparations," in *Critical Race Theory,* ed. Kimberle Crenshaw, Neil Gotanda, Gary Peller and Kendall Thomas (New York: New Press, 1995), p. 74.

acknowledgment of a past wrong, a 'repayment of a debt,' and hence, like an apology, the redressing of the moral balance or the restoring of the status quo ante culpum."[12]

More generally, the expressive feature of reparations is to make public society's *own* liability concerning the wrongs it has wrought upon a group or individuals. It is to offer an unqualified and unambiguous *apology* to the wronged parties (or their successors) without presumption of forgiveness or mercy. Moreover, it is to acknowledge, in a public way, the moral wrongness of the act(s) in question and to never forget them. For as George Santayana encourages, those who do not remember the errors of the past are doomed to repeat them. The expressive feature of reparations is articulated by Jeremy Waldron when he writes: "Quite apart from any attempt genuinely to compensate victims or offset their losses, reparations may symbolize a society's understanding not to forget or deny that a particular injustice took place, and to respect and help sustain a dignified sense of identity-in-memory for the people affected."[13] Insofar as reparations have their expressive functions, they send a message to citizens (and noncitizens alike) about the importance of building and strengthening social solidarity toward justice and fairness. In this way, the justification of reparations is forward looking.

Moreover, there are at least two sorts of arguments that might be given for reparations: end-state arguments and historical ones. A. John Simmons clarifies the difference between these kinds of reparations arguments:

> Historical arguments maintain that whether or not a holding or set of holdings is just (that is, whether or not we are entitled to or have a moral right to our holdings) depends on the moral character of the history that produced the holdings. We must see how holdings actually came about in order to know who has a right to what. End-state arguments maintain that the justice of holdings (and our rights to them) depends not on how they came about, but rather on the moral character of the structure (or pattern) of the set of holdings of which they are a part.[14]

Briefly, reparations can be supported on the ground that they truly respect the actions (inactions and attempted actions, as the case may be) of history in the sense that they try to correct significant imbalances of power or fortune that result from undue force or intrusion, fraud, or other gross forms of wrongdoing. Moreover, reparations disrespect as being morally

12. Feinberg, *Doing and Deserving*, p. 76.

13. Jeremy Waldron, "Superseding Historic Injustice," *Ethics* 103 (1992): 6.

14. A. John Simmons, "Historical Rights and Fair Shares," *Law and Philosophy* 14 (1995): 150–51.

arbitrary any statute of limitations pertaining to the kinds of cases in question.[15] This is especially true where the extent of the facts of guilt, fault, harm, and identity of the perpetrators and victims are unambiguous. Whether it is a crime occurring forty or four hundred years ago, justice requires that significant wrongdoings are compensated in manners that would do justice to the idea of proportional compensation for damages in cases where the perpetrator(s), victim(s) and damages are provable by current legal standards (beyond reasonable doubt, for example, in criminal cases, and by the preponderance of evidence in tort cases). With reparations, then, both the balance of human reason and history must be our twin and primary guides to the truth of whom (or what) owes what to whom (or what), and why. For my current purposes, it is assumed that the law ought to follow these guides. The argument for reparations to Native Americans insists that reparations ought to be made when a right has been infringed by way of significant injustice[16] (In assessing the plausibility of precisely this sort of argument, David Lyons points out that it relies on the ideas of original acquisition and legitimate transfer of land).[17] Thus the justification for reparations is essentially backward-looking, though it might involve aspects of considerations that are forward-looking.

The foregoing suggests the following reparations argument:

(1) As much as is humanly possible, instances of clear and substantial historic rights violations ought to be rectified by way of reparations;

(2) The U.S. government has clearly committed substantial historic rights violations against millions of Native Americans;[18]

(3) Therefore, the historic rights violations of the U.S. government against Native Americans ought to be rectified by way of reparations, as much as humanly possible.

The basis for (1) might be a desert-based (retributivist) one that insists that there is either a perfect duty or an imperfect duty to rectify past injustices of a substantial nature. Or, to the extent that it is humanly possible to rec-

---

15. Of course, this claim is unproblematic in cases involving murder, as the United States itself recognizes no legal statute of limitations in murder cases. For a refutation of a variety of arguments in favor of a moral statute of limitations on injustice, see Roberts, "The Morality of a Moral Statute of Limitations on Injustice."

16. MacCormick, "The Obligation of Reparations," p. 179.

17. Lyons, "The New Indian Claims and Original Rights to Land," p. 252. Indeed, it is a historical, rather than an end-state, argument for reparative justice.

18. These acts amount to a series of intentional actions that were crimes, torts, and/or contract violations.

tify substantial wrongs for which a wrongdoer is responsible, the wrong-doer ought to rectify the wrongdoing. The locution, "as much as humanly possible" in (1) and (3) is meant to capture the idea of reparations being proportional to the harms they are meant to rectify.

Objections to the Reparations Argument and Replies

If the reparations agument is plausible, then wherever there is significant injustice there is at least a prima facie reason to believe that such injustice deserves compensation or rectification. Moreover, where the facts of the guilt, fault, harm, and identity of the perpetrators and victims are clear, reparations ought to be pursued for the sake of corrective justice.[19] Hence, there is a presumptive case in favor of reparations to Native Americans by the U.S. government, given the substantial wrongs many Native Americans have experienced at the hands of the United States.

Precisely what is/was the harm perpetrated against Native Americans? At the very least, it is the following. To the extent that Will Kymlicka is correct when he argues that cultural membership is crucial for self-respect,[20] and to the extent that a Rawlsian liberalism is correct in arguing that cultural membership is a primary good,[21] the particular cultural membership that is crucial to *their* self-respect is/was undermined for Native Americans by force and fraud. The campaigns against various Native American nations by the U.S. military serve as examples here. One specific instance of U.S. crimes against the Lakota Sioux was the massacre at Wounded Knee, which in turn culminated in the retaliatory violence against the U.S. military at Little Big Horn. Examples of U.S. torts against Native Americans are the fraudulent takings of lands, often followed by the U.S. government's refusal to honor its treaties made with various Native American nations. Yet for all of the several instances of unjustified violence and other crimes, torts and contract violations committed by the U.S. against various Native Americans, few, if any, apologies or reparations have been issued by the

19. For a discussion of the concept of corrective justice that is helpful in the context of reparations, see Jules L. Coleman, "Corrective Justice and Wrongful Gain," *Journal of Legal Studies* 11 (1982): 421–40.

20. Will Kymlicka, *Liberalism, Community, and Culture* (Oxford: Oxford University Press, 1989), p. 165. Discussions of Kymlicka's argument are found in John Tomasi, "Kymlicka, Liberalism, and Respect for Cultural Minorities," *Ethics* 105 (1995): 580–603; Robert Murray, "Liberalism, Culture, Aboriginal Rights," *Canadian Journal of Philosophy* 29 (1999): 109–38.

21. John R. Danley, "Liberalism, Aboriginal Rights, and Cultural Minorities," *Philosophy and Public Affairs* 20 (1991), p. 172.

U.S. government. These are some reasons that form the presumptive case for reparations to Native Americans.[22] But such a presumption can be overridden if it can be shown that considerations against such reparations outweigh the strength of the prima facie case for them where the instances in question are not "hard cases."[23] Hence it is important to consider the plausibility of various of the strongest objections to reparations to Native Americans: the objection from historical complexity, the objection to collective responsibility, the objection from inter-nation conquests, the objection from historical and normative progress, the affirmative action objection, the no Native American concept of moral rights objection, the objection from the indeterminacy of Native American identity, the historical reparations objection, the objection from social utility, the religious freedom objection, the acquired rights trumping original lands rights objection, the supersession of historic injustice objection, the anti-private-property-rights objection, and the counterfactual objection. To the extent that such objections are defeasible, the presumptive case for such reparations gains strength, and the reparations argument gains plausibility.

The Objection from Historical Complexity

Given the above understanding of the nature of reparations, are reparations to Native Americans by the U.S. government morally required? Ought the U.S. government to provide reparations to Native Americans? A number of arguments can be marshaled against the imposition of reparations, and they deserve close scrutiny. First, there is the *objection from historical complexity*. This objection avers that history contains far too many and complex situations of conflict such that it would be impossible to figure out all of the injustices that would putatively require reparations. Where the perpetrators of the evils are dead and cannot be punished for their horrors it would be sheer dogmatic idealism to think that respecting rights requires or even permits the kind of complex legal casework that would be required to rectify all past wrongs. To award reparations to the wronged party or her

22. Another reason might concern factors of distributive justice: the continual failure or refusal of a government to recognize in the form of compensation its harms against some of its constituents often results in the social alienation and violence that erupt in society as a result (at least in part) of such nonrecognition. For such nonrecognition of a government's harms leads many to believe that the government supports the status quo of what happened to the victims.

23. For a discussion of hard cases in the context of law, see Ronald Dworkin, *Taking Rights Seriously* (Cambridge: Harvard University Press, 1978), chapter 4.

descendants would end up forcing innocent parties (perhaps the descendants of the wrongdoers) to pay for what they themselves did not do.[24] Among other things, the objection from historical complexity seems to assume that past injustices should not forever burden future putatively "innocent" generations.[25] The objection from historical complexity challenges (1) of the reparations argument, suggesting that there are some instances of historic injustice that ought not to be rectified by way of reparations.

The Principle of Morally Just Acquisitions and Transfers

In response to this objection to the reparations argument, it might be pointed out that the inability to figure out with precise accuracy *all there is to know* about *every case* that putatively involves reparations hardly prohibits a juridical system from awarding some measure of significant reparations where cases are clear (based on unambiguous historical records, for example). Even if it were true that a full-blown policy of reparations would involve reparations to Native Americans by not only the U.S. government, but by the governments of Spain, Portugal, England, France, the Netherlands, among others, and even if it proved overly difficult to figure out the extent to which each said government contributed to harms against Native Americans, this would hardly show that clear cases of U.S. harms to Native Americans ought not to be compensated by the United States. Moreover, though the parties to a putative case of reparations would involve those who themselves did no harm to the victims in question, such "innocent" parties who currently reside on or "own" lands that were once resided on by Native Americans are in violation of the principle of morally just acquisitions and transfers:

> *Whatever is acquired or transferred by morally just means is itself morally just; whatever is acquired or transferred by morally unjust means is itself morally unjust.* [26]

24. A version of the argument from historical complexity seems to be articulated by Loren Lomasky when he writes: "It is undeniably the case that virtually all current holdings of property descend from a historical chain involving the usurpation of rights. It does not follow that those holdings are thereby rendered illegitimate, morally null and void." Loren Lomasky, *Persons, Rights, and the Moral Community* (Oxford: Oxford University Press, 1987), p. 145. A similar view is articulated, but not endorsed, in A. John Simmons, "Original Acquisition Justifications of Property," *Social Philosophy & Policy* 11 (1994): 74–75.

25. This assumption will be taken up in discussing the objection to collective responsibility, below.

26. This principle bears a keen resemblance to the principle of just acquisitions, transfers and rectification found in Robert Nozick, *Anarchy, State, and Utopia* (New York: Basic

Basically, the intended meaning of this principle is that to the extent that property is acquired or transferred in a morally justified way (i.e., without force, fraud, or other kinds of coercion or deceit), the acquisition or transfer of that property carries with it a genuine moral claim or entitlement to occupy it without interference from others. To the extent that the principle of morally just acquisitions and transfers is violated, there is no legitimate claim or entitlement to occupy the property being acquired or transferred. Thus the principle need not specify ownership rights to property. In this way, then, it is neutral concerning the matter of property rights of ownership between political liberals and Marxists. This point of clarification precludes a Marxist-style objection that reparations to Native Americans are not morally justified in that they are contingent on Native Americans having original land rights, which themselves are dubious on moral grounds. For the principle of morally just acquisitions and transfers does not support reparations to Native Americans by the United States because Native Americans had property *ownership* rights to the lands, but because Native Americans had property *sovereignty* or *occupancy* rights therein.[27]

Although the locutions "morally just" and "morally unjust" are somewhat vague, relatively clear cases of unjust acquisition or transfer, for instance, exist: when such acquisitions or transfers occur as the result of significant nonvoluntariness (the violent use of force, for example) on the part of those relinquishing property,[28] when acquisitions or transfers involve fraud,[29] or severe misunderstanding between principal parties.[30] In the

---

Books, 1974), p. 150. However, the principle of morally just acquisitions and transfers makes no particular theoretical commitments to Nozick's entitlement theory or its implications.

Writing on the recovery or repossession of stolen or lost property, Immanuel Kant argues that those who acquire such property have a responsibility to "investigate" the historical chain of acquisitions and transfers of the property, and if, unbeknownst to her, the property she deemed she purchased legitimately was the actual possession of another, then "nothing is left to the alleged new owner but to have enjoyed the use of it up to this moment as its possessor in good faith." Immanuel Kant, *The Metaphysical Elements of Justice*, 302, in Kant, *The Metaphysics of Morals*, trans. and ed. by Mary Gregor (Cambridge: Cambridge University Press, 1996), p. 82.

27. Note that the matter of property *ownership* is not at issue here. Rather, *sovereignty* over land, a notion consistent with Native American worldviews, is at issue. For more on property and sovereignty, see Thompson, "Historical Injustice and Reparation," pp. 313–29.

28. For descriptions of examples of the taking of Native American lands by force and violence, see Debo, *A History of the Indians of the United States*, pp. 47, 87, 96, 118, 297, 304–5, 317, 320.

29. For descriptions of examples of the taking of Native American lands by fraud, see Debo, *A History of the Indians of the United States*, pp. 89, 106, 118, 207, 261, 320–21, 379.

30. For descriptions of examples of the taking of Native American lands by misunder-

case of Native American lands (then a part of the United States) most of which were taken from them forcibly by the U.S. military at the direction of the U.S. president Andrew Jackson and other U.S. officials (many of which lands were encroached upon illegally by U.S. citizens or civilians), there is no question who the wrongdoer was (the U.S. government, along with its citizen trespassers) and who the harmed parties were (Native Americans of various nations). In other cases, Native Americans were believed to have "given away" their land to invaders, interpreted as such, presumably, because of the hospitality of the Native peoples toward the invaders. In such cases, the questions are not who is the guilty party and who was the victim, but precisely how ought the victims to be "reparated" for the wrongdoings. In still other instances, such as our own, U.S. citizens have purchased in good faith lands from other non-Native peoples to which the former may not in fact have an overriding moral right. That a person purchased in good faith a stolen item in no wise entitles him to that item, as even the law stipulates. She who is truly entitled to the item has a right to it, and that right must be respected by all who take seriously what morality requires. Note that this argument is *not* contingent on the status of well-being of either the perpetrators or the victims of the evils inflicted that might require reparations. For reparations are morally required even if, say, the United States and its citizens were not well-off and if Native Americans were indeed relatively better-off. Reparative justice does not depend on the ability of perpetrators of wrongdoing to enrich their lives by inflicting wrongdoings on others. It is concerned primarily with rectifying past injustices regardless of whether or not perpetrators have been enriched at all by their wrong-doings. Thus the attempt of the objection from historical complexity to defeat (1) fails.

The Objection to Collective Responsibility

This raises the issue of collective moral retrospective liability responsibility[31] of, say, the U.S. government for severe wrongs committed in *its* name

standing, deliberate or otherwise, see Debo, *A History of the Indians of the United States,* pp. 76, 190–91.

31. For discussions of the concept of collective responsibility, see J. Angelo Corlett, *Responsibility and Punishment* (Dordrecht: Kluwer Academic, 2001), chapter 7; Feinberg, *Doing and Deserving,* chapter 8; Peter French, *Corporate and Collective Responsibility* (New York: Columbia University Press, 1984); *Responsibility Matters* (Lawrence: University of Kansas Press, 1990); Virginia Held, "Can a Random Collection Be Morally Responsible?" *Journal of Philosophy* 67 (1970): 471–80; "Corporations, Persons, and Responsibility," in *Shame, Responsibility, and the Corporation,* ed. Hugh Curtler (New York: Haven, 1986); "Group Re-

or on *its* behalf against Native Americans. *The objection to collective responsibility* challenges the morality of reparations to Native Americans on the grounds that it is problematic to hold the current U.S. government and its citizenry morally accountable for wrongs committed by previous generations of people who acted or failed to act, as the case may be, to harm Native Americans and on behalf of the U.S. government, its agencies, and/or on behalf of themselves as actual or putative U.S. citizens. Thus the objection to collective responsibility challenges (2) of the reparations argument insofar as (2) seeks to hold the U.S. *government* responsible for certain substantial wrongs against Native Americans.

However, the objection to collective responsibility falls prey to at least two weaknesses. First, the fundamental documents that form at least the basis of U.S. government are still those which govern the United States. Even though the atrocities committed against Native Americans generations ago were not the direct responsibility of today's U.S. citizens, the fact is that the U.S. government has persisted over time, and still exists.

Furthermore, it is plausible to think that when the U.S. army and government committed genocidal acts of violence against various Native American nations they rendered the United States collectively guilty and at fault because such acts were committed knowingly, intentionally, and voluntarily. Thus *we* (since it is *our* government, acting on *our* behalves) *are* justified in inferring that they were both causally responsible and morally liable (culpable) for those harms committed by them against the Native American nations.[32] Additionally, though legally speaking it is not required that a guilty party apologize to the victim(s) of its wrongdoing(s), the extent of the harms committed by the U.S. government against various Native American nations would seem to suggest that an apology is needed. If this is true, then it would appear that both U.S. governmental (collective) feelings and expressions of guilt and remorse are suggested. That is, we would expect that the U.S. government would, in some official manner, express its genuine feelings of guilt and remorse to Native Americans,

---

sponsibility for Ethnic Conflict," *Journal of Ethics* 6 (2002): 157–78; *Journal of Ethics* 6:2 (2002); Larry May, *The Morality of Groups* (Notre Dame: University of Notre Dame Press, 1987); *Sharing Responsibility* (Chicago: University of Chicago Press, 1992); Burleigh T. Wilkins, *Terrorism and Collective Responsibility* (London: Routledge, 1992).

32. Joel Feinberg argues that there is a kind of collective responsibility, namely vicarious responsibility, which derives from the process of authorization. See Joel Feinberg, *Doing and Deserving*, p. 226. Thus when U.S. president Andrew Jackson, duly elected by the U.S. citizenry, commands the U.S. army to conduct the policy of "Indian removal" even by violent force, vicarious responsibility accrues to the United States and its citizens. Presumably, such responsibility, insofar as it entails culpability, would accrue at least until adequate reparations are made to the various Native American nations that were victimized by the said policy and others akin to it.

publicly renouncing its history of racially motivated oppression and holocaust against Native Americans and vowing that it never occur again. Of
course, a clear record of governmental policies should reflect a support for
such genuine feelings of guilt and remorse.

It is reasonable, then, to hold *it* (the U.S. government) accountable for
its past wrongdoings, pending some adequate argumentation in support
of the morality of a statute of limitations on trying and punishing/com-
pensating such crimes.[33] If it was just "discovered" that a corporation committed a gross wrongdoing (including murders) in 1900, would not justice
dictate that the courts seek rectification in such a case, especially if that corporation is still in operation? The reasoning behind this might be either
that the putatively guilty corporation is simply deserving of being forced
to compensate some parties for the wrongdoing in question (a retributivist
rationale) and/or that the corporation has gained an unfair advantage in
committing such acts. In either case, where matters are clear, past wrongs
of such magnitude as what happened to many Native Americans require
that justice be realized and there appears to be no adequate reason why
past wrongs against Native Americans by U.S. governmental representatives should not be treated in a similar manner as those in which we treat
gross corporate wrongdoings that result from corporate representatives'
actions or inactions.[34] As for the individuals or aggregate mobs who committed theft, violent crimes, and other illegal acts against Native Americans, in some cases some criminals' transfers of assets/fortunes can be
traced to current U.S. citizens or institutions, thereby providing a source
of reparations. Of course, one who inherits what has been acquired or
transferred to her hardly deserves what she inherits if possession of it is in
violation of the principle of morally just acquisitions and transfers. The
burden of argument, then, seems to be on those who would suggest that
there is a moral statute of limitations on injustice. Furthermore, this burden of argument must be satisfied absent question-begging and/or self-
serving reasoning.

A second problem with the objection to collective responsibility is that
the principle of morally just acquisitions and transfers renders irrelevant
the issue of whether or not the current U.S. government and its citizenry
can legitimately be held accountable for the past injustices committed
against Native Americans. In other words, the principle of morally just acquisitions and transfers renders otiose the objection to collective respon-

33. Such arguments are examined and found quite unwarranted in Roberts, "The
Morality of a Moral Statute of Limitations on Injustice."

34. For discussions of corporate responsibility, see Corlett, *Responsibility and Punishment*,
chapter 8.

sibility. And the principle does this in the following way: if, say, most or all of the lands currently occupied by the U.S. government and its citizens are in fact occupied in violation of the principle, then it matters not whether current occupants of those lands are actually liable for the illegitimate transfer of the lands. What truly matters here is whether or not the lands in question have indeed been transferred legitimately. Since most or all of them have not been legitimately transferred to current occupants, then no such occupants can have a legitimate and overriding moral claim to the lands they occupy. The problem of collective responsibility simply does not affect this fact. It is a red herring given the plausibility of the principle of morally just acquisitions and transfers. This rebuttal to the objection to collective responsibility relies on a "weak" form of compensation.[35]

The significance of these replies to the objection to collective responsibility is that one provides a link between the U.S. government and many of the serious wrongs committed against Native Americans, satisfying the legal criteria of privity, standing, and nexus, each of which is necessary to establish a legal case for reparations. The second reply renders the objection to collective responsibility impotent insofar as Native Americans' moral rights to the lands in question are concerned. Thus the objection to collective responsibility fails to defeat (2) of the reparations argument, unless, of course, it can be shown by way of independent argument that there is a moral statute of limitations on injustice.

The Objection from Internation Conquests

Related to the objection from historical complexity is the *objection from internation conquests*. This argument states that reparations to Native Americans are not warranted because such peoples themselves are guilty of violating the principle of morally just acquisitions and transfers, and against other Native Americans! A case in point, it might be argued, is the Lakota's driving-off several Crow, Kiowa, and other Native American nations from land, which was then considered to belong to or to be justifiably inhabited by the latter Native American nations, respectively. Thus the historical complexity of the violations of the principle of morally just acquisitions and transfers is of such a magnitude that it is unclear, historically speaking, who is genuinely and morally entitled to the lands in question. The objection

---

35. For a distinction between weak and strong forms of compensation, see Bigelow, Pargetter, and Young, "Land, Well-Being, and Compensation," pp. 336–37. Bigelow, Pargetter, and Young argue for compensation in a strong sense as a reply to the objection to collective responsibility.

from inter-nation conquests challenges the assumption of the reparations argument that the Native Americans wronged by the U.S. government (and its citizens) are the rightful occupants to the territories in question.

However, there are at least two replies to the objection from internation conquests. First, only a minority number of Native American nations engaged in conquest behavior.[36] Even when the Lakota did engage in conquest of Native American lands, it did so *after* the European invaders had long since succeeded in pitting several Native American nations against each other as a way of eventually fulfilling manifest destiny.[37] The majority of Native American nations were peaceful, and when some did engage in internation violence, it was not, arguably, for purposes of conquering, but rather for reasons of retributive justice or in self-defense.[38] Thus the most that can be said for the objection from internation conquests is that where history is clear about which Native Americans violated the principle of morally just acquisitions and transfers, only those Native peoples who did not violate this principle in their acquisition or transfer of land are plausible candidates for reparations. Of course, by far most Native Americans would qualify for reparations by this standard.

Second, even *if* no existing Native Americans did qualify for reparations because of their violating the principle of morally just acquisitions and transfers, it would not logically follow that anyone *else would* have a genuine and overriding moral claim to the lands of North America. This is true due to the widespread violation of the moral principle in question by the governments and "explorers" who preceded those of us who currently reside on the lands. Either some Native Americans have valid moral claims/interests sufficient to ground their respective moral rights to North American lands, or no subsequent non–Native American residents do, except for a possible *few* cases where a *genuine* transfer of land transpired between Native Americans and others.

The Objections from Historical and Normative Progress

The *objection from historical progress* states that groups experiencing harms at the hands (or weaponry) of others have in many cases triumphed over such problems. Examples here include several African Americans. There is,

36. Debo, *A History of the American Indians of the United States,* chapter 1.
37. Ibid., pp. 67, 74.
38. Ibid., chapter 1.

then, no need for reparations to Native Americans. As history progresses, so will the well-being of Native Americans.

However, the objection from historical progress suffers from the error of supposing that those who deserve reparations are somehow beyond the pale of reparative justice in that history itself "compensates," in one way or another, even severely wronged groups. This sort of fatalism runs counter to our moral intuitions about rights and justice. Justice should not wait for the wheels of historical inevitability to turn, especially since the doctrine of historical inevitability is in itself morally odious and unconvincing.

A more sophisticated version of the objection from historical progress is the *objection from normative progress*. This objection holds that victims of severe wrongdoings of the distant past *should* simply rise above their respective circumstances which, though caused by others unjustly, can be overcome. The lives and messages of Mohandas K. Gandhi and Martin Luther King, Jr., respectively, serve as grist for the mill of this argument, which sees reparations as a crutch for those who are too slothful to make their own ways in life, perhaps blaming others for their own shortcomings. So even if history is clear about many cases of injustice toward Native Americans, and even if it is untrue that those who experience evil at the hands of others do not succeed, reparations are not morally required in that a genuinely good life can and should be attained by such persons nonetheless. This is especially the case in the "land of opportunity" (the United States).

In reply to the objection from normative progress, it must be pointed out its rather excessive insensitivity concerning the ways in which history influences humans as individuals and as groups. For the injustices experienced in the past clearly have some significant bearing on a person's or group's ability to realize virtue in the present and in the future. It is certainly important for the victims of wrongdoing to attempt to "get on with their lives" and not be *overly* concerned about the injustices they or their ancestors have experienced in the past. But this is a social psychological consideration; it hardly defeats any moral claim or entitlement to reparations. Furthermore, the abilities of members from different ethnic groups victimized by oppression might differ remarkably. For instance, while it may be true that African Americans have, as a group, made continual and rather impressive strides toward flourishing, Native Americans as an ethnic group (more precisely, as a set of subethnic groups) have languished.[39]

39. I say "flourished" and "languished" because some might argue plausibly that African Americans have sold their souls to succeed in a society that stripped them of what is most valuable in life and hence cannot truly be said to flourish, while Native Americans, many of them, have decided to remain alienated from the society which is substantially responsible for the evils perpetrated against what is most important to Native Americans: their land and culture. For what profit it someone if they should gain material prosperity while losing

The objection from normative progress rather naively assumes that those who have experienced the most horrible forms of oppression ought to rise above it and get on with their lives, just as many African Americans have flourished in areas such as medicine, politics, business, education, athletics, music, entertainment, and so forth. However, there are good reasons that explain why African Americans can and do flourish in U.S. society, while Native Americans find it rather difficult to do so. While African Americans have had much or all of their original African heritage stripped from them during slavery, they were nonetheless able to create their own new heritage based on their experience as African Americans. As displaced people, African Americans were forced through acculturation to give up their former heritage as they were forced to become slaves on U.S. soil. But Native Americans still reside on (albeit small) sections of what was once *their* territory, and many see no need, nor do they have the desire, to adopt the ways of a people whose very values included the inflicting of evil on Native Americans. While African Americans found themselves being a part of a newly developing heritage of displaced survivors bent on succeeding in a new environment as unwilling foreigners, Native Americans as a class see themselves as having the greatest moral claim to the lands of North America as it was theirs in the first place. For African Americans, liberation from slavery, and later on, equal rights, were ways of gaining an "improved" lifestyle that was in accord with the way they were acculturated into the Christian religion, which remains the dominant and most accepted form of religion in U.S. society. Moreover, slaves were often valued rather highly, even if as mere means to the end of a slaveholder's profit, and they never had reason to think of themselves as having a legitimate moral claim to the land on which they resided either as slaves or as African Americans.

For Native Americans, however, there was a genuine sense that they were invaded by hostile forces that sought to displace them in the name of European religion and values. Native Americans were not deemed as being useful to the European invaders, especially given that Native Americans cherished, above all, their land and culture. Most Native Americans do not believe it would be honorable to concede their great cultures to those who took the land illegitimately, and who had values that would do to that land irreparable damage. Had the Native Americans been enslaved *as* were many Africans and stripped of their original culture,[40] then one might

one's land and culture? For a discussion of why African Americans as a group have flourished while Native Americans have, by comparison, languished in U.S. society, see chapter 6 of this book.

40. Many Native Americans were enslaved as such, as we read in Brown, *Bury My Heart at Wounded Knee,* pp. 2, 4, 14, 204; Debo, *A History of the Indians in the United States,* pp. 43, 47, 49–50, 67, 74, 77, 119, 162, 165, 269.

expect that Native Americans would "flourish" in U.S. society. For an ethnic group that has been deprogrammed of its original culture and successfully reprogrammed into the culture of the dominant group is in general
in a better sociological and psychological position to "succeed" in terms of
what the dominant group deems valuable. But instead of "merely" being
enslaved by the European invaders, which would have been evil enough,
those Native Americans who were enslaved or deprogrammed and acculturated in "Indian boarding schools" were often hunted like buffalo, the
basic goal of which was, rather ironically, to make room for a society which
declared that it respected the rights of all humans.[41] Native American economic structures, many of which took centuries to build and stabilize, were
destroyed by the effects of the European invaders. It is no wonder that native peoples as a class languish, and that despite U.S. material "prosperity."[42] The objection from normative progress hardly counts as a good
reason to reject as morally unrequired reparations to Native Americans.

The Affirmative Action Objection

There is another objection to reparations: the *affirmative action objection.*
This argument states that reparations are otiose given the existence of af-
firmative action in the hiring of underrepresented groups in the United
States, typically, those which have been victimized by racial discrimination.
Such support of historically wronged/underrepresented groups takes the
form of affirmative action programs. With affirmative action programs in
place, there is no need for reparations policies to Native Americans since
Native Americans qualify for affirmative action programs.

However, affirmative action legislation is designed to assist in the providing of equal opportunities in employment and education for Native
Americans, African Americans, and other minority groups. Yet in the case
of employment opportunities, it would seem that affirmative action alone

41. One of the most disappointing ironies of U.S. history is that the class of people who
most boldly declared equality for all humans acted so inhumanely toward some of the most
noble of humans. Moreover, the fact that the United States has *yet* to even apologize for such
inhumane behavior sets it apart as being, in a genuine way, significantly more evil than most,
if not all, countries in history.

42. Let us also not forget the significance of linguistic complications which go toward
explaining the difficulty of the Native American voices to be heard and respected by invaders. As N. Scott Momaday argues, "One of the most perplexing ironies of American history is the fact that the Indian has been effectively silenced by the intricacies of his own
speech, as it were. Linguistic diversity has been a formidable barrier to Indian-white diplo-
macy." See N. Scott Momaday, "Personal Reflections," in *The American Indian and the Problem of History*, ed. Calvin Martin (Oxford: Oxford University Press, 1987), p. 160.

serves as a cruel form of mockery when construed as compensation for the numerous and harsh civil rights violations of these groups by the U.S. government and its citizens. Moreover, if distributive justice is the reason for the grounding of affirmative action, then affirmative action cannot serve as a challenge to reparations. For the recipients of such programs earn the wages or salaries they receive. This can hardly be seen as a legitimate form of compensation for damages. Affirmative action programs, whatever their legitimacy status, cannot and should not be construed as a form of reparations.[43] As pointed out in previous chapters, to think that affirmative action programs can take the place of reparations to Native and African Americans is to commit a category mistake by conflating two essentially distinct policies with distinct functions.

The No Native American Concept of Moral Rights Objection

Yet another objection to reparations, especially in the cases of Native American nations, is that the Native Americans had no conception of rights as entitlements to the lands in question. As John Locke argues, Native Americans lived in a state of nature and had no government that would adjudicate rights claims to land and other property.[44] I shall refer to this as the *no Native American concept of moral rights objection*. It follows, according to this argument, that reparations to Native Americans are not required because lands were acquired from those who did not even believe in rights, not to mention land rights. Moreover, the objection continues, invaders acquired moral rights to at least some of the lands, though such rights may not have justified the violent and evil ways in which such lands were taken. (This part of the objection is developed below in the "acquired rights trumping original land rights objection.") The no Native American concept of moral rights objection is a complex one and is aimed at specific kinds of cases of putative reparations, such as those said to accrue to Native Americans.

In reply to this objection, it must be pointed out that it is a fallacy of reason to think that simply because someone does not believe that they possess *X* that they in fact do not have *X*. Many persons who do not enjoy the

---

43. A similar point is made in chapter 7 of this book. Also see Boxill, "The Morality of Reparation," p. 271.

44. John Locke, *The Second Treatise of Government* (Indianapolis: Bobbs-Merrill, 1952), sections 14, 28, 30, 34, 36, 37, 41–43, 48–49, 108–9. For a helpful assessment of Locke's views on the political status of Native Americans, see Tully, "Aboriginal Property and Western Theory: Recovering a Middle Ground," pp. 158f.

moral right, say, to a good education often do not understand that they have such rights. But it is hardly true that such persons do not have such rights, morally speaking. For they might simply be ignorant or fearful of claiming such rights, especially in the face of coercive force and antagonistic propaganda. Thus the argument that Native Americans should not be awarded reparations for past injustices due to the claim that Native Americans had no notion of rights is beside the point. The real issue here is whether or not the balance of human reason requires that reparations be awarded to Native Americans.

But even if it were true that the moral requirement of reparations to Native Americans is contingent on Native Americans, many of whom held some concept of rights, one must ask which rights concept is required? Given that philosophers have not themselves settled on a singular notion of rights[45] (indeed, many doubt the very sense of rights talk itself!),[46] it can hardly be argued that reparations to Native Americans are required only if there is a singular notion of rights among Native Americans. So it appears that the question here is whether or not Native Americans, or at least many of them, had some working idea of rights, especially rights to the lands on which they resided and that which in most cases was subsequently and forcibly taken from them. On this score, E. Pauline Wilson, a Mohawkan poet, writes:

> Starved with a hollow hunger, we owe to you and your race.
> What have you left to us of land, what have you left of game,
> What have you brought but evil, and curses since you came?
> How have you paid us for *our* game? how paid us for *our* land? . . .
> You say the cattle are not ours, your meat is not our meat;
> When *you* pay for the land you live in, *we'll* pay for the meat we eat.
> Give back *our* land and *our* country, give back *our* herds of game;
> Give back the furs and the forests that were *ours* before you came; . . . [47]
> But they forget we Indians *owned* the land

---

45. For a sample of some of the leading contemporary thinking about the nature, value and function of rights, see Joel Feinberg, *Social Philosophy* (Englewood Cliffs: Prentice-Hall, 1973); *Freedom and Fulfillment: Philosophical Essays* (Princeton: Princeton University Press, 1992), chapters 8–10; Will Kymlicka, ed., *The Rights of Minority Cultures* (Oxford: Oxford University Press, 1995); Lomasky, *Persons, Rights, and the Moral Community* (Oxford; Oxford University Press, 1987); L. W. Sumner, *The Moral Foundations of Rights* (Oxford: Oxford University Press, 1987); Judith J. Thomson, *The Realm of Rights* (Cambridge: Harvard University Press, 1990); Carl Wellman, *A Theory of Rights* (Totowa: Rowman & Littlefield, 1988); *The Proliferation of Rights* (Boulder: Westview, 1999).

46. J. Waldron, *Nonsense Upon Stilts* (London: Methuen, 1987), p. 44.

47. From "The Cattle Thief," in E. Pauline Johnson, *Flint and Feather: The Complete Poems of E. Pauline Johnson (TEKAHIONWAKE)* (Ontario: PaperJacks, 1972), 13–14. My emphasis on the use of "our" and "ours."

From ocean unto ocean; that they stand
Upon a soil that centuries agone
Was *our* sole kingdom and *our right alone.* . . .
By *right*, by birth we Indians *own* these lands,[48]

Other Native Americans expressed notions of rights, in particular, rights
held against invaders of their lands. Sitting Bull asked, "What treaty that
the whites have kept has the red man broken? Not one. What treaty that
the white man ever made with us have they kept? Not one. Where are *our*
lands? Where are *our* waters? Who owns them now? Is it wrong for me to
love my own?"[49] Old Tassel, in a letter to the South Carolina governor
(1776) stated that "we are the first people that ever lived on this land; it is
ours."[50] In a letter to John Ross, Aitooweyah, The Stud and Knock Down
wrote: "We the great mass of the people think only of the love of our land
. . . where we were brought up . . . for we say to you that our father who sits
in Heaven gave it to us."[51] In 1860, Ross advised the Cherokee council that
"our duty is to stand by *our rights*, . . . " and he wrote to Ben McCulloch that
"our country and our institutions are our own. . . . They are sacred and
valuable to us as are those of your own . . . I am determined to do no act
that shall furnish any pretext to either of the contending parties to over-
run *our country* and destroy *our rights*."[52] Isaac Warrior of the Senecas once
said that "then we always thought . . . when we ran away we did nothing,
and *always consider the land we have as ours yet*, and we want to stand there
yet."[53] Ten Bears of the Comanches once said that "I want no blood upon
my land to stain the grass. I want it clear and pure, and I want it so that all
who go through among my people may find peace when they come in and
leave it when they go out."[54] Satanta added: "A long time ago this land *be-
longed to our fathers*; but when I go up the [Arkansas] river I see camps of
soldiers on its banks. These soldiers cut down *my timber*, they kill *my buffalo*;
and when I see that it feels as if my heart would burst with sorrow."[55] Towa-
conie Jim of the Wichitas once said that "we have always thought *our lands
would remain ours*, and never be divided in severalty, and *it can never be done*

48. From "A Cry from an Indian Wife," in Johnson, *Flint and Feather*, pp. 15–17, emphasis added.
49. Quoted in J. Angelo Corlett, "Moral Compatibilism: Rights, Responsibility, Punishment, and Compensation." Ph.D. dissertation, Department of Philosophy, University of Arizona, 1992, p. 224, emphasis added.
50. Debo, *A History of the Indians in the United States*, p. 86.
51. Ibid, p. 124.
52. Ibid., p. 171.
53. Ibid., p. 181.
54. Ibid., p. 219.
55. Ibid., p. 220.

with our consent. The Government treats us as if we had no rights, but we have always lived at our present place, and that is *our home.*"[56] Certainly these words contain at least a pre-reflective notion of rights as entitlements to sovereignty over natural resources, for those, that is, who acquire them legitimately and care for them responsibly. So it is simply false, and perhaps even unusually insulting, to think that rights are indicative of a civilized society and that Native Americans were too barbaric to have and understand some notion of rights which would be recognizable today.

Moreover, as James Tully insightfully points out, various Native American nations indeed had governments which recognized equality and trust in negotiations and treaties between parties, and European invaders themselves (at least many colonists) recognized Native Americans as being sovereign nations with whom treaties could and should be negotiated and signed.[57] Hence the baselessness of Locke's rather naive analysis of Native American peoples as having no governments that articulate and protect property rights, including land rights.

It is false, then, to claim that the moral requirement of reparations is contingent on the wronged party having a sense or conception of rights that would ground the reparations, and it is also false of many Native Americans in particular that they had nothing akin to a contemporary notion of rights, broadly construed. One wonders why the constant cries for Native American rights to be respected were ignored by the majority of the European invaders and especially by the U.S. government and its citizenry, each of whom proclaimed to respect the rights of all humans. One plausible answer is that the treatment of Native Americans by most European invaders was nothing short of racist in their construing and treating them as "savages," a racism motivated perhaps by fear, ignorance, a sense of self-superiority European invaders obtained from, among other things, certain religious beliefs.

The Objection from the Indeterminacy of Native American Identity

Another objection to the awarding of reparations to Native Americans is the *objection from the indeterminacy of Native American identity.* This argument states that, even if there is no moral statute of limitations on otherwise legitimate Native American claims to reparations, such reparations are

56. Ibid., p. 302.
57. Tully, "Aboriginal Property and Western Theory: Recovering a Middle Ground," pp. 169–79.

unwarranted because of the overly difficult task of determining the boundaries of ethnic group membership in general, and of Native American tribal affiliations in particular.[58] For example, does it make moral sense to provide reparations to those who are, say, 10 percent Cherokee and 90 percent European American? What are the boundaries of ethnic group identity for purposes of reparations in particular and corrective justice more generally?

However, the objection from the indeterminacy of Native American identity is too pessimistic concerning the abilities of history, the law, and Native Americans themselves to trace ethnic ties within and between Native peoples. Today's Native American nations (such as the Navajo or Diné nation in Window Rock, Arizona, or Six Nations in Brantfort, Ontario, Canada) keep reasonably successful or accurate track of membership within their respective nations. Thus to the extent that a person is able to be clearly identified as someone belonging to a particular Native American nation (or to more than one nation, for that matter), and to the extent that that nation (or members of it) are owed reparations, that is the extent to which each member of the nation, as a descendant of the victims of gross forms of wrongdoing, are deserving of reparations. It is irrelevant to the moral status of reparations (or the moral desert notion of reparations) that such reparations might impinge on the privacy of persons in regards to their ethnicities, or that a "Balkanization" of ethnic groups might ensue. Insofar as the boundaries of Native American identity are concerned, perhaps these possible problems are, in the end, insoluable in any absolutely precise or totally uncontroversial sense. But these factors hardly render unrequired reparations to Native Americans. For many Native Americans are 50 percent or greater Native Americans of one or more such nations. And the fact that some people's Native American identity is dubious in no way serves as a reasonable consideration to refuse reparations to those who are clearly of substantially Native American ethnicity and who are otherwise deserving of them. Indeed, chapters 2–3 and 6–7 provide a plausible account of how we might identify ourselves, ethnically speaking, and for precisely these sorts of purposes. The genealogical conception of ethnic identity serves as a reasonably accurate model of ethnic identification.

Furthermore, the difficulties in defining precisely the boundaries of Native American identity hardly justifies the current occupation of lands once used and settled by Native Americans by non–Native Americans where

58. This issue is raised in relation to reparations to African Americans. See Boris Bittker, "Identifying the Beneficiaries," in *Reverse Discrimination*, ed. Barry R. Gross (New York: Prometheus, 1977), pp. 279f.

such land possession violates the principle of morally just acquisitions and transfers. To the extent that this principle is violated in the chain of transfers of lands that have a trail to Native Americans and the taking of their lands and lives by, say, the U.S. military, then it is in no way justified for current non–Native American residents of the lands to claim anything more than a mere prima facie right to the lands.

The Historical Reparations Objection

Yet another objection to reparations to Native Americans is that reparations have already been paid to Native American nations in the past for wrongs committed by the U.S. government. I shall refer to this objection as the *historical reparations objection*. In the case of those awarded to Native Americans by the United States, there are the examples of the state of Georgia's restoration of many Cherokee landmarks, a newspaper plant, and other buildings in New Echota, and the state of Georgia's repealing of its repressive anti–Native American laws of 1830. (It took until 1962 for this to occur, however.) Moreover, in 1956 the Pawnees were awarded more than $1 million in a suit they brought before the Indian Claims Commission for land taken from them in Iowa, Kansas, and Missouri. In 1881, the Poncas were compensated by Congress for their ill-treatment by the Court of Omaha, Kansas. For the illegal seizure of the Black Hills in 1876, then owned by the Sioux, compensation was paid. In 1927, the Shoshonis were paid over $6 million for land illegally seized from them (the amount was for the appraised value of *half* of their land, however). There are a few other instances of reparations to Native Americans, as history tells us.[59]

However, the historical reparations objection is based on evidence of reparations to a few Native American nations for property rights violations. There is a threefold difficulty here. First, such reparations were hardly sufficient to serve as anywhere close to adequate compensations for the property, "maltransfers," damages, and other malfeasances in question. Furthermore, the objection ignores completely the question of reparations for undeserved violence in the form of human rights violations against Native Americans, much of such violence was inflicted on various Native Americans by the U.S. military. Finally, it ignores the fact that the vast majority of property rights violations and civil rights violations against Native Americans in general are as of yet *un*compensated. Not unlike the objection from historical progress, the historical reparations objection, then, seems to be more of a non sequitur than a genuine concern.

59. Debo, *A History of the Indians in the United States*.

The Objection from Social Utility

There is another objection to the argument for reparations to Native Americans, and it concerns whether or not the awarding of reparations to Native Americans by the United States would significantly decrease overall social utility. It would render the United States and its citizens—not to mention Native Americans themselves—worse off. For, as Locke argues, the European-based commercial system makes life better for everyone than the primitive hunting and gathering ways of life enjoyed by the Native American nations.[60] I shall refer to this as the *objection from social utility*. This utilitarian-based concern is that, strictly speaking, the awarding to Native Americans of the lands that were acquired from them in violation of the principle of morally just acquisitions and transfers would surely mean the dissolution of the United States as we know it, as mostly each U.S. citizen resides on land which would, presumably, be relinquished to Native peoples should reparations be enforced. The economic, political, and social implications of this action would be unthinkable, even if the awarding of reparations in this fashion were required by the balance of human reason. So social utility requires that reparations not be awarded because of the undue disruption that would certainly be experienced by the majority of citizens of each of the countries in question. Where would such citizens go if forced by, say, international law, to vacate the premises? Which countries would be in economic and political positions to admit these newly homeless persons? Thus reparations to Native Americans are morally unjustified, it is argued, because they would violate some acceptable principle of social utility.

However, the objection from social utility does not take seriously what people deserve and what retributive justice requires. For even if, strictly speaking, the balance of human reason permitted or required reparations that would then force U.S. citizens from the land on which they reside, this would not mean that the moral prerogative of the reparations in question would lead to the disbanding of the current citizens of the United States. For Native peoples might very well settle for sovereignty rights to the existing lands, yet lease such lands to the rest of the inhabitants. This mode of reparations would most likely dissolve the United States as we know it. But perhaps the United States, insofar as it was founded on the clear, repeated, and intentional violations of the content of the principle of morally just acquisitions and transfers, deserves to be dissolved in favor of taking

---

60. Locke, *Second Treatise on Government*, sections 34, 37, 40–43. For an assessment of Locke's view, see Tully, "Aboriginal Property and Western Theory: Recovering a Middle Ground," pp. 161f.

much more seriously (than it currently does) morality and justice. None-theless, the sovereignty over certain lands by Native Americans to others satisfies the concern for morality and justice in that it gives back to Native peoples the lands to which they had and have ultimate ("trumping") moral rights. But it also does not unduly affect those currently living on those lands in violation of the principle of morally just acquisitions and transfers. For they are not left without a place of residence, evading the aforemen-tioned concern. (But they would be alienated from what is not really theirs to begin with, morally speaking.) Thus the objection from social utility does not pose an insoluble problem for reparations to Native Americans, though at least one strict form of reparations to Native Americans does im-ply the dissolution of the United States as we know it. The citizens of the United States would become highly dependent on the goodness of the Na-tive American nations. Of course, history shows that most, if not all, Native peoples are not the kinds of people with whom one has to worry regard-ing good will and cooperation. A lengthy history of upheld treaties with the United States speaks loudly to this effect. If any party is not to be trusted along these lines, it is surely the U.S. government and its "patriotic" citi-zenry.

Furthermore, there is something misleading about the objection from social utility as it applies to reparations to Native Americans. The objection is that the majority of persons now residing in the United States would be significantly and adversely effected by the awarding of such reparations to a minority of persons, all in the name of some "ideal" of retribution. Yet the argument fails to recall that on the invasion of such lands centuries ago by Europeans, the clear majority of residents were Native Americans! Re-call that there were *hundreds* of such nations, many of which were thriving societies. The objection from social utility seeks to argue that reparations to Native Americans would pose social utility problems for current U.S. cit-izens. This objection, at least in some contexts, represents a rather insen-sitive attitude toward the crimes committed by the U.S. military against various Native Americans. Moreover, if the informational content of the same argument is indexed to the times in which Native American lives and lands were improperly acquired by the U.S. government, then considera-tions of social utility might well favor a policy of reparations to Native Amer-icans as a (then) numerical majority whose rights were violated by certain (then) numerical minority of invaders. Thus we cannot without indepen-dent and plausible argumentation simply assume that current U.S. citi-zens, say, count as the primary index of social utility maximization. For when social utility maximization is indexed to the times in which Native American lands and lives were lost to, say, Andrew Jackson's military campaign to fulfill manifest destiny, then Native Americans are the ones who (cumulatively speaking) count as the index of social utility maximization. After all, if the objection from social utility works against the awarding of reparations to Native Americans by indexing what counts as social utility maximization to what maximizes happiness for today's residents of the lands in question, then by parity of reasoning it works against attempts to compensate U.S. citizens should, say, a more populous China succeed in conquering the United States by way of genocide. After all, if what is most important is the maximization of social happiness or such for the greatest number of persons, then what truly maximizes a majority group of conquerors will often, if not always, trump the rights of those of the conquered minority groups. This sort of "ethic" appears indistinguishable from a policy of "might makes right," hardly to be taken seriously by a moral philosopher. If it demonstrated anything at all, the objection from social utility shows the futility of an act utilitarian standpoint in taking seriously the rights of minority members of society. This point about act utilitarianism, of course, is not novel.[61]

The Religious Freedom Objection

Closely related to the objection from social utility is the *religious freedom objection,* one which objects that reparations to Native Americans are morally unjustified because they would lead to the dissolution of the United States, which was founded on the principle of religious liberty for all. Since this principle is sound, whatever would pose a significant problem for it must be rejected. Since the dissolution of the United States would spell the demise of its protection of liberties of various religious groups within U.S. borders, substantial reparations to Native Americans are unjustified.

But the religious freedom objection fails to see the bitter irony in what it claims to support. For the United States was established, among other things, to secure religious liberty, yet in the process it ran roughshod over the religious freedom of hundreds of Native American nations! Moreover, as if that were not sufficient, the United States still engages in such duplicity.[62] Thus the religious freedom objection cannot be used to thwart reparations to Native Americans without exposing the crudest form of U.S.

61. That considerations of social utility might *favor* (rather than disfavor) reparations to those deserving of them is argued in Matsuda, "Looking to the Bottom: Critical Legal Studies and Reparations," pp. 74f.

62. See Burleigh Wilkins, "A Third Principle of Justice," *Journal of Ethics* 1 (1997): 355–74.

hypocrisy. Furthermore, even if the religious freedom objection works, it supports Native American reparations, as such reparations would surely serve to secure religious freedom for the descendants of Native Americans.

The Acquired Rights Trumping Original Land Rights Objection

Some would argue that certain rights can be acquired where previously there were no such rights. In particular, some would object to the moral requirement of reparations to Native Americans on the grounds that the U.S. descendants of the European invaders are not themselves morally accountable for the evils inflicted on earlier Native peoples in America, thus escaping the pale of moral retrospective liability responsibility on which such reparations are said to be based. Those who currently reside on putatively U.S. soil and who are not Native Americans did not secure the land illicitly. Furthermore, it is argued, recent generations of U.S. citizens have actually acquired moral rights to the lands on which they reside.[63] What grounds such rights? To be sure, many U.S. citizens have mixed their labor with the land in the forms of building/purchasing homes and working the land.[64] This Lockean point regarding what one has a right to is said to ground the moral rights of contemporary U.S. citizens to "their" land. In addition, one might argue that what the supporters of reparations to Native Americans neglect to see is that there is more to this matter than mere original land acquisition rights. There are also the issues of merit and desert. Arguments for reparations to Native Americans based on original land acquisition are implausible given that they ignore the fact that current non-Native peoples have since acquired rights to the lands based on their acquiring such lands legitimately. Because property (including land) rights change over time, argues David Lyons, today's Native Americans would probably not have rights to their ancestors' lands even had they not been stolen from them by the U.S. government. Thus reparations to Native Americans by the U.S. government for the past injustices

63. This argument is set forth and defended in Lyons, "New Indian Claims and Original Rights to Land," pp. 252f.

64. See Locke, *The Second Treatise of Government*. For a helpful discussion of Locke's positions on rights and other political concepts, see A. John Simmons, *The Lockean Theory of Rights* (Princeton: Princeton University Press, 1992); *The Edge of Anarchy* (Princeton: Princeton University Press, 1993). Locke's line of reasoning has been plausibly refuted in Robert Nozick, "Distributive Justice," *Philosophy and Public Affairs* 3 (1973): 7of. See also Jeremy Waldron, *The Right to Private Property* (Oxford: Oxford University Press, 1988), chapters 6–7; "Two Worries About Mixing One's Labor," *Philosophical Quarterly* 33 (1983): 37–44.

are unwarranted.[65] I shall refer to this as the *acquired rights trumping original land rights objection*.

But the acquired rights trumping original land rights objection is flawed, and for several reasons. First, reparations do *not* require that those who pay them are morally accountable for the wrongdoing that justifies—or even requires—them. This point was addressed when answering the objection from historical complexity and the objection to collective responsibility. Suffice it to add that, as Joel Feinberg argues, there are cases of collective liability where there is no fault distributed amongst members of a collective.[66] Even apart from collectives, however, "a person may incur legal liability even though they were not in any sense responsible for the event that triggered the liability. Restitutionary liability of an innocent, passive recipient of a mistaken payment or beneficiary of fraud is a good example. There may . . . be both responsibility without legal liability, and legal liability without responsibility."[67] Second, a ruthless invader can steal land and then mix her labor with it and thereby, according to the argument, gain rights to the stolen land. This might serve well the purposes of invaders seeking to establish their own putative democracy. Yet this is hardly morally justified. Furthermore, that invader's selling her ill-gotten land to an "innocent" party is a clear violation of the principle of morally just acquisitions and transfers. In a similar way, then, the mixing of one's labor with the land is insufficient to ground a moral right had by U.S. citizens to the lands in question. Furthermore, as Waldron argues,

> the Lockean image of labor (whether it is individual or cooperative) being literally embedded or mixed in an object is incoherent. . . . For it would be impossible to explain how property rights thus acquired could be alienable—how they could be transferred, through sale or gift, from one person to another—without offense to the personality of the original acquirer.[68]

So something else must be true to make plausible the claim that current U.S. citizens have overriding moral rights to the lands on which they reside. But what would that be, except that one must inherit or acquire land *without* it being the case that the principle of morally just acquisitions and transfers is violated? One cannot legitimately inherit or deserve what has

65. Lyons, "The New Indian Claims and Original Rights to Land," pp. 254f. Lyons argues, astonishingly, that the genuinely compensable wrongs against Native Americans by the U.S. government might be more recent acts of discrimination against them, rather than the historical injustices of murders and illegitimate takings of their lands (Lyons, "The New Indian Claims and Original Rights to Land," pp. 268–71).

66. Feinberg, *Doing and Deserving*, pp. 248f.

67. Peter Cane, *Responsibility in Law and Morality* (Oxford: Hart, 2002), p. 1.

68. Waldron, "Superseding Historic Injustice," p. 17.

been acquired or transferred by way of immorality or injustice. As Christine M. Korsgaard argues, "If a theft or swindle succeeds, we do not take it that the new distribution of property is legitimate."[69] Finally, if some U.S. citizens have moral rights to "their" lands by "just" inheritance,[70] then why would we not think that original land rights of Native peoples in turn accrue to current Native Americans? This would mean that the real question of which set of moral rights claims/interests "trumps" another's boils down to, among other things, whether or not there was a violation of the principle of morally just acquisitions and transfers concerning what is now deemed by many to be U.S. territory.

It might be argued, perhaps instead of there being a moral statute of limitations on injustice, that there is a justified limitation of time placed on rights claims, and that the limitation on the claim of a right to reparations has expired for Native Americans to justly claim their rights to the lands. In U.S. law, this is referred to as the *Laches* doctrine: if there is a significant amount of time that passes without a wronged party's attempting to claim its right to something, then the claimant loses its right to that thing. Or, at the very least, the right "fades" over time.[71]

But this line of reasoning neglects the historical reality that at several points in time various Native American nations have publicly claimed their land rights—even to the U.S. government! That such claims were made repeatedly and not respected is a matter of historical fact, and that the claims of many Native Americans were not respected fails to count as evidence for the claim that the opportunity to claim the right to reparations has truly expired.[72] For many Native Americans satisfied the condition in question. But their pleas were simply ignored or turned away. We must bear in mind that an unjust legal system's failure to uphold Native American claims to lands (and compensation for crimes constituting violence to persons, among other things) hardly serves as a rational foundation for a moral (or

---

69. Christine M. Korsgaard, "Taking the Law into Our Own Hands: Kant on the Right to Revolution," in *Reclaiming the History of Ethics: Essays for John Rawls*, ed. Andrews Reath, Barbara Herman, and Christine M. Korsgaard (Cambridge: Cambridge University Press, 1997), p. 307.

70. That inheritance is justly and fairly delimited by principles of justice is argued in John Rawls, *A Theory of Justice* (Cambridge: Harvard University Press, 1971), pp. 277f.; *Collected Papers*, Samuel Freeman, ed. (Cambridge: Harvard University Press, 1999), pp. 142f.

71. A similar point is found in Waldron, "Superseding Historic Injustice," p. 15.

72. As noted above, U.S. law recognizes no statute of limitations in cases of murder. Thus neither the moral statute of limitations objection to reparations to Native Americans (rejected earlier) nor the *Laches* doctrine in U.S. law count against reparations to Native Americans in instances where murders of Native Americans were perpetrated by the U.S. Government and representatives of its agencies in the fulfilling of their duties as official representatives of the U.S. government.

even a legal) statute of limitations on Native American claims concerning what they deserve as compensation for such wrongdoings. Reparations to Native Americans in the United States are either morally required or they are not, regardless of the fact that morally corrupted legislative and judicial systems were put in place to (among other things) bias decisions against Native American claims, thus supporting the idea of the expiration of the statute of limitations on Native American land claims. Furthermore, that contemporary U.S. citizens are not causally responsible for the past wrongs committed against Native Americans in no way nullifies the fact that today's lands are, in the main, occupied by those who have acquired them through a chain of possessions that is in clear violation of the principle of morally just acquisitions and transfers. For as was pointed out in the refutation of the objection to collective responsibility, that one has not wronged Native Americans in some direct way hardly justifies ones being in the possession of stolen or ill-gotten property. Thus there needs to be a reason other than the one provided by the statute of limitations advocates that would ground the acquisition of moral rights to lands now occupied by U.S. citizens.

Some might argue that the Lockean proviso grounds the rights of current U.S. citizens to the lands on which they reside in that Native Americans in the distant past had more land than they could use, and that the Native Americans had no right to deprive European "invaders" of their settlement of North American lands that were not in use by Native Americans.

However, this line of reasoning is problematic for the following reasons. First, most of the land acquired by the European invaders (including the U.S. government) was by way of force and fraud against Native Americans (not to mention, non–Native Americans!). So even if Native Americans had an obligation (based on the Lockean proviso) to share some of the North American lands with others, it does not follow that the lands had to be shared with those who dealt Native Americans injustices of the harshest orders. This holds whether the invaders were conquering "explorers" or "mere settlers." The possible difference between these two groups in terms of their putative collective moral liability for harms against Native Americans does not diminish the fact that each group played a crucial role in the unjust acquisitions and transfers of lands that were inhabited by Native Americans.

Second, the Lockean proviso states that one has a right to X to the extent that there is enough and as good of X for others.[73] However, U.S.

---

73. See Locke, *Second Treatise on Government,* section 27; Robert Nozick, *Anarchy, State and Utopia* (New York: Basic Books, 1974), pp. 175–82; A. John Simmons, *The Lockean Theory of Rights* (Princeton: Princeton University Press, 1992), pp. 278f.

history is replete with examples of Native Americans *welcoming with open arms* European invaders, under the assumption, no doubt, that something like the principle of morally just acquisitions and transfers would not be violated in the course of the latter groups' settling the lands. So Native Americans, by and large and from the outset of the invasion of the Americas, acted in congruence with the Lockean proviso both in terms of their dealings with non–Native Americans and in terms of their dealings with most other Native Americans. Yet history tells the complicated and dismal stories of injustices Native Americans experienced in losing their lands, often times violently to European invaders, hardly a moral foundation for current U.S. claims to North American lands.[74]

Furthermore, it is unclear whether the Lockean proviso was violated by Native Americans as a whole. Considering that there were hundreds of such nations in North America, and that many of them were nomadic, it is not at all certain that there was sufficient land and resources for them to share with Europeans.[75] This is especially plausible if one accords to Native Americans the same moral and legal rights to have families and to meet the needs of expanding families (including the need for additional land). Thus it is difficult to see how original rights of Native Americans to the lands and resources in question are trumped by subsequent European putative rights to the same lands and resources for reasons of the Lockean proviso.

The Supersession of Historic Injustice Objection

Furthermore, there is the *supersession of historic injustice objection* to reparations, articulated by Waldron. The basic idea here is that "changing circumstances can have an effect on ownership rights notwithstanding the moral legitimacy of original appropriation."[76] Applied to the Native American experience, the argument runs as follows. There have been historic injustices committed against Native Americans, as we all know. But historical circumstances have changed, and situations where resources are scarce, such as now, are those in which the future generations of those who themselves wronged Native Americans are morally *entitled* to share resources

74. Furthermore, it has been argued that it is reasonable to hold that the Iroquois indeed acquired rights to some North American lands, and on a Lockean basis! See John D. Bishop, "Locke's Theory of Original Appropriation and the Right of Settlement in Iroquois Territory," *Canadian Journal of Philosophy* 27 (1997): 311–38. See also Naomi Zack, "Lockean Money, Indigenism, and Globalism," *Canadian Journal of Philosophy (Supplementary Volume)* 25 (1999): 32f.

75. See Thompson, "Historical Obligations," pp. 320–21.

76. Waldron, "Superseding Historic Injustice," p. 24.

(including land) with Native Americans. Thus the initial injustices by past generations of European invaders and the U.S. military (among others) against Native Americans is superseded by changing circumstances. "Claims about justice and injustice must be responsive to changes in circumstances," as Waldron argues.[77] So the issue of historic injustice, though an important one, is superseded by the fact that inhabitants of lands are required to share it with others under conditions of scarcity of resources. After all, "the aboriginal inhabitants would have had to share their lands, whether the original injustice had taken place or not."[78] Waldron writes,

> If circumstances make a difference to what counts as a just acquisition, then it must make a difference also to what counts as an unjust incursion. And if they make a difference to that, then in principle we must concede that a change in circumstances can effect whether a particular continuation of adverse possession remains an injustice or not. . . .
> . . . It may be that some of the historic injustices that concern us have not been superseded, and that, even under modern circumstances, the possession of certain aboriginal lands by the descendants of those who expropriated their original owners remains a crying injustice. My argument is not intended to rule that out. But there have been huge changes since North America and Australasia were settled by white colonists. . . . We cannot be sure that these changes in circumstances supersede the injustice of their continued possession of aboriginal lands, but it would not be surprising if they did.[79]

There are problems, however, with the supersession of historic injustice objection to reparations to Native Americans. Although the argument admits that European invaders (and the U.S. government, more specifically) had no rightful claims to lands that they expropriated from Native Americans, the argument seems to say that later generations of at least some of those European invaders gained land rights based on the premise that under conditions of scarcity, resources must be shared by all occupants of a territory (a version of the Lockean proviso). Yet the fact is that such conditions of scarcity would, so far as history informs us, have not likely existed if not for the doings of the European invaders themselves! There was certainly significant land and resources (buffalo, for instance, and other food sources) for the millions of Native Americans prior to the invasion of North America by Europeans and prior to the massacres of various Native Americans by the U.S. military. Nor is there uncontroversial evidence to suggest

77. Ibid., p. 25.
78. Ibid., p. 25.
79. Ibid., pp. 25–26.

that there is a high probability that there would have been a scarcity of such resources among Native Americans absent natural disasters and European invaders. So in effect the argument seeks to ground the future generations of European invaders' putative moral claims to the lands on which they reside on the fact that those whose ancestors by and large created a problem of resource scarcity have a moral claim to the lands over and above those who once possessed the land without scarcity of resources. (This does *not* imply, however, that there was enough for Native Americans to share with others—even if they wanted to do so.)

But why not infer from history and morality a rather different conclusion, namely, that at best current non–Native Americans possess trumping or overriding moral claims to whatever property they legitimately own which is *on* the land belonging to the descendants of those from whom the European invaders expropriated it? Is this not the more intuitively sensible inference, given historical circumstances? How, then, can we say that the violations against Native Americans are "superseded," as Waldron avers? Simply because such evils occurred long ago? Hardly. For neither the *Laches* defense nor statutes of limitations seem plausible, morally speaking. Would we dare infer that a thief who breaks into my home, takes me hostage, and resides there for months on end, eating my food, making himself "at home" in various other ways in turn somehow gains a right to the home, even if he should assume some of the household chores (after all, he is a rather tidy thief and does not like to live in a messy place)? Would we not say that he is a thief, and that no matter how much he makes himself at home, that he has made himself at home in *my* home, and that he is to be arrested, tried, and if found guilty by way of due process, then he is to be punished and made to compensate me for damages? And would we not say of the great, great grandson of that thief who inherited the house and the land on which it rests that it is *not* really his house or land, even though he is not at fault for its being stolen property? Why, then, do we not conclude similarly in the case of reparations to Native Americans? I say "similarly" in that those who currently reside on U.S. lands do so while they themselves are not causally responsible for the crimes perpetrated against Native Americans by the U.S. military. Thus compensation, not punishment, is what is at issue regarding reparations to Native Americans. The supersession of historic injustice objection, then, surely has little to recommend it.

The Anti-Private-Property-Rights Objection

The previous discussion pertained to the matter of whether or not reparations to Native Americans by the U.S. gvernment are morally required.

However, there is a line of argument that would challenge the very basis of the discussion, it would appear. It is that the fundamental flaw in the previous discussion, especially as concerns the pinciple of morally just acquisitions and transfers, is that it wrongly assumes the plausibility of the notion of private property rights, something that Karl Marx, among others, sought to refute (especially in terms of original acquisition of land rights). The Marxian line of reasoning might take the form of a regress argument, challenging the validity of each land or property transfer to and from private parties such that—in the end—there is no moral basis for or justification of original acquisition rights to land (in the ownership sense, not in the occupation sense on which my articulation of Native American rights to land depends). Thus to the extent that the concept of private property rights (whether ownership or sovereignty rights) is problematic, so is the entire line of reasoning of the previous discussion supporting reparations by the U.S. government to Native Americans. I shall call this the *anti-private-property-rights objection* to reparations to Native Americans.

In reply to this concern, several points might be made in order to neutralize its argumentative force. First, even if sound, this criticism is not open to a defender of U.S. capitalism in that U.S. capitalism is contingent on the plausibility of the notion of private property rights. So if it turns out, for example, that Marx is correct in his call for "the abolition of landed property" (1869), then it would follow that no U.S. citizen (or the U.S. government, for that matter!) has a moral right to *any* land, in particular, to the land on which she (or it) currently resides. Thus this Marxist-style concern about the morally problematic nature of property (land) rights and of the original acquisition of it is *not* open to the defender of the U.S. or its citizens from paying reparations to Native Americans.

Second, even if it turns out that the concept of property rights is null and void, especially as it pertains to land, it would not follow that reparations by the U.S. government are not owed to Native Americans. For though the arguments for land-based reparations might become problematic, such reparations might be justified on the basis of the Native American holocaust itself.[80] It is hard to imagine that Marx would object that the victims of racist oppression in the form of genocide ought not to receive their compensation from the capitalist aggressors. So even if Marxist arguments against the ownership of land are plausible and win the day, it hardly follows that they in turn defeat the claim that reparations by the U.S. government to Native Americans are morally required on the basis of severe *civil* rights violations. One need not argue, by the way, that property

80. Just as many people use the term *holocaust* as a synonym for the Nazi genocide of Jews, I use the term *holocaust* as a synonym for "genocide" here and elsewhere in this book.

rights, or rights more generally, are the core of an adequate moral and political philosophy. For rights (and their correlating duties) are at best merely part of what is needed and desired for a plausible moral and political economy. Nothing that I have argued herein assumes a solely rights-based morality or political economy, though my defense of reparations (in terms of land) against various objections to them assumes the significance of property (land) rights.

Third, *to the extent that* the concept of property (land) rights is plausible, it would appear that this same concept both supports the moral viability of U.S. capitalism (if it does at all) and condemns it on moral grounds in that U.S. capitalism is founded on the genocide of Native Americans. What the principle of morally just acquisitions and transfers and the preceding discussion of various arguments against reparations to Native Americans show is that the concept of property rights condemns (not supports) U.S. capitalism, morally speaking. To the extent that the United States was established on the intended and voluntary genocide of various Native American nations, U.S. capitalism is condemned on moral grounds. And this moral condemnation can hardly, except on the crudest of act-utilitarian grounds, be rescued by an appeal to the relative economic productivity experienced by the United States in recent years. Nor can the moral evils of the United States be somehow erased or neutralized by the ignoring of the Native American holocaust in favor of appeals to alleged or actual progress that the United States has made in terms of democratic civil rights reforms. For no amount of reform can itself serve as compensation for the degrees and kinds of physical harms of a holocaust when that holocaust remains un-rectified.

The Counterfactual Objection

There is a final concern with policies of reparations to Native Americans. Waldron notes a counterfactual difficulty regarding reparations:

> The present surely looks different now from the way the present would look if a given injustice of the past had not occurred. Why not therefore change the present so that it looks more like the present that would have obtained in the absence of the injustice? . . .
> The trouble with this approach is the difficulty we have in saying what would have happened if some event (which did occur) had not taken place.[81]

81. Waldron, "Superseding Historic Injustice," pp. 7–8.

Waldron adds that the problem of reparations becomes even fuzzier when we factor into the rectificatory scheme the matter of human choice. For given the fact that humans do have some choices, this makes it quite problematic to figure out how the present situation might be readjusted to best approximate the scheme of things had a particular injustice not taken place. Besides the matter of whether or not such human choices can rightly have normative import and to be nonarbitrary, argues Waldron, "Ultimately, what is raised here is the question of whether it is possible to rectify particular injustices without undertaking a comprehensive redistribution that addresses all claims of justice that may be made."[82] I shall refer to this as the *counterfactual objection.*

In reply to Waldron's concerns about counterfactual aspects of reparations, it might be argued that it hardly counts against the moral requirement of reparations to, say, Native Americans that the subsequent redistributive scheme of compensatory justice would lead to a proliferation of rights claims to historic injustices pertaining to the settlement and development of North America. Even if it were true that few such claims could or would be settled adequately, this does nothing to count against the claim that reparations are required as a matter of moral principle. Nor does it somehow render senseless the multidimensional aspects of the expressive functions of reparations to Native American nations. Furthermore, in the case of Native American nations, there are records of leaders of such nations declaring their unambiguous aversion to and despising of most anything to do with "manifest destiny" and other social, political, and cultural features of the "American experiment." Historical records provide a keen understanding of the culture and beliefs of Native American peoples, and we can be sure that what is important to them is at least the returning of their land to them, even though the land is hardly in the condition in which it was seized from them. That it is impossible to return to Native American nations what was once theirs and in the same condition as it was when it was taken from them by force and fraud is not a good enough reason to think that it is not morally required to return such lands to them, however damaged.[83] Moreover, to my knowledge there is nothing in Native American history or culture to suggest that Native Americans would have freely chosen to give up their lands to anyone who would do to the lands what European settlers by and large did to it.

Although the counterfactual approach to reparations is indeed a problem

---

82. Ibid., p. 13.

83. For a discussion of how reparations might accrue in such circumstances, see Tyler Cowen, "Discounting and Restitution," *Philosophy and Public Affairs* 26 (1997): 168–85.

for reparations policies, it says nothing about the moral requirement of reparations themselves, except that, like matters of punishment and compensation in general, rectificatory justice is at best imprecise. The counterfactual objection to reparations to Native Americans would seem to imply that punishment and compensation themselves are too problematic even for most contemporary courts to handle, as evidence and argumentation is rarely unambiguous in interpretation. Yet this is surely an implication few would find plausible. Imprecision and Herculean cases are hardly excuses for the law's turning its head from the need for justice. So the counterfactual objection against reparations to Native Americans does not show that reparations are not morally required, or that they are not feasible as a legal means of compensating (to some significant extent) those who deserve them.

If the objections to reparations to Native Americans are specious for at least the reasons noted, and if the principle of morally just acquisitions and transfers is plausible and applicable to the Native American experiences, then the balance of reason suggests at least the prima facie plausibility of some policy of reparations to Native Americans. Moreover, it is incumbent on the supporter of such reparations to devise a plausible policy of reparations. Although a full-fledged theory and policy of reparations to Native Americans is beyond the scope of this book, a few points can be noted along the lines of how reparations to Native Americans might accrue.

It should be acknowledged that various of the nations that constitute Native Americans as a broad set of ethnic groups have varying degrees of experiences with oppression at the hands of the European invaders, and that a principle of proportionality must be used to distinguish variant levels of reparations to different Native American nations, that is, where history is clear about the differences in evil experienced by them. In general, however, whether it be the Diné, the Cherokees, the Mohawks, the Six Nations, the Senecas, or other Native American nations, sufficient evils have been perpetrated against them by the U.S. government that would require some form of compensatory reparations of a significant measure.[84] One obvious reason for this is noted by G. Sher: "In the case of . . . Indians, . . . we may indeed have enough information to suggest that most current group members are worse off than they would be in the absence of some initial wrong."[85] Yet it is unnecessary to impose a standard of strict proportionality that the law cannot uphold even in much easier cases. After all, one

84. This is not to deny that certain corporate or other business parties played roles in the "American Holocaust" of Native Americans. The development of railroads, telegraph and certain other industries did play such roles.

85. G. Sher, *Approximate Justice* (Totowa: Rowman and Littlefield, 1997), p. 15.

possible strategy is to argue that even if compensating for such wrongs would not restore full justice to Native Americans, it would at least bring Native Americans substantially closer to justice than they are currently.

Some Possible Reparations Policies

What sorts of specific compensatory measures ought to be imposed and against whom? Let us consider the plausibility of a range of possible policies of U.S. reparations to Native Americans. I will consider a number of such possible policies, from some of the more demanding ones to some of the least demanding. I assume that the crimes of unjust land takings, murders, and political repression by the U.S. government contain a minimal amount of moral and historical ambiguity: that the identities of the collective perpetrators, victims, and those targeted for reparations are knowable within reasonable clarity and precision.[86]

Strict Justice, the Complete Restitution of Lands and Compensation for Personal Injuries/Loss of Personal Property.

It might be argued that, strictly speaking, morality and justice require the complete return of the lands of North America that were gotten from Native peoples in violation of the principle of morally just acquisitions and transfers. Such a measure of reparations would not only return all such lands outright to Native peoples, but would require the U.S. government (along with British, Dutch, Spanish, French and Canadian governments, among others) to pay native peoples significant sums of money as compensation for damages for the crimes (murders, rapes, mayhems, and robbery by the thousands) committed against Native Americans in the "settling" of the "New World." It is plausible to believe that at least trillions of dollars would be rightly owed to Native Americans by these governments (perhaps respectively, especially considering punitive damages, unpaid interest accrued, and penalties!), each of which participated in the massacre and near complete genocide of all Native Americans over periods of generations. This form of reparations to surviving Native American nations would surely bring to economic demise each of the governments paying such reparations and would tilt rather severely the balance of global

86. Each of the following possible policies of reparations is consistent with *each* of the reparations standards found in Cowan, "Discounting and Restitution," pp. 171–75. Also assumed is a principle of proportional compensation according to which compensation in the form of reparations must be commensurate to the harms inflicted on Native Americans by the U.S. government and its agencies/institutions.

economic power in favor of Native Americans (and other indigenous peoples receiving similar such settlements).

In response to this proposed policy of reparations, it might be argued that a certain utilitarian consideration outweighs strict retributive justice, namely, that the millions of U.S. citizens not be made significantly worse-off in the process of rectifying past wrongs committed against native peoples. This is especially true since those who would be made worse-off are the clear numerical majority of people residing in the United States. Considerations of utility require that a less extreme and demanding policy of reparations be adopted. Thus the argument from social utility, refuted above, is reinvoked here.

But one question is whether or not such U.S. citizens are in a moral position to deny the legitimacy of a policy that would place them in economic ruins. The reason why such citizens are not in a moral position is that they are residing on lands to which they have no genuine and overriding moral right, that is, a moral right that (all things considered) trumps other competing moral claims to and/or interests in the lands in question. Does Andrew, who knowingly or unknowingly purchases or otherwise receives stolen property, have a moral claim to it? If so, does Andrew's moral claim trump the moral right of the victim (the original moral right holder of the property) to the same? Consider the following example of a wealthy person whose *entire* fortune was contingent on and amounted to that which she inherited in violation of the principle of morally just acquisitions and transfers. Even if she is not morally entitled to that which was obtained unjustly, is she not entitled to the fruits of her labor/investments above and beyond the basic value of the inheritance?[87] Even if it is true that she mixed her labor with some of the ill-gotten fortune to increase the fortune over time, her increase in fortune might be offset by the balance of leasing or interest payments owed for the land ill-acquired or the fortune acquired unjustly. Yet we would not think it correct that she remain in possession of "her" fortune, but that she return it to the rightful heir or owner, namely the person who has a valid moral claim to the fortune.

Complete Restitution of Lands

Another policy of reparations to Native Americans would be the complete restitution of lands to them. Although it is impossible to return to particular Native American nations the lands that were theirs originally due to the fact that some such nations no longer exist, it would be possible to provide Native American nations, *as a coalition,* all such lands that were acquired

---

87. This issue is raised in Coleman, "Corrective Justice and Wrongful Gain," p. 421.

or transferred in violation of the principle of morally just acquisitions and transfers. Presumably, this would mean that most or all U.S. occupied lands would be transferred to Native American nations, and that Native Americans would, as a coalition, become a sort of "landlord" over those who currently reside on the lands.[88]

One difficulty with this proposed policy of reparations is that it does not account for the crimes against persons and is thus an insufficient form of reparations to Native Americans who as a group not only lost their native lands, but also were in many cases enslaved, killed, suffered severe damage to forms of livelihood, and so forth. So the restitution of lands to Native Americans simply repays them for the lands which is theirs by moral right. However, it does not compensate them for the damage to the land and resources, nor for the crimes against persons committed against them by the U.S. government.

Complete Compensation for Harms to Persons and Property

Another policy of reparations to Native Americans would involve complete compensation for harms against Native Americans and their personal property. This would surely entail the payment of billions of dollars over several years, especially in light of the millions of such native persons who were murdered, mutilated, tortured, and enslaved, and those who survived but often had their belongings and livelihoods ruined by marauding U.S. citizens (even by the U.S. army!). A complete compensation program for Native Americans would likely involve a continual payment of a substantial sum of money to Native American nations, with the idea that such payments would in themselves hardly serve as adequate compensation for the crimes perpetrated.

The difficulty with this form of reparations is that it does nothing to provide restitution to native peoples for their land that was taken from them in violation of the principle of morally just acquisitions and transfers. In fact, such a "complete" compensation policy leaves untouched the very social structure and government and forces that subdued the Native Americans in the first place, standing as a continual reminder of how evil can mock true justice. Even compensation with restitution of lands is hardly adequate for justice in this case. The same would follow, then, regarding policies of partial compensation for harms to persons and property, partial restitution of lands, partial compensation for harms to persons and property, and partial compensation for lands.

88. A restricted version of this policy is proposed in Thompson, "Historical Obligations," p. 328.

The "Buffalo Commons" Proposal

Short of complete restoration of lands and/or compensation for personal injuries of Native Americans, there lies another proposal. It is the partial but significant restoration of lands to Native Americans, lands that have, it is argued, never played an important role in the economic viability of the United States. Thus the restoring of such lands to Native Americans by way of reparations would pose no real threat to the U.S. economy. This is what has been referred to as the "Buffalo Commons" proposal:[89]

> What you end up with is a huge territory lying east of Denver, west of Lawrence, Kansas, and extending from the Canadian border to southern Texas, all of it "outside the loop" of United States business as usual.
>
>   The bulk of this area is unceded territory owned by the Lakota, Pawnee, Arikara, Hidatsa, Mandan, Crow, Shoshone, Assiniboine, Cheyenne, Arapaho, Kiowa, Comanche, Jicarilla, and Mescalero Apache nations. There would be little cost to the United States, and virtually no arbitrary dispossession or dislocation of non-Indians, if the entire Commons were restored to these peoples.[90]

The reasons given in favor of this proposal are twofold. First, it provides Native Americans a means of tangible sovereignty and self-determination. Secondly, it provides "alternative socioeconomic models" for possible adaptation by those who are not Native Americans.

Of course, this proposal, however reasonable in its attempt to not disrupt the lives of U.S. citizens, is grossly inadequate as a form of reparations for the remainder of the territories taken by force and fraud from Native Americans. Nor does it begin to compensate Native Americans for the murders and other personal injuries inflicted on them by the U.S. government. Nonetheless, the Buffalo Commons proposal is a reasonable attempt to balance the application of some plausible principle of utility to current U.S. society over against the demand for some degree of rectification for injustice to Native Americans. Although reasonable, the Buffalo Commons proposal is insufficient as a means for providing adequate reparations to Native Americans.

Substantial Reparations Tax

The previously discussed policies of reparations to Native Americans would come in the form of court-ordered settlements. But that is not the only way in which such reparations might be made. Instead, a tax might be levied

---

89. Ward Churchill, *From a Native Son* (Boston: South End Press, 1996), pp. 528–30.
90. Ibid., p. 529.

on U.S. citizens, one that would be paid to various Native American nations. A substantial tax might amount to, say, 25 percent of each non–Native American's annual gross income in perpetuity.

An objection to this substantial reparations tax might be that it is overly substantial and demanding on U.S. citizens. However, it is hard to understand this concern in light of the fact that current U.S. citizens are residing on lands to which they have no moral right, given the foregoing arguments. Sometimes justice and morality demand what we in our less honorable moments find too difficult to do. If anything is problematic about the nature and scope of the substantial reparations tax, it is rather that it is insufficiently substantial, not that it is overly substantial.

Minimal Reparations Tax

A minimal reparations tax might amount to, say, 1 percent of each U.S. citizen's gross annual income. But if the substantial reparations tax is properly deemed as insufficient to adequately compensate for the harms committed against Native Americans by the U.S. government, then surely this minimal reparations tax would be nothing more than an insult to Native Americans and to justice and fairness itself.

The points of criticism of each of the above sketched reparations policies are meant to convey the idea that the fact that the U.S. citizenry does not desire to compensate Native Americans for the wrongs that the U.S. Government has committed against the latter shows a certain amount of moral ineptitude on the part of the U.S. citizenry in general. Moreover, if the principle of morally just acquisitions and transfers is correct in regards to the Native American experiences, then one is hardly in a moral position to deny the plausibility of any of these policies of reparations so long as they are acceptable to Native Americans. For neither policy is adequate to compensate Native Americans for the wrongs their people have suffered at the hands of the very government that persists today. Yet one wonders why, except for reasons of racism and lack of moral character, even today most U.S. citizens would balk at even the hint of a *minimal* reparations tax to cover a fraction of the costs of arguably the worst evils ever perpetrated by a modern government.

If the arguments against reparations to Native Americans in the United States are defeasible for the reasons given herein, then the presumptive case in favor of reparations to Native Americans gains strength. Barring further argumentation that would render morally problematic such reparations, then, a case for such reparations has been made along the following lines. To the extent that history is unambiguous concerning the extent of guilt, fault, wrongdoing, and the identities of perpetrators and victims of historic injustices, policies of reparations to Native Americans should be enacted according to some fundamentally sound principle of proportional compensation.

If the foregoing analysis is sound, then one hope that the United States has of dragging itself out of the mire of its own perpetration of historic injustices against Native Americans is for it to institute adequate policies of reparations to Native Americans. Even so, such policies must receive far more commitment by the U.S. government than the treaties made by the U.S. government with Native American nations had received in the past. What is also needed is a national sense of shame-based guilt[91] and collective remorse[92] for the roles that the U.S. government and its citizenry played in founding the United States. Yet if such shame requires a higher-level self-consciousness,[93] this might well be precisely what U.S. society lacks, providing its critics with ammunition for claims of the fundamental immorality of the United States in general. For a society that is based on unrectified injustice is itself unjust. But a society that simply refuses to admit its unjust history toward others not only remains unjust on balance, but serves as a stark reminder of the unabashed arrogance of its unspeakable badness.

91. For an account of collective feelings of guilt, see Margaret Gilbert, "Group Wrongs, Guilt Feelings," *Journal of Ethics* 1 (1997): 65–84. For a more recent account of the concept of collective guilt, see Margaret Gilbert, *Sociality and Responsibility* (Totowa: Rowman and Littlefield, 2000), chapter 8.

92. For an account of collective remorse, see Margaret Gilbert, "Collective Remorse," in *War Crimes and Collective Wrongdoing*, ed. Aleksandar Jokic (London: Blackwell, 2001); Gilbert, *Sociality and Responsibility*, chapter 7.

93. Gabrielle Taylor, *Pride, Shame, and Guilt* (Oxford: Oxford University Press, 1985), p. 67.

9

Reparations to African Americans?

On 26 April 2002, three federal lawsuits were filed in New York seeking reparations to the approximately 35 million African Americans for the enslavement of Africans in the United States. Over sixty companies are targeted by the suits, including Aetna Insurance Company, FleetBoston Financial Services, and the railroad company, CSX. Aetna's own company documents reveal that about 33 percent of its initial one thousand policies were written on the lives of slaves, while slave labor was used to build portions of the rail lines for companies like CSX that currently use them. The settlements sought by the suits do not include cash for African Americans. Rather, they include a variety of social programs that would benefit African Americans. The suits are built on a rationale that the consequences of slavery are still having a negative impact on several millions of such persons today, long after slavery.[1] Is there any merit whatsoever to such claims? If so, how much merit is there? Regardless of the legal merit of such claims, what are the *moral* implications of such historic injustices that might be used to ground legal claims for reparations to African Americans today?

Having in the previous chapter argued in favor of the reparations argument as it applies to the case of Native Americans (as a conglomerate of ethnic groups), I shall now consider to what extent a slightly modified version of the same argument might ground the case of reparations to African Americans.[2] But prior to engaging this problem, it is important to explore

---

1. Larry Neumeister, "Three Federal Lawsuits Filed in New York Seek Reparations for Slavery," *Associated Press*, 26 April 2002.
2. By "African Americans," I mean those of African descent whose ancestors were en-

some preliminary matters of significance, including some ways in which the problem of reparations to African Americans differs from the problem of Native American reparations.

But it is crucial to first separate the question of whether or not reparations to African Americans are morally required from the question of which *policies* of reparations would be justified if it turns out that such reparations are required in the first place. The reason why this is an important distinction is that there are certain objections to reparations to African Americans that seem to conflate the two questions, unwarrantedly assuming, for instance, given the problem of *how* to exact reparative justice, that it somehow follows that reparations to African Americans are unnecessary. Such an inference would follow, it might be assumed, from " 'ought' implies 'can.' " But even if it were the case that no proposed reparations policy to date is plausible for whatever reasons, it would not follow logically that African Americans are not owed reparations of a *just* nature. To think otherwise would be to fallaciously infer that our supposed inability to work through the problem of how to award reparations logically implies something about what African Americans deserve, in this case, as a matter of corrective justice through compensation. For this reason, we must not confuse the question of the moral requirement of reparations to African Americans with the question of how, if such reparations are indeed morally required, they ought to be awarded. The former is a question of deserved compensation based on injustices experienced by African Americans and their forebears, the latter is a question of how such reparations, assuming they are deserved, are to be awarded to African Americans. The same conceptual point holds just as well in the case of reparations to Native Americans discussed in the previous chapter. With this point in mind, I now turn to the matter of how some issues of reparations to African Americans differ from some issues of reparations to Native Americans.

One obvious difference between the experiences of Native and African Americans is that while Native Americans experienced both gross human rights violations and massive land theft at the hands of both the U.S. government and several of its citizens, African Americans for the most part experienced the former (but not the latter) by way of the slave trade. In fact, there is a real sense in which the human rights violations of African American slavery were somewhat less severe than those suffered by Native

---

slaved in the United States, though an extended use of the category might include all such persons whose African ancestors were enslaved throughout the Americas: North, Central, and South.

Americans. Not only were several Native Americans enslaved as were (by definition, all) African Americans' ancestors, and not only were both groups the victims of brutal forms of acculturation (for the former it took the form of Indian boarding schools, for instance; for the latter it took the form of infesting African slaves with various forms of insidious "Christian" religion, however well-intentioned, in the guise of missionary work with "savages"),[3] but as a general rule African slaves were not the subjects of massive killings or of a genocide as were Native Americans. Instead, they were treated, however inhumanely, as the valuable "property" they were deemed by southern slave masters. So there is a sense in which reparations to Native Americans, if based on a principle of proportionality of reparations to harms and wrongs inflicted, ought to be greater than reparations paid to African Americans. For not only did Native Americans as a set of nations suffer the loss of an entire continent of land and natural minerals and other resources to the United States (as well as to Canada, Mexico, Brasil, Colombia, Guatamala, Peru, and other countries), but the loss of lives and other forms of human sufferings experienced by them are not even rivaled by the horrendous evils of U.S. slavery of Africans. With this understanding, it is nonetheless helpful to investigate philosophically the plausibility of claims to African American reparations for slavery of Africans in the United States. For it is quite clear that the evils experienced by Native and African Americans stand in a class by themselves relative to harms and wrongdoings experienced by other groups at the hands of the U.S. government.[4]

Another difference between the cases of Native and African American oppression is that the Native American experiences often, but not always, involved treaties and their being broken by the U.S. government, while U.S. enslavement of Africans involved no such treaties with the slaves themselves. This is explained by the fact that treaties are made between governing bodies, and African slaves in the United States did not constitute a governing body. Nor were they considered by most U.S. citizens and the U.S. government as sufficiently human to merit treaty negotiations. Perhaps this is one reason why African Americans posed less of a perceived threat to manifest destiny than did Native Americans, as suggested in chapter 5.

3. Robert Berkhoffer, Jr., *Salvation and the Savage* (New York: Atheneum, 1965).

4. This is not to suggest that Native and African Americans are the only groups worthy of consideration for reparations from the U.S. government. Rather, it is to suggest that a fair-minded reading of U.S. history seems to place these two groups in a category apart from all others relative to evils experienced by the U.S. government on what is deemed by most as being U.S. territory.

The Argument for Reparations to African Americans

There are a variety of ways in which one might argue in favor of reparations to African Americans, whether or not such claims involve cash settlements, social programs, or some combination thereof. First, such reparations might be sought from *private parties* (e.g., individuals, corporations, and companies) for the unjust enrichments, harms, and/or wrongdoings resulting from the institution of *slavery*. Second, reparations might be sought from *private parties* for the unjust enrichments, harms, and/or wrongdoings resulting from *Jim Crow*. Third, reparations might be sought from *private parties* for the unjust enrichments, harms, and/or wrongdoings resulting from *both slavery and Jim Crow*. Fourth, reparations might be sought from the *U.S. government (and its citizens)* for the unjust enrichments, harms, and/or wrongdoings resulting from *slavery*. Fifth, they might be sought from the *U.S. government* for the unjust enrichments, harms, and/or wrongdoings resulting from *Jim Crow*. Sixth, reparations might be sought from the *U.S. government* due to the unjust enrichments, harms, and/or wrongdoings of *slavery and Jim Crow*. Even more ambitiously, reparations might be sought from *both private parties and the U.S. government* for unjust enrichments, harms, and/or wrongdoings resultant from *slavery*. Moreover, reparations might be sought from *both private parties and the U.S. government* for the unjust enrichments, harms, and/or wrongdoings resultant from *Jim Crow*. Finally, and perhaps most ambitiously, reparations might be sought from *both private parties and the U.S. government* for the unjust enrichments, harms, and/or wrongdoings resultant from *both slavery and Jim Crow*. Although plausible cases might be able to be made along each of the above lines (perhaps with varying degrees of success), I shall concentrate my attention on the case for the sixth option: the case for reparations to African Americans against the U.S. government for the unjust enrichments, harms, and/or wrongdoings of both slavery and Jim Crow. I construe my arguments for this option to be supportive of the most ambitious one, namely, the case for reparations to African Americans from both private parties and the U.S. government because of the unjust enrichments, harms, and/or wrongdoings of both slavery and Jim Crow.

Recall the reparations argument from the previous chapter herein modified for the case of African Americans:

(1′) As much as is humanly possible, instances of clear and substantial historic rights violations ought to be rectified by way of reparations;

(2′) The U.S. government has committed substantial historic rights violations against millions of African Americans;[5]

(3′) Therefore, the historic rights violations of the U.S. government against African Americans ought to be rectified by way of reparations, as much as humanly possible.

As with the argument for reparations focusing on Native Americans, there are challenges that might be raised to the move from (2′) to (3′) in the above argument. I shall consider the following such objections: the objection from historical complexity; the objection to collective responsibility; the objection from historical and normative progress; the affirmative action objection; the objection from social utility; the supersession of historic injustice objection; the anti-private-property-rights objection; and the counterfactual objection. It is important to note that in the case for reparations to African Americans, the objection from inter-nation conquests, the no Native American concept of moral rights objection, the objection from the indeterminacy of Native American identity, the historical reparations objection, the religious freedom objection, and the acquired rights trumping original land rights objection (each discussed in chapter 8 in terms of reparations to Native Americans) are either irrelevant, or are answerable quite transparently when taken from the Native American experience and applied to the African American experience.

It is interesting to note that the relevant set of objections, unlike the objections to Native American reparations, does *not* include objections involving land claims by African Americans. Nor does it involve claims to national sovereignty. Thus there is a sense in which the reparations argument pertaining to the African American experience is simpler (not simple, but simpl*er*) than the case of Native American reparations. For in the case of Native American reparations, it would seem that any reparations settlement that did not involve a substantial return of land to them is grossly unjust, especially in light of the plausibility of the principle of morally just acquisitions and transfers (discussed in chapter 8), and the importance of land to Native Americans' philosophies and religions are concerned. Yet in the case of African Americans, reparations might well be made in the form of cash settlements much akin to (though in far more substantial financial terms than) the case of Japanese Americans for the harms and wrongs done to them by the U.S. government during World War

---

5. These acts amount to a series of intentional actions that were crimes, torts, and/or contract violations.

II. African American reparations might well take the form of social programs, though this might depend on whether or not sufficient amounts of cash settlements accrue. But as noted in chapters 6–7, one must be ever mindful to not conflate reparations with social programs such as those of the affirmative action variety. On the other hand, if they are required on moral grounds, reparations must be proportional to the harms dealt to the enslaved ancestors of African Americans. And it is dubious that social programs, though helpful, would even approach the doorstep of adequacy as rectification for slavery and Jim Crow.

Moreover, given the genealogical conception of ethnic identity articulated and defended in chapter 7, there seems to be no need to take seriously any objection regarding the determinacy of African American identity (except, of course, where the actual setting of percentage of genealogical tie to an ethnic group is concerned). And since there is (to my knowledge) no record of reparations to African Americans by the U.S. government, the historical reparations objection is irrelevant. Thus I will consider the plausibility of those objections to reparations to African Americans concerning matters of historical complexity, collective responsibility,[6] historical and normative progress, affirmative action, social utility, supersession of historic injustice, private property rights, and counterfactual problems.

An important similarity between Native and African American reparations cases (should reparations be owed) is that each group would appear to have a case not only against the U.S. government, but also against other colonial governments and powers such as Portugal, Spain, England, the Netherlands, France, the Roman Catholic church, various Southern Baptist churches, and a number of other extant countries and organizations that played substantial roles in the transatlantic slave trade and/or the colonization of the Americas, and/or the founding and sustaining of Jim Crow. So if the respective cases for Native and African American reparations go through as they target the United States, then they might well also succeed if they target those other conspirators to and/or perpetrators of racist evils. With the recent founding of the International Criminal Court (ICC), perhaps arguments can be brought to it that might force the United States to eventually come to terms with its unquestionably evil foundations. Given the fact that reparations to African and Native Americans in any adequate sense have simply been refused or denied generation after generation, perhaps the final court of appeal is the ICC. But the effectiveness of the ICC will in the end rest on its ability to carry out its sanctions.

6. As in previous chapters, I mean by this term collective retrospective moral liability responsibility.

The main question before us in this chapter is whether or not the United States in particular owes reparations to African Americans for the brutality of slavery in the United States. However, it is not only the physical and psychological brutality of slavery that is at issue, but the wrongful gain by way of forced labor power and the surplus labor value that it brings illicitly to slaveholders in particular, and to an entire U.S. economy more generally, and the incessant refusal over generations of the U.S. government to rectify its injustices against African Americans by way of slavery. I refer to this argument as a "Marxist" one in that it is based primarily, though not exclusively, on the illicit (because forced) labor power of Africans and the illicit (because forced) extraction of labor value from their labor power,[7] which then illicitly (because forced from the slaves) enriched not only slaveholders, but the southern and U.S. economies more generally. But as I shall argue, this Marxist argument hardly depends on whether or not anyone—slaveholder or not—actually benefited from the forced labor power of U.S.-enslaved Africans.

It is important, moreover, to point out that it is not only the injustice of African American slavery (e.g., slavery of Africans in the United States) that is at issue, but also Jim Crow and all of the significant ramifications of segregation throughout the entire United States for generations subsequent to slavery.

The Objections from Intergenerational Justice and to Collective Responsibility

I concur with Bernard Boxill and Howard McGary that what is relevant to the case for African American reparations by the U.S. government is a plausible case for collective moral liability responsibility, along with the historical fact of human rights violations. But each of these points must lead to the conclusion that, say, the current U.S. government owes reparations to contemporary African Americans for the said atrocities of the distant and more recent past.

The conditions necessary and sufficient for collective moral responsibility have been articulated and defended.[8] Elsewhere, I have provided an

7. Those familiar with Karl Marx's criticism of capitalism recognize this point as derivative of his claim that capitalism illicitly extracts labor value from forced labor power of workers. For discussion of Marx's critique of the exploitation of labor in the capitalist system, see G. A. Cohen, *History, Labour, and Freedom* (Oxford: Oxford University Press, 1988), part 3.

8. For an analysis of the general conditions of collective moral liability responsibility,

analysis of the conditions under which collective moral liability responsibility accrues. Besides, fault and guilt, conditions of collective intentionality (construed as acting according to ones own beliefs and wants), knowledge and voluntariness must also be satisfied to some meaningful extent, and the degree to which a collective is morally liable for a harm and wrongdoing is the extent to which it ought to be punished or forced to compensate the victim(s). As we shall see below, fault and guilt accrue to the U.S. government in its complicity or contribution to U.S. slavery and Jim Crow. And that the U.S. government acted according to its wants and desires, with virtually unfettered voluntariness and with knowledge of the foreseeable consequences of its actions and policies is hardly questionable. So there is little doubt that the U.S. government bears the brunt of liability for the harms and wrongdoings of past generations of slavery and Jim Crow. That current U.S. citizens would end up paying for such reparations (should they be morally required) is congruent with the points made in chapter 8 that both collectives and individuals can sometimes be held liable for wrong doings—even though they are not at fault or responsible for the harms that eventuate from them.

However, even assuming the plausibility of the notion of collective moral responsibility, it simply will not suffice to show that there were indeed evils that were perpetrated against African Americans, even by the U.S. government, without also linking the normative case for reparations to the present day.

So even if it is true, as Boxill argues of African American slavery, that:

> the slaves had an indisputable moral right to the product of their labor; these products were stolen from them by the slave masters who ultimately passed them on to their descendants; the slaves presumably have conferred their rights of ownership to their descendants; thus, the descendants of slave masters are in possession of wealth to which the descendants of slaves have rights; hence, the descendants of slave masters must return this wealth to the descendants of slaves with a concession that they were not rightfully in possession of it,[9]

McGary is correct in claiming of Boxill's argument that:

---

see J. Angelo Corlett, *Responsibility and Punishment* (Dordrecht; Kluwer Academic, 2001), chapter 7. For an analysis of collective moral liability responsibility as it pertains particularly to reparations to African Americans, see Howard McGary, *Race and Social Justice* (London: Blackwell, 1999), chapter 5. Other discussions of collective responsibility are found in Larry May and Stacey Hoffman, eds., *Collective Responsibility* (Savage: Rowman and Littlefield, 1991).

    9. Bernard Boxill, "The Morality of Reparations," *Social Theory and Practice* 2 (1972): 117.

it fails to show how whites who are not the descendants of slave masters owe a debt of justice to black Americans. In order to argue that the total white community owes the total black community reparations, we must present an argument that shows how all whites, even recent immigrants benefited from slavery and how all blacks felt its damaging effects.[10]

Although I find the cumulative effect of both Boxill's and McGary's arguments convincing, their implied "unjust enrichment argument," though it is quite helpful in establishing a case for collective moral liability responsibility to provide reparations to African Americans, is not necessary for establishing the case for African American reparations. For even if no slave master (or a descendant of one) ever benefited from the enslavement of Africans or the racist treatment of their descendants in the U.S., reparations might nonetheless be owed to African Americans today. But how might this be the case? And precisely by whom or what ought the reparations to be paid, and to whom, and what kind and how much reparations ought to be awarded?

Prior to examining in depth the aforementioned objections to African American reparations, it is important to gain a perspective on the implications of a certain line of reasoning regarding the matter. Consider the "objection from intergenerational justice," which states that justice between generations is problematic because those who pay reparations at time t_{n+1} for significant injustices at t_n must be the ones directly guilty and at fault for the harms and wrongs done to the group for which reparations are requested. Intergenerational (reparative) justice is problematic because it violates precisely this rule, making allegedly innocent parties pay for what other guilty parties did in harming and wronging others. It is clear how this objection underlies a concern about collective moral liability responsibility. Indeed, the objection from intergenerational justice seems to be the foundation of the objection to collective moral responsibility.

It is important to understand, however, that if the objection from intergenerational justice counts against reparations to African Americans, then by parity of reasoning it also counts to a significant degree against reparations to Israel by Germany prior to the genocide of Jewish persons by the Nazi regime during the World War II era. Not only does it count in some significant measure against the case for reparations to Israel by Germany, but it also counts against the case for reparations to certain Japanese Americans by the United States for the internment of many Japanese Americans during the same era. The reason that the objection from intergenerational

10. Howard McGary, "Justice and Reparations," *Philosophical Forum* 9 (1977–78): 253.

justice counts in some significant measure against these historic acts of reparations is that—even though many German and U.S. citizens who bore the fiscal brunt of such reparations were actually alive as adults during the oppression of Jewish persons during the Nazi attempt to extinguish them and during the U.S. internment of Japanese Americans—millions of "innocent" German and U.S. citizens ended up paying the reparations in each case, citizens who themselves were children, or not even born at the time of the atrocities in question. Thus there is a violation of the principle that forms the bedrock of the objection from intergenerational justice, namely, *that those who are innocent must not suffer harm or be forced to compensate for harms they did not cause.* There is indeed a regress argument at work here, one that attempts to render problematic any attempt to justify reparations to Israel and Japanese Americans in that some allegedly innocent (German and U.S.) parties ended up paying the fiscal brunt of the reparations payments, persons who in some cases could not have had anything whatsoever to do with the evil events in question.

Moreover, it might be argued that political liberalism's claim that individual persons, *and only individual persons,* qualify as moral agents who are morally liable to praise or blame for what they do voluntarily, intentionally, and epistemically poses a challenge to any view of reparations that holds that such reparations are based on intergenerational justice and collective moral liability responsibility. Thus what is needed is a defense of the conception of collective moral liability responsibility that would in turn ground reparative justice claims against the U.S. government and its citizens who would end up bearing the burden of such reparations, intergenerationally speaking.

With these points made, is it true that "we must present an argument that shows how all whites, even recent immigrants benefited from slavery and how all blacks felt its damaging effects?" Although I shall argue that such an argument is not necessary, I believe that the strongest case for reparations owed to African Americans lies precisely along the lines that Mc-Gary suggests. Thus even though it is, as I shall argue, unnecessary to show that anyone was unjustly enriched by slavery or Jim Crow in order to prove the case for African American reparations, doing so is surely sufficient to make the case. And the sufficiency of the case seems to depend on the strength of the argument for collective moral responsibility, intergenerationally speaking.

Against the claim that the unjust enrichment argument is needed to prove the case for African American reparations, it should be understood that it is entirely possible that there are significant numbers of people who benefited *accidentally* from the enslavement of Africans in the United States. Yet if someone benefited in such a manner—even from an evil such as race-based slavery—it is unclear whether or not the persons enriched by it are guilty or even at fault and ought therefore to pay reparations for slavery. Would it not be more sensible, morally speaking, to hold account- able only those who, according to the general line of the unjust enrich- ment argument, benefit *non*accidentally from the evil? I believe that this is what McGary has in mind with his words, however, so I do not see that this point refutes, but rather attempts to significantly clarify and support, his general line of argument.

There is another reason why the unjust enrichment argument is prob- lematic, however well-intentioned. It is that persons might owe reparations to a group even if the persons did not benefit from a particular injustice that forms the basis of the group's receiving reparations. An example of this sort of case would be, say, a European American slave master whose "empire" ended up, largely due to slavery, ruining him forever. Perhaps the forcing of others to do labor for his family and such was far outweighed by his mis- management of his slaves, social and political pressures against slavery at the time of his having slaves, and other factors. Yet simply because this slave mas- ter, perhaps owing to his own incompetence as a master of slaves, did not ben- efit from his having slaves hardly means that he is not morally responsible for his having slaves. Or, consider the example of an individual act of civil dis- obedience to U.S. slavery by one who not only refuses to support with her taxes the United States (or even state or local governments) but who also lives a holistic lifestyle of protest against the "peculiar institution." This citizen hardly benefits from U.S. slavery of Africans, but is rather in protest opting out of whatever significant ways in which she might benefit. Thus we need not demonstrate that those responsible for providing reparations to African Americans were those who benefited from the harms and wrongs against African Americans that would justify such reparations. For an incompetent slave master's not benefiting from slavery hardly exempts him from what he owes based on Boxill's argument that he has deprived slaves of the value of their labor, unforced, and one who protests incessantly and holistically U.S. slavery of Africans benefits, it seems, in no interesting way from it. Other- wise, the unjust enrichment argument would seem to imply that those who benefited most from U.S. slavery ought to be held most accountable for paying their fair share of reparations, for instance, more of the reparations amount than those who benefited significantly less than they. Moreover, when all is said and done, the amount of reparations owed according to this scheme would only be as much as the amount of fiscal benefit to those guilty and at fault for slavery. Yet this amount might not reflect the amount of reparations owed based on the amount of labor value stolen from the slaves. In turn, this scheme of reparations would make African American reparations contingent on the successes and failures of the market of slave holdings, rather than on the value of the labor stolen from the slaves. Since it seems more intuitively plausible to award reparations on the basis of labor value stolen forcibly from slaves, the amount of reparations ought to reflect *this* fact. Yet this would seem to imply that, though establishing the plausibility of claims to unjust enrichment from slavery and Jim Crow are indeed helpful in making the case for reparations to African Americans, we *need not* demonstrate the plausibility of the unjust enrichment argument.

But what precisely would establish, on moral grounds, the plausibility of the reparations argument concerning African Americans? I argue that it is, as Boxill implies, the illicit taking by force and/or fraud of the surplus labor value of the slaves. It is at this point of argument that the principle of morally just acquisitions and transfers plays a fundamental role in the reparations argument for African Americans as it does in the case of Native American reparations. For *whatever is acquired or transferred by morally just means is itself morally just, and whatever is acquired or transferred by morally unjust means is itself morally unjust.* (This is the principle of morally just acquisitions and transfers, discussed on pages 155ff. of this book.) Forced labor power and the extraction of value from it is morally unjust and must be rectified by way of compensation and/or punishment. Since the U.S. government supported the institution of slavery of Africans by permitting slavery to go virtually unchecked for generations, it is responsible for the harmful effects of slavery and liable to pay reparations to descendants of the slaves should such descendants exist or have trusts in their names. Further harms to African Americans accrued as the federal and various state governments institutionalized racism (by way of Jim Crow) against generations of African Americans. This much can serve as the locus of agreement, however, between supporters of African American reparations and their detractors. For detractors might concur that the stealing of the labor power and hence surplus labor value from the slaves entitles reparations to slaves, but to no one else. Thus an argument is needed that establishes on moral grounds reparations to contemporary African Americans, not simply to their forebears who were enslaved or who were victims of Jim Crow.

Boxill provides the basis of such an argument when he states that "the slaves presumably have conferred their rights of ownership to the products of their labor to their descendants." Yet it is precisely at this point where objections to the reparations argument might be challenged as it pertains to African Americans. It might be argued that the very idea of inheritance is morally arbitrary and has no basis in a morally sound system of social living (perhaps because, it might be argued, it violates strict notions of moral desert and responsibility). Be this as it may, it seems that Boxill's point is made in light of the way the legal system works in the United States: *given that inheritance is recognized by U.S. law,* it would seem to follow that the stolen value of the slaves' labor ought to be recognized, naturally, as inherited by the heirs of slaves, who would by (my) definition be African Americans. I too share Boxill's assumption and shall not here take on the task of challenging the morality of inheritance systems under U.S. law. Yet it is important to recognize that should such systems in the end fail on moral grounds, Boxill's argument runs aground on such problems (as does my own argument here). But then so would the legal practice of inheritance more generally, wreaking significant havoc in U.S. society.

However, my argument for reparations to African Americans does not simply depend for its overall plausibility on matters of inheriting certain rights to compensation to one's descendants. The primary focus of my argument is that to the extent that U.S. slavery and Jim Crow led to widespread injustices to African slaves in the United States and African Americans (their descendants), reparations are owed African Americans by the U.S. government on moral grounds because it is the same governmental systems that harmed African slaves as that which either permitted or enacted and enforced Jim Crow, and that exists today as that which has yet to pay reparations even though formal and informal democratic demands for reparations have been made since Reconstruction. Reparations to African Americans, not unlike those to Native Americans, are debts unpaid by an *existing perpetrator,* namely, the U.S. government.[11]

It is at this juncture where the argument for collective moral responsibility (of the U.S. government) must be provided in order for the case for reparations to African Americans to be most plausible. And there are various ways in which the case for collective moral liability responsibility for reparations to African Americans accrues in that the same U.S. government that perpetrated the evils of the past on African (and Native) Americans exists *today.* Thus the continuity through time of the U.S. government defeats the idea that collective moral liability responsibility fails to accrue to the current U.S. government. First, at the level of the most fundamental principles of law, U.S. constitutional law, it might be argued that from generation to generation the U.S. Supreme Court has upheld the fundamental values of the U.S. Constitution and Bill of Rights such that, as Ronald Dworkin has argued, the Supreme Court justices engage in a constant, albeit Herculean, task of interpreting the Constitution as a near

11. This is not meant to imply that there are not private parties that or who also owe reparations to African Americans based on the extent of their contributory fault or liability for African slavery in the United States and/or for Jim Crow.

"seamless web" in light of interpretive extralegal principles.[12] Indeed, the highest level of U.S. government never seems to challenge the basic principles embedded in the Constitution, but instead uses such principles to guide decision-making on a variety of problems in U.S. society.

Second, not only does the U.S. government support and not challenge the fundamental legitimacy of the principles and values embedded in the Constitution, but by far the majority of U.S. citizens do the same. And this is true intergenerationally speaking! Indeed, the typical response to anti–U.S. terrorism is that "we must protect our way of life," meaning that the "freedoms" explicit and implicit in the Constitution and Bill of Rights are to be protected, even by way of retaliatory violence and war. And fortunately, the actions and stated attitudes of so many U.S. officials and citizens speak strongly to this effect. Scarcely would more than a small minority of U.S. citizens in U.S. history serve as counterexamples along these lines. *From generation to generation, then, there is collective support and implementation of the various values deemed important in the documents the contents of which form the very basis of life in U.S. society.* This is intended to support the claim that contemporary collective moral liability responsibility obtains concerning the U.S. government and its citizens to the extent that conditions of collective intentionality, knowledge, and voluntariness are satisfied intergenerationally, though collective fault and guilt need not, as was argued in the previous chapter concerning reparations to Native Americans. For various collective decision-making processes in U.S. society not only preserve from past to current generations of U.S. society the fundamental norms, values, and folkways based on foundationally defining documents of the putative democracy, but this in turn preserves the essential identity of the country as a political unit over time. If this is true, and I can scarcely imagine anyone who would deny that the *U.S. as a political unit has survived over time,* then why would it not be thought—except by some politically liberal individualist superstition that only individual persons can be moral agents—that U.S. society as a whole inherits, not only the benefits, but the *debts* of its past?

Although it is certainly true that few, if any, U.S. citizens would support the enslavement of Africans in the United States or even Jim Crow and

12. Ronald Dworkin, *Law's Empire* (Cambridge: Harvard University Press, 1986). For critical discussions of Dworkin's theory of legal interpretation, see Andrew Altman, "Legal Realism, Critical Legal Studies, and Dworkin," in *Philosophy of Law,* ed. Joel Feinberg and Hyman Gross, 5th ed. (Belmont: Wadsworth, 1995), pp. 176–91; J. Angelo Corlett, "Dworkin's *Empire* Strikes Back!" *Statute Law Review* 21 (2000): 43–56; Timothy Endicott, "Are There Any Rules?" *The Journal of Ethics* 5 (2001): 199–220; J. L. Mackie, "The Third Theory of Law," in *Philosophy of Law,* ed. Feinberg and Gross, pp. 162–68.

their horrendous results, few U.S. citizens and leaders did much at all to recognize the injustice sufficient to even take seriously the possibility of reparations to African Americans, or to newly freed slaves. This points to a kind of complicity in the continual refusal in the face of constant demands throughout history to award some meaningful justice to those who were harmed severely by the U.S. government and U.S. society.

Additionally, the unjust enrichment argument serves to emphasize the fact that most, if not all, U.S. citizens have been in some significant measure unjustly enriched by slavery and Jim Crow. For example, Aetna Insurance Company, various and sundry tobacco companies, textile companies, and real estate companies engaged in racist and oppressive practices that supported not only slavery, but other forms of anti-African American oppression that unjustly enriched shareholders, employees, managers, and others. Moreover, millions of U.S. citizens were provided rights and privileges that few, if any, African Americans were accorded until recent years. And these rights were systematically denied to African Americans for *generations,* taking the U.S. government until the Civil Rights Act of 1964 to *begin* to correct. To think that millions upon millions of non–African Americans have not been unjustly enriched at the expense of African Americans from 1775 until most recently is to make a mockery of the facts of U.S. history. There was undoubtedly collective or societal support of U.S. slavery and Jim Crow to the extent that without such support those institutions would not have "succeeded" in the ways that they did (at least for whom they did succeed). Until the 1960s, few non–African Americans stood against such racism. One must recall that bad Samaritanism can serve as a form of moral negligence supportive of intentionally harmful wrongdoing.

Thus it is clear how the argument for collective moral responsibility supports the unjust enrichment argument for reparations to African Americans. At various levels of U.S. society, there was in fact governmental and societal support for the enslavement of Africans and Jim Crow. Such injustices should be rectified by way of reparations, rectified by the same government and society that intergenerationally oppressed African slaves and their ancestors. For as Joel Feinberg has so persuasively argued, *the folkways of a society can sometimes reflect the fault of a group's wrongdoing.* Quoting Dwight Macdonald, Feinberg points out that:

> the constant and widespread acts of violence "against Negroes through the South, culminating in lynchings, may be considered real "people's actions," for which the Southern whites bear collective responsibility [because] the brutality . . . is participated in, actively or with passive sympaty, by the entire white community." The postbellum Southern social system, now

beginning to crumble, was contrived outside of political institutions and only winked at by the law. Its brutalities were "instrumentalities for keeping the Negro in his place and maintaining the supraordinate position of the white caste." Does it follow from this charge, that "Southern whites [*all* Southern whites] bear collective responsibility?" I assume the ninety-nine percent of them, having been shaped by the prevailing mores, wholeheartedly approved of these brutalities. But what of the remaining tiny fraction? If they are to be held responsible, they must be so vicariously, on the ground of their strong (and hardly avoidable) solidarity with the majority. But suppose a few hated their Southern tradition, despised their neighbors, and did not think of themselves as Southerners at all? Then perhaps Macdonald's point can be saved by excluding these totally alienated souls altogether from the white Southern community to which Macdonald ascribes collective responsibility. But total alienation is not likely to be widely found in a community that leaves its exit doors open; and, in a community with as powerful social enforcement of mores as the traditional Southern one, the alienated resident would be in no happier position than the Negro. Collective responsibility, therefore, might be ascribed to all those whites who were not outcasts, taking respectability and material comfort as evidence that a given person did not qualify for the exemption.[13]

To those who might argue that Feinberg's words, if plausible, only apply to European American southerners who supported and were unjustly enriched by slavery and Jim Crow, it might be pointed out that the U.S. government and citizens who were not southerners continually played the role of bad Samaritans in refusing for *generations* to outlaw and enforce the prohibition of such evils. This implicated morally the entire United States for slavery and Jim Crow. Moreover, it must be remembered that segregationism was alive and well throughout the entire U.S. society for generations. From housing to voting rights, to opportunities for education and hiring practices, it was clear and evident that African Americans and even former slaves were not accorded the dignity that was promised all persons under the Constitution and Bill of Rights. It appears, then, that the principle of morally just acquisitions and transfers applies to the case of African American reparations, yet in a somewhat different way than it does to the case of Native American reparations. Unjust enrichment was experienced by most every U.S. citizen in every generation of U.S. history, as the cumulative effects of superior advantages in U.S. society placed European Americans far ahead of African Americans insofar as basic human rights and equal opportunities for life, liberty, and the pursuit of happiness are concerned.

13. Joel Feinberg, *Doing and Deserving* (Princeton: Princeton University Press, 1970), pp. 247–48.

It simply will not do, morally speaking, for one to argue that reparations are not owed because today's U.S. citizenry is "innocent" of any act of slavery or oppression against African Americans. For this line of argument ends up as a "might-makes-right" mentality, as it assumes without argument that a government that for generations ignored and denied demands for justice has rightful cause for not paying what it owes to those against whom it has committed atrocities such as slavery and Jim Crow. Ever since Reconstruction there have been demands for justice to African Americans, often in the form of reparations arguments. So the same governments that harmed African slaves and their descendants via Jim Crow stand to pay what they owe to African Americans. Here I mean by such governments those of the southern states, and even the U.S. government to the extent that it aided and abetted in the oppression of slaves and/or African Americans.[14]

If the foregoing is correct, then it seems that reparations to African Americans are grounded in the historical fact that reparations for slavery were requested but never granted during and subsequent to Reconstruction, and that Jim Crow was not only oppressive of African Americans living (especially) in the southern states, but that such oppression was aided and abetted by the U.S. government in significant ways. One among many specific ways in which the U.S. government aided and abetted the enslavement of Africans in the United States was by way of its enacting and enforcing the Fugitive Slave Laws whereby a southern slave master could recapture and reenslave his fugitive "property" by way of the federal court system.[15] The U.S. government was a bad Samaritan[16] in that it was grossly negligent as it for generations stood by and permitted southern states to flourish not only under slavery, but under Jim Crow. Recall also that it took the federal government *over a century* subsequent to U.S. slavery to pass (and eventually enforce!) civil rights legislation, primarily to combat Jim Crow and other forms of racist segregation throughout the United States. That the U.S. government was a bad Samaritan along these lines is important, as

14. This is not meant to imply that northern or western state governments were innocent in the oppression of African Americans, as each had its own way of enforcing racist policies and/or practices of housing, education, and employment discrimination against them.

15. For a discussion of how the federal courts decided such cases, see Robert Cover, *Justice Accused* (New Haven: Yale University Press, 1975); Ronald Dworkin, "Review of Robert Cover, *Justice Accused*," *Times Literary Supplement*, 5 December 1975.

16. For discussions of Bad Samaritanism, see Joel Feinberg, "The Moral and Legal Responsibility of the Bad Samaritan," in *Freedom and Fulfillment* (Princeton: Princeton University Press, 1992), pp. 175–96; and John Kleinig, "Good Samaritanism," in *Philosophy of Law*, ed. Feinberg and Gross, pp. 529–32.

such bad Samaritanism serves as part of the moral basis for the claim of reparations owed by the same government responsible, in one way or another, for both the evils of slavery and of Jim Crow, and how much reparations are owed. Assumed here, of course, are the ideas that governments have duties to respect and protect the basic human rights of their respective citizens, and that individuals and governments have duties to assist those in need insofar as such assistance does not pose a serious threat to their own well-being. Concerning the case at hand, it is implausible to think that the U.S. government was not a bad Samaritan as it very well could have acted in various ways to provide adequate justice to slaves and former slaves, and to African Americans for the effects of Jim Crow, and to hold accountable states that failed to comply with civil rights legislation that should have been enacted and enforced immediately subsequent to slavery in the United States. After all, the U.S. government has the military might to ensure its results anywhere within "its own territory." No coalition of southern states could begin to challenge the U.S. military, especially after the devastating loss (by the South) of the Civil War. This placed the federal government in a particularly powerful position vis-a-vis the South. It is clear that there were reasons why it took so long to pass and enforce Civil Rights legislation. That such reasons are adequate, morally speaking, is quite unclear. Assumed here is the plausibility of the claim that massive and significant human rights violations ought to be handled adequately and as soon as humanly possible, implying that the federal government's handling of human rights violations against African slaves and African Americans was nothing less than morally inept.

Yet with all of this said and done, there is a rather nagging curiosity concerning the issue of why reparations to African Americans is so greatly resisted in the United States.[17] For even if it were conceded, contrary to the previous line of argumentation, that the enslavement of Africans on U.S. soil did not justify reparations to the descendants of such slaves today, there remains a series of queries that tend to suggest the fundamental racism that U.S. citizens have toward African Americans. For might it not be much more plausible on moral grounds to base reparations to African Americans on the depths and almost permanent racist effects of generations of segregation throughout the United States? And is it not true that many millions of African Americans who have experienced the bitter hand (fist?) of

---

17. For a discussion of this particular issue, see Rodney C. Roberts, "Why Have the Injustices Perpetrated against Blacks in America not Been Rectified?" *Journal of Social Philosophy* 32 (2001): 357–73; Laurence Thomas, "Morality, Consistency, and the Self: A Lesson From Rectification," *Journal of Social Philosophy* 32 (2001): 374–81; Bernard Boxill, "Power and Persuasion," *Journal of Social Philosophy* 32 (2001): 382–85.

Jim Crow's oppression are still alive? And would it not also be true that what Japanese Americans experienced at the hands of the U.S. government was not nearly as harmful as what African Americans experience(d), both in terms of the very kinds of racist oppression and in terms of duration? And would not such facts suggest that, just as the United States willingly apologized[18] and provided reparations to certain Japanese Americans, so too ought the United States to do so to African Americans? Moreover, should not the amount of reparations to African Americans be substantially larger than that which has been provided to certain Japanese Americans? This would follow from both the kinds of anti-African American racist oppression and the duration of it.

One concern here is that my argument fails to consider that U.S. reparations to *certain* Japanese Americans were just that, e.g., reparations to only those Japanese Americans who actually suffered in the internment camps during World War II as opposed to all Japanese Americans as a collective. However, my argument for African American reparations can easily accommodate this concern. For what might be done is that the U.S. government award reparations to only those African Americans who have suffered significant harm under Jim Crow. Even today, this amounts to a substantial number of those who were forced to live under conditions of a much larger, much more brutal and lasting "concentration camp:" U.S. segregationist society (north, south, east and west).

Perhaps it is this final point that makes most U.S. citizens recoil at the very idea of reparations to African Americans. But this simply exposes what is really at work in U.S. society, especially in light of the arguments, the facts underlying them, and how a lesser case of racist harm against some Japanese Americans was handled compared to the incessant refusal of U.S. society to even take seriously reparations to even some African Americans. The inference to the best explanation here seems to emerge as insidious racism, a racism which seeks to cloak itself in the guise of sophisticated philosophical argumentation, argumentation that is not, by the way, applied to the Jewish (Israeli) and Japanese American cases by parity of reasoning. It is obvious that U.S. citizens do not believe that African Americans deserve reparations, and for at least the reason that amounts to the objection from intergenerational justice. Holding to the plausibility of this objection is not in itself constitutive of racism against African Americans. However, holding this view as a reason against providing reparations

18. For philosophical analyses of the nature of an apology, see J. Angelo Corlett, *Responsibility and Punishment* (Dordrecht: Kluwer Academic, 2001), chapter 6; Jeffrie G. Murphy, *Character, Liberty, and the Law* (Dordrecht: Kluwer Academic, 1998).

to African Americans for the harms of Jim Crow experienced by contemporary African Americans who experienced Jim Crow while simultaneously supporting reparations to many Japanese Americans for much lesser oppressive harms seems to demand an explanation as to why such a view is not racist toward African Americans. Sociologically speaking, perhaps it is a case of a society's supporting, however begrudgingly, the injustice they can *afford* to compensate, rather than supporting the full range of what is owed due to their government's evil actions. But it also seems to be a blatant instance of simply expressing significant respect to those whom most citizens feel respect, while denying significant respect to those whom most citizens believe are not worthy of it.[19]

However, yet another concern might be raised about the argument for collective moral responsibility as it is used to bolster the unjust enrichment argument for reparations to African Americans. It challenges the points that have been made, above, regarding the generational support (or lack of nonsupport) of most U.S. citizens of slavery and Jim Crow. The most that can be said in favor of reparations to African Americans, the objection might aver, is that *some* of today's U.S. citizens, namely, those who actually contributed to the harms and wrongdoings in question (Jim Crow, as no U.S. slaveholders are alive today) are morally liable for reparations and ought to be forced to pay them. However, this hardly shows that the *United States* owes reparations to African Americans. Again, today's U.S. citizen, it is argued, is hardly responsible for what happened to African slaves and African Americans in the distant past, as the objection from intergenerational justice states. For the U.S. government is *not* the same government as it was when those atrocities were perpetrated. Different persons compose the government, and the citizenry is *not* the same. Moreover, this is evidenced by the fact that almost everyone in U.S. society recognizes a significant moral progress that has accrued along the lines of its now condemning such evils as totally unjust.

In reply to this version of the objection from intergenerational justice, it is important to consider that whether or not a society owing reparations to a group it has harmed and wronged *recognizes its role in harming and wronging the group* is not a necessary condition of that society's owing reparations to the group. For in the case of the United States paying reparations to certain Japanese Americans, it was surely not the case that the United States as a whole recognized that it owed reparations to certain Japanese Americans. The anti-Japanese fervor in the United States at that time was rampant, and millions of U.S. citizens despised Japanese ("American" or not)

---

19. I borrow this point from Bernard Boxill.

for the events at Pearl Harbor in 1941. The point here is that a society can be incorrect, because it is not infallible in its moral judgments, about whether or not it owes reparations to a group it has harmed. This is especially true of evil societies. Indeed, this is in part what makes some societies evil! No matter how "civilized" a society appears (or proclaims itself) to be, it cannot be genuinely civilized, what John Rawls would deem a "decent" or "reasonably just" one, if it fails to rectify its past evils, no matter how far in the past it perpetrated them. Otherwise, *it is incumbent on the critic of this point to devise a non-self-serving and non-question-begging argument that would establish a moral statute of limitations on historic injustice.* As was pointed out in the previous chapter and it bears repetition here, the burden of proof is on those who support a moral statute of limitations on injustice to provide non-question-begging and non-self-serving arguments that would explain its soundness. Otherwise, such a notion is not to be accepted by the epistemically responsible person. And as we discovered in the previous chapter, attempts at that feat are sorely lacking in plausibility.

Second, as Feinberg so astutely points out, though moral guilt and fault do not transfer from one generation to the next, liability does (in some cases). In general, collective liability accrues in cases where the conditions of collective solidarity, prior notice, and opportunity for control are satisfied to some meaningful extent. However, he argues,

> An exception . . . is suggested by the case where an institutional group persists through changes of membership and faultless members must answer for harms caused, or commitments made, by an earlier generation of members. Commitments made in the name of an organized group may persist even after the composition of the group and its "will" change. When, nevertheless, the group reneges on a promise, the fault may be that of no individual members, yet the liability for breach of contract, falling on the group as a whole, will distribute burdens quite unavoidably on faultless members.[20]

Now to this line of argument of Feinberg's it might be objected that only individual persons count as moral agents who are liable to blame or praise for what they do, fail, or attempt to do. And it is this politically liberal point that haunts the argument for collective moral responsibility, and which undergirds the objection to collective responsibility.

But it is precisely this objection to collective responsibility that must be challenged, and for at least two reasons. First, political liberalism's insistence on the claim that individual persons, *and only individual persons*, are moral agents is highly contestable. For if we assume that only individual

20. Feinberg, *Doing and Deserving*, p. 249.

moral agents are those who have rights, and can be held liable to blame or praise, then it would imply that groups do not have rights to compensation for harms experienced. It would also imply that there can be no collective responsibility for wrongdoing. For there is only individual wrongdoing, and only individuals who are harmed deserve compensation for their harms experienced. That individual persons are moral agents is accepted by liberals and their critics alike. Yet since the liberal adds the highly con-troversial claim that *only* individual persons are moral agents, he or she owes a plausible argument for the claim that only individual persons are those who can either harm and wrong others or be the victim of harm and wrongdoing and be owed compensation. It is difficult to surmise precisely what an argument for such a claim would amount to, that is, if the argu-ment is not self-serving or question-begging. This ought to make one rather wary of the liberal doctrine of individualism, that is, unless and un-til such a view can be substantiated by plausible argument. Epistemically speaking, the claim that only individual persons are moral agents is *not* basic, self-evident, or self-justifying external to the politically liberal frame-work.

However, not only is there no plausible argument in favor of the politi-cally liberal claim that only individual persons count as moral agents, but Feinberg has provided at least a prima facie case for collective personhood. Although Feinberg states that his analysis is intended to be a legal one, there is reason to think that it is morally grounded (e.g., justified by the balance of reason, on his view). Applying Feinberg's words (quoted above) to the case of African Americans and reparations, it might be argued that the U.S. government and society have persisted throughout time, from one generation to the next, from its inception to the present day. At no time whatsoever have more than a "tiny fraction" of U.S. citizens *not* been sig-nificantly enriched unjustly as the result of the enslavement of Africans in the United States and Jim Crow, as already explained, however briefly. Given the truth of the principle of morally just acquisitions and transfers, and given the *im*plausibility of a moral statute of limitations on historic in-justice, it would appear that there is indeed a plausible case in favor of the moral liability of U.S. citizens and their government for what their forebears and their government did to Africans and African Americans throughout the generations.[21] Thus, contrary to the objection to collective

21. It becomes increasingly astounding, on moral grounds, how it is that so many mil-lions of U.S. citizens and government officials take such pride in their own political fore-bears and how the United States was founded as a putative democracy, yet when a link from such citizens and leaders to the evil pasts of slavery and Jim Crow are concerned, such citi-zens and leaders suddenly disavow any link to such historic evils.

responsibility, there is doubt about the plausibility of the liberal claim about exclusive individual moral agency, as well as some significant reason, especially in light of the doubt about liberal individualism, to think that in some cases collective moral liability accrues even in the absence of collective fault. For there is a real sense in which U.S. citizens, in a plethora of ways, act, neglect to act, or attempt to act (and have throughout U.S. history) such that their cumulative lives, together and separately, amount to a context in which sociality leads to collective responsibility.[22]

The Objection from Historical Complexity

The previous line of reasoning addresses straightforwardly the objection from intergenerational justice, which underlies the objection to collective responsibility. But in answer to the objection from historical complexity, it might be replied that, though U.S. history is complex as regards to the enslavement of Africans and Jim Crow oppression of African Americans, there is nonetheless extraordinary historical evidence of the *fact* of U.S. oppression of both groups, along with continual pleas for reparative justice ever since the "Forty Acres and a Mule" suggestion was made and declined during Reconstruction. That every detail of every case of African and African American oppression is unavailable to us because of lost records and the complexities of U.S. history is hardly a good reason for the U.S. government to deny reparations to African Americans. The libraries of volumes of critical U.S. history serve as a resounding reminder of the *fact* of U.S. oppression of these groups. So the objection from historical complexity, not unlike the objection to collective responsibility, is as implausible in the case of reparations to African Americans as it is in the case of reparations to Native Americans.

The Objections from Historical and Normative Progress

Ought African Americans to simply abandon any concern for reparations and instead become "successful" citizens, thereby making such reparations unnecessary as the objections from historical and normative progress aver? Is not U.S. history replete with examples of tremendous successes of

22. For an analysis of collective responsibility in terms of collective guilt, see Margaret Gilbert, "Group Wrongs and Guilt Feelings," *Journal of Ethics* 1 (1997): 65–84; *Sociality and Responsibility* (Lanham, Md.: Rowman and Littlefield, 2000); "Collective Guilt and Collective Guilt Feelings," *Journal of Ethics* 6 (2002): 115–43.

African Americans, as noted in chapter 5, in various areas of life? The insensitivity of this line of reasoning belies a sort of ignorance of what justice entails. First, it blindly assumes that all African Americans have (or should have) a desire to remain "successful" within the society that has systematically oppressed it over several generations. Second, it unwarrantedly assumes that justice ought to pertain at all to the economic or social status of victims of oppression or other forms of wrongdoing. *To the extent that reparations are to accrue to African Americans, they accrue to them regardless of their respective economic or social statuses.*

The Affirmative Action Objection

But what of the affirmative action objection? As was pointed out in chapter 8 with the case of Native American reparations and in chapter 6 in the context of affirmative action for Latinos, to think that affirmative action is an instance of reparations is a category mistake, especially if what one means by "affirmative action" is preferential treatment of African Americans in employment hiring. For in such cases, recipients of affirmative action programs *earn* their wages, whereas reparations are a group's *un*earned compensation for being harmed and wronged. This consideration undercuts the plausibility of the affirmative action objection to the reparations argument concerning African Americans.

The Supersession of Historical Injustice Objection

Furthermore, Waldron's incredible supersession of historic injustice objection (discussed in the previous chapter) fails in the case of African American reparations for the same reason that it fails in the case of Native American reparations. For its fundamental plausibility is contingent on the moral justifiedness of a moral statute of limitations on injustice. Yet Waldron provides no argument whatsoever in defense of a moral statute of limitations on historic injustice, making his underlying assumption, along with his objection, unwarranted.[23] Unless and until plausible arguments are provided in favor of a moral statute of limitations on injustice, then there is no good reason to accept such a claim, especially

---

23. For a critical assessment of philosophical arguments given for a moral statute of limitations on injustice, see Rodney C. Roberts, "The Morality of a Moral Statute of Limitations on Injustice," *Journal of Ethics* 7 (2003): 115–38.

since, contrary to Thomas Reid, beliefs are not innocent until proven guilty.[24]

The Objection from Social Utility

How might the objection from social utility, the anti-private-property-rights objection, and the counterfactual objection regarding the reparations argument for African Americans fare? The objection from social utility avers that if the U.S. government pays adequate reparations to African Americans, then the sheer cost of the reparations would bankrupt the United States, as in the case of reparations to Native Americans. This in turn would send millions of U.S. citizens into abject poverty. Why should the majority of U.S. citizens who are neither African nor Native Americans have to be inconvenienced and plunged into the abyss of poverty and despair by paying reparations to a minority number of citizens? It is, on utilitarian grounds, immoral to provide reparations to any group when the payment of adequate reparations would spell the demise of the majority of people in society.

In reply to this line of utilitarian argument, it is helpful to remind ourselves of how poorly such an argument fared in the case of reparations to Native Americans (chapter 8). Basically, the objection from social utility insists that the disutility experienced by the majority of U.S. citizens as the result of their paying reparations to African Americans (those who lived under Jim Crow) and their forebears (under U.S. slavery) outweighs the harms and wrongdoings done to African slaves and African Americans under Jim Crow. But the magnitude of the respective harms between contemporary U.S. citizens who are not African Americans and African Americans is incomparable, even in light of the fact that there are far fewer African Americans than others in the United States. So on basic grounds of social utility alone, it is unclear that the paying of reparations to African Americans would eventuate in a society that is worse-off than it would be otherwise, all things considered. The objection from social utility self-servingly assumes that the "poverty" of several millions of U.S. citizens is clearly greater than the poverty and enslavement (and all that was involved in slavery) of millions of African slaves in the United States. And since reparations to African Americans would eventuate in the former scenario of poverty of millions of U.S. citizens who are not African Americans, then reparations are to be denied on grounds of social utility maximization.

24. J. Angelo Corlett, *Analyzing Social Knowledge* (Totowa, N.J.: Rowman and Littlefield, 1996), chapter 5.

But surely it is questionable to think that "poverty" by today's U.S. standards is anything remotely akin to the horrendous evils of that "peculiar institution"! And if this is plausible, then on what grounds can the objection from social utility warrant nonpayment of reparations to the harms incurred by African Americans and their forebears? Furthermore, even if it is assumed for the sake of argument that social utility is *not* maximized (for all U.S. citizens) economically by way of paying reparations to African Americans, it hardly follows that social utility is not maximized by payment of reparations, *all things considered.* For if *unrectified evil is evil still,* and if the United States refuses to pay adequate reparations to African Americans for its evil treatment of them, then the evil that accompanied the founding and sustaining of the United States in the forms of slavery and Jim Crow stand to condemn the United States as evil. Such moral evil is of a magnitude so significant that it is difficult, if not impossible, to imagine how any amount of economic welfare of U.S. citizens could outweigh the nonpayment of reparations to victims of U.S. oppression. So if the objection from social utility is to be marshaled against the reparations argument as it pertains to African Americans, then it must be marshaled nonselectively concerning what counts as social utility, including, of course, considerations of moral guilt and responsibility for evil. And it is far from obvious that the economic hardships likely to accrue to other U.S. citizens from their paying adequate reparations to African Americans outweigh the historic evils experienced by millions of African Americans and their forebears. Thus the objection from social utility is neutralized, if not defeated, by certain utilitarian considerations themselves.

The Anti-Private-Property-Rights Objection and Counterfactuals

The anti-private-property-rights objection to African American reparations states that the very notion of private property rights is something Africans lacked until they were captured, sold, traded, enslaved, and acculturated into U.S. society. Insofar as reparations are matters of private property rights (e.g., to stolen surplus labor value), they are morally unjustified because they do not represent anything indigenous Africans would have cherished had they not been acculturated to accept the idea in the first place. Note how the anti-private-property-rights objection is fused with Waldron's counterfactual objection, which states that reparations to African Americans are unjustified because it is impossible to calculate in what condition African Americans *would* have been had such historic evils *not* occurred.

In reply to this rather strange line of argument proffered against reparations to African Americans, it must be clarified that *normative ethics* does *not* require that such a standard be satisfied in order for reasonably approximate damages to be awarded to a deserving party. In the case of African Americans, as we have already seen, it is reasonable to think that a fairly accurate calculation can be made of the wages stolen (forcibly withheld) from African slaves by slave masters, along with the kinds of punitive damages for all kinds of basic human rights violations that were inflicted on African slaves in the United States, and on their descendants in the United States. The calculation, when inflation, compounded interest, punitive damages, and penalties for nonpayment are taken into account, might well range into the trillions of dollars. Yet all of this can be done without having to solve some counterfactual problem. For whether the counterfactual problem is a real problem, it is certainly *not* a difficulty for normative ethics in determining reparations to African Americans, except on the unreasonable assumption that complete and absolutely perfect rectification of African Americans is required in order to justify the said reparations. However, if approximate justice is what such reparations seeks to effect, then the counterfactual objection (as well as the anti-private-property-rights objection) seems to be a red herring. For we need not resolve matters of perfect justice in every possible world in order to mete out approximate justice in *this* world. This is important for my line of reasoning in that it is normative, yet aimed at a reasonably just legal system for its enforcement.[25]

Some Possible Reparations Policies

Having argued in favor of reparations to African Americans by the U.S. government, and having defeated or neutralized various leading objections that might be made to the reparations argument concerning African Americans, it is helpful to explore some ways in which such reparations might accrue. First, it is noteworthy that many have argued in favor of affirmative action or preferential treatment as a legitimate form of reparations to African Americans.[26] Indeed, this chapter started with a summary of a legal suit that seeks precisely this kind of "reparations" to African Americans. However, as I have argued in chapters 6–8, to construe affirmative

25. The same can be said plausibly concerning Native Americans.
26. One recent example is found in Howard McGary, *Race and Social Justice* (London: Blackwell, 1999): 100–104.

action or preferential treatment as a form of reparations is a category mistake since affirmative action in many forms amounts to programs of preferential treatment the benefits of which are *earned* by recipients, whereas this is not true of reparations. Furthermore, it is a grand confusion to suppose, as most do, that descendants of U.S. slavery who deserve reparations for their ancestors' human rights being violated (in millions of instances, for the durations of their entire lives!) are to be adequately compensated by *earning* their salaries by way of positions awarded them by way of preferential treatment.[27] For it violates principles of what a victim of harm and wrongdoing *deserves* in *proportion* to damages suffered by the victim.

Unlike possible policies of reparations to Native Americans that ought to consider ways in which substantial acres of land as well as monetary damages be awarded to Native Americans, reparations to African Americans ought not involve U.S. territory since the moral entitlement to such territory belongs by and large to Native Americans, as argued in the previous chapter. So in this regard, reparations to African Americans are relatively simple as they involve some amount of monetary compensation as in the cases of Germany's reparations to Israel and the United States' reparations to certain Japanese Americans.

To argue, as some do, that programs of social welfare or such might be considered as reparations to African Americans not only runs the risk of the category mistake just mentioned, but it also presumes that African Americans ought to or must integrate into the very society the government of which has served as their most ardent oppressor since its very inception. Surely justice cannot require—or even presume—that victims of racist evils ought even to desire to coexist alongside those whose government has oppressed them so badly, without compensation after centuries of brutal human rights violations! This being the case, reparations to African Americans ought not to assume an integrationist posture. And given that the amount of reparations owed to African Americans would be the amount owed for the estimated costs of labor power and value stolen by coercion from the millions of African slaves in the United States and all human rights violations at the hands of the U.S. government and various state governments, it is plausible to assume that African Americans would have sufficient funds to successfully segregate themselves from their U.S. oppressors once and for all. There is no question that thousands, perhaps millions, would desire precisely that.[28]

27. Importantly, McGary does *not* make such an assumption.

28. This general line of argument can also be applied to the Native American case for reparations.

Strict justice might well require that the U.S. government pay to African Americans as a group (by way, say, of an African American elected congressional body) all of the monies owed African Americans for the evils of slavery and of Jim Crow. Since "ought" implies "can," such payments could not be made in a lump sum any time in the foreseeable future. So some sort of annual "tax" would need to be assessed against those who are not predominantly Native and/or African Americans, given the genealogical conception of ethnic identity advanced and defended in earlier chapters. The overall amount of reparations owed would be calculated and then paid over, say, fifty to one hundred years,[29] including compounded interest, penalties for previous nonpayment, inflationary factors, and perhaps even punitive damages. Admittedly, as in the case of Native American reparations, no amount of reparations will truly suffice for the evils wrought on oppressed peoples. But this is hardly a good reason for not making an honest effort to do the right thing in paying some substantial amount to the descendants of slaves and those who were victimized by Jim Crow. Concerns about the possible corruption of African Americans actually distributing the reparations monies need not concern us any more than, say, German citizens have a legitimate concern about how Israel ought to distribute reparations payments received from Germany. Moreover, any suggestion that significant parcels of land be set aside for African Americans as part of a reparations agreement would run afoul of legitimate Native American moral rights to the land.

There is no question that the United States could no longer survive as it now does should it finally own up to what it owes in reparations to African Americans (and to Native Americans). But as we saw, the objection from social utility neither negates the reparations argument in the Native American case, nor in the African American case. Whatever suffering accrues to the United States as the result of its paying fair amounts of reparations to Native and African Americans might be seen rightly as the moral cost of constructing a putatively civil society while murdering and otherwise oppressing untold millions of Native and African Americans. If such suffering due to the cost of paying reparations spells the demise of the United States as we know it, then perhaps the costs would serve as a reminder to

29. In perpetuity payments of reparations to Native and African Americans run the danger of such ethnic groups being diluted over time (relative to whatever percentage of ethnicity is required for public policy purposes) such that members of the oppressed groups in question receive lesser percentages of reparations payments. I suggest, then, that an adequate amount of reparations be paid to each group within a century so that more of those who experienced some of the historic evils can benefit from reparations. On the other hand, if reparations payments end up being inadequate in sum, then it would seem fair to make such payments accrue in perpetuity.

the rest of the world as to how *not* to build a society. It must be borne in mind that the United States as a perpetrator of severe evils on these groups is not in a moral position to complain about whatever harms it is now forced to endure as the result of its paying adequate reparations to Native and African Americans. Indeed, reparations seem to be the moral cost of the United States to attempt to redeem itself from the dredges of immorality in which it alone has placed itself, generation after generation, by simply refusing to pay what it owes to those whom it has murdered, enslaved, and otherwise oppressed.

In this chapter, I have articulated the reparations argument for African Americans. Then I considered an array of objections to the argument, many of which were applied from the case of reparations to Native Americans in chapter 8. Along the way, some similarities and differences between the cases for reparations to African and Native Americans were noted. In the end, it was concluded that not only are reparations owed to Native Americans, but to African Americans also.

As Raimond Gaita writes, "Communities take pleasure and pride in the fact that injustices have been acknowledged and overcome, and that reparation has been made when it is possible. Such pleasure in justice is necessary if people are lucidly to love their community, country, or nation."[30] Perhaps motivated by some complex array of self-serving biases that in turn lead U.S. citizens and their government to repeatedly deny reparations for some of the most horrendous evils in the history of the world, reparations have not been paid to African Americans. This is somewhat surprising, given that so many U.S. citizens and governmental leaders declare loudly that the United States is the best country in the world. But once again, if *unrectified evil is evil still,* and if the United States is responsible for the oppression of African Americans and their forebears, then the United States owes it to African Americans to adequately rectify the evils, however approximately and tardily. Time may heal all wounds, but it hardly erases unrectified evil and severe injustice! And the United States cannot by any stretch of the imagination continue to rightly claim to be a morally legitimate country unless and until it rectifies adequately its past evils. For *the evils of the past do not wither with the mere passing of time.* Rather, they cling to one's being with incessant fury until that moment when the attempted flight from one's evil deeds has ended with evil catching up with one, at times only to terrorize the evildoer with unimaginable vengeance.

30. Raimond Gaita, *A Common Humanity* (London: Routledge, 1998), p. 85.

Conclusion

In the preceding chapters, I have sought to provide connections between the concepts of race, ethnicity, racism, and reparations in ways that have not previously been done in philosophy. I attempted to clarify primitive race theories and what it means when most people use racialized discourse. Discontent with metaphysical analyses of race because they do not provide the law or public policy analysts with means by which to compensate ethnic or racialized groups for racist harms they have experienced, I provided a genealogical conception of Latino identity (and then the genealogical conception of ethnic identity) that grounds the classification of ourselves into ethnic groups for purposes of public policy administration, medical research, self-esteem, and group pride.

With a working notion of ethnic group membership in mind, I analyzed the nature of racism as a complex array of motivations and kinds, based ultimately on normal human cognition. Racism was defined not only doxastically as prejudice, but also involving an accompanying discrimination. Although not all persons are racists all of the time (I doubt that anyone is [e.g., thinks and behaves like] a racist all of the time), most everyone is (e.g., thinks and behaves like) a racist some of the time. Because of the various kinds and motives of racism, the racism in question need not always involve institutions, power, or hatred as is commonly believed. This better explains the pervasiveness of racism in the world today. For if it were true, as most philosophers argue, that only certain kinds of people are racists, then the dissolution of racism would be relatively simple. But unfortunately, racism is much more deeply imbedded in our cognitive architecture. And because we tend to act, fail to act, or attempt to act on our beliefs/attitudes, racist beliefs can and often do end up being racist in one way or another. As experimental social cognitive psychologists inform us, the failure of us to self-monitor when we classify ourselves and others into ethnic groups can and often does lead to racist actions, inactions, or attempted actions, as the case may be. Until philosophers understand this fact about racism, they will continue to believe that the "system" is responsible for what they call ("institutional") racism. If institutional racism were truly all there was to racism, it would be easier to rid the world of racism. But things are not so simple as those who construe racism as institutional power aver. That is only one kind of or motivation for racism. The cognitive-behavioral theory of racism sheds new philosophical light on the complex nature of racism with the hope that if we know more fully what racism is, we are in a better position to own up to *our own* contributions to its persistence in our world.

Two of the world's most horrendously evil forms of racism are the genocide of hundreds of Native American nations (the American holocaust) and the enslavement of Africans (and some Native Americans) by the United States, along with Jim Crow. What inspires this book is the desire to address such racist evils. Hence the need for both adequate working concepts of ethnic classification and of racism. But while many believe that affirmative action programs suffice to handle the historic problems of racial injustice, I argue that affirmative action programs ought to be restructured to account for the degrees of racist harms perpetrated in the past by the U.S. government.

If one is concerned about justice and proportional compensation as a means of rectification, however approximate, for historical harms and wrongdoings, then affirmative action ought never to be conflated with reparations. In the United States, reparations ought to be reserved for the most horrendous forms of evil such as the racist evils inflicted by the U.S. government on Native and African Americans. Affirmative action programs might well serve as means of promoting goals of distributive justice for various disadvantaged ethnic groups. But even here there needs to be a sense of degrees of greater or lesser states of disadvantage between such groups. A fair-minded reading of U.S. history would seem to show that Native and African Americans are far more disadvantaged (due to racist oppression) than all other groups. Thus affirmative action programs ought to reflect this fact and award greater benefits to members of more disadvantaged groups than they do to members of less disadvantaged groups. And this includes awarding affirmative action benefits (say, in hiring) differentially to women over men within ethnic categories. However, to this point of U.S. history, affirmative action programs have actually lumped all disadvantaged groups together into one category, with each receiving the same benefits as the others. This does violence to the crucial differences that exist between groups insofar as the extent to which each has been harmed by the U.S. government. Since disadvantaged groups ought to receive benefits comparable to the harms they experienced at the "hands" of the U.S. government, then the affirmative action policies ought to be revised to reflect this principle of proportionality in public policy administration. If this is not done, and matters remain as they are, then one morally problematic and tragic result of a well-intentioned set of policies is that European American women, who have long since served as one of the oppressors of people of color in the United States, will continue to benefit more than any other group that receives affirmative action.

As far as reparations are concerned, it seems morally appalling that the United States would award reparations to certain Japanese Americans for suffering in the U.S. internment camps of the World War II era while denying any reparations whatsoever to African Americans suffering under Jim Crow, perhaps the largest internment camp in the world, and denying anything akin to adequate reparations to Native Americans for the genocidal theft of much of an entire continent! After all, Jim Crow outlasted the Japanese internment camps by generations, and there are those alive today who could still benefit from such reparations. Furthermore, anti-Japanese-American racism pales in comparison to either anti-African American racism or anti-Native American racism, an historical and moral fact too often not understood or appreciated by most people. That such reparations are nonetheless denied in such cases bespeaks of a kind of racist indifference toward Native and African Americans that pervades the very essence of the United States at nearly every level of social being.

The problem of reparations for U.S. racist harms and wrongdoings to Native and African Americans is typically discussed in terms of the historic evils of genocide and enslavement of the former, and of enslavement of the latter, along with Jim Crow's oppression of African Americans. This book has set forth a simple, yet compelling, reparations argument for Native and African Americans. Moreover, it has sought to defend the reparations argument against seemingly all manner of objection, none of which turned out to be unproblematic. Such objections ended up being either irrelevant, self-serving, or in some crucial way unsupported by argument. Yet lacking a sound objection to the reparations argument, it would seem that there is very good reason indeed to think that Native and African Americans are deserving of and ought to receive reparations from the U.S. government. If this is true, then it behooves us to consider rationally what reasonable forms such reparations might take. In the case of Native Americans, I noted a cluster of possible reparations policies, explaining how inadequate each one was, and why. In the end, the most realistic reparations policy will *not* be the one most deserved, as most U.S. citizens are morally unwilling to do what is right or good in the first place.

Unfortunately, it becomes a miraculous feat of morality to simply attempt to persuade citizens of the most powerful country in the world that its own unrectified evil makes it evil still. Moreover, the only way in which the United States could even hope to not remain evil is if its historic evils are rectified in some adequate way(s). Yet the only way in which such evils can be rectified seems to be by the United States providing some substantial amount of reparations to both Native and African Americans.[1]

It is one thing for a society to proclaim itself to be the greatest society in the world; it is quite another thing for it to live up to such a bold pronouncement. Technological innovations and high standards of living for its own citizens must not blind one to the vicious costs of such "gains" in terms of human oppression. After all, would there even be a U.S. society had not it not received substantial "assistance" from other countries that settled unjustly the continent by force and fraud,[2] thereby violating the principle of unjust acquisitions and transfers? And would there be a U.S. society had not it not waged a genocidal war against Native Americans for the sake of expansionism? Would the economic strength of the Old South been strong without the forcibly stolen surplus labor value from African slaves? There is no doubt, morally speaking, that nearly whatever goodness there is found in the United States today is contingent on the unpaid bills of reparations it owes for such infringements of basic human rights. And no amount of passage of time alone can possibly place a moral statute of limitations of such injustices, especially since it was the U.S. government that continually denied requests (even demands!) for justice for such inhumanities.

Quite simply, it is morally impossible for U.S. society to be the greatest country in the world if it exists and even thrives off of the evils its government has perpetrated on others. Without such evils it would not even exist. Perhaps what many U.S. patriots and supporters believe is that the United States is the greatest country in the world, but not at all in a moral or ethical sense. Or perhaps what they mean by their unabashed patriotism

---

1. I do not assume here that these two groups or clusters of groups are the only ones deserving of reparations from the U.S. government. Rather, it is that they represent the clearest cases for reparations and of the greatest amounts of reparations.

2. The point here is that the intrusion of European invaders from "all sides" posed a many-faced enemy too daunting for even the greatest coalition of Native American nations to resist successfully.

and support is that such oppression was necessary for the United States to arise and stand as the world's pillar of democracy. But such amoral or self-serving patriotism is just that and is irrelevant to any discussion of the morality of unrectified evil. If the United States fails to own up to its great debts to Native and African Americans, then morally speaking, what it itself deserves, quite disappointingly, is far worse than what it experienced on 11 September 2001. For the world has no need for self-aggrandizing patriots of one of the most evil countries in human history posing as a defender of goodness and rightness while ignoring the fact that its materialistic flourishing has been at the cost of its thorough commitment to rectify adequately some of the most horrendous of evils the world has ever witnessed. The very least that the United States and its citizens ought to do concerning war crimes tribunals (as well as the sessions of the newly established International Criminal Court) is to sit in utter silence and render not even the hint of judgment until the United States rises to the moral occasion of coming to real terms with its own unrectified evils. Otherwise, U.S. citizens and leaders would appear very much akin to the person (spoken of in one of the parables of Jesus of Nazareth) who sought to point out a sliver in someone else's eye, while having a *beam* in his own! Moral hypocrisy should have no place in the world, and neither does immorality in the form of unrectified evil.

It is this author's hope that the United States will awaken to this plea for rectificatory justice and at least begin to make some sincere effort to compensate Native and African Americans. For such an effort would at least remove the United States from the ethical burden of evil that it faces (self-recognized or not) as the result of its own doing. Then certain other countries must face similar roles they played in the oppression of others and commence to pay their respective debts for such injustices. But let us start with the simpler cases first and watch and wait to see if the United States even owns up to its unpaid debt.

There is of late growing discussion of the ethics of reconciliation in light of mounting global conflicts. But it is morally presumptuous to think that there can be reconciliation without reparations in cases of unrectified evil. We must come to understand that, though reconciliation is a worthy goal, certain things must obtain in order for true reconciliation to accrue. In the case of injustices against Native and African Americans, genuine reconciliation requires at the very least adequate reparations that include apologies to each group. By "adequate reparations" I mean those adequate in light of the quality and quantity of the evils inflicted on Native and African Americans, not what is deemed affordable or adequate by parties forced to pay the reparations quite apart from an appreciation of the horrors of the historic evils experienced by these groups. However, lacking adequate reparations and apologies, there neither can nor should be peace. Yet without peace there can be no genuine reconciliation. Nor should there be. Finally, that adequate reparations and apologies are necessary conditions of genuine reconciliation between the United States and Native and African Americans hardly means that they are sufficient. For it is always a moral prerogative of morally virtuous victims to forgive their perpetrators.[3] And especially in cases of long-term unrectified evils ranking amongst the worst in human history, it would be the height of moral presumption to think for even a moment that reconciliation should automatically follow adequate reparations and even the most sincere of apologies by the United States. For the moral duty of perpetrators to rectify their wrongdoings (especially evils) in no way whatsoever implies a moral duty of victims to either forgive or desire to reconcile with their perpetrators. What can be hoped for, in the end, is that the United States would at least commence to do the right things by Native and African Americans. Perhaps over time, adequate reparations and apologies would accrue, followed by whatever responses deemed morally appropriate by these oppressed groups. In any case, the United States is not in a moral position to complain should adequate reparations and genuine apologies be met with no desire to forgive and reconcile.

A most grievous question remains: is it ever too late for the U.S. government to do the right things by way of Native and African Americans? It is sincerely hoped that it is not. For the next exhortation for justice for these and other groups might not, it is feared, be as peaceful as the one found in this book.[4]

3. J. Angelo Corlett, *Responsibility and Punishment* (Dordrecht: Kluwer, 2001), chapter 6.
4. J. Angelo Corlett, *Terrorism: A Philosophical Analysis* (Dordrecht: Kluwer, 2003).

Selected Bibliography

Acuña, Rudolph. *Occupied America*. 3d ed. New York: Harper Collins, 1988.

Adam, Herbert. "Anti-Semitism and Anti-Black Racism: Nazi Germany and Apartheid South Africa." *Telos* 108 (1996): 25–46.

Adler, Mortimer, ed. *The Negro in American History*. 3 vols. New York: Encyclopedia Britannica Educational Corporation, 1969.

Aksiuchits, Viktor. "Westernizers and Nativists Today." *Russian Studies in Philosophy* 31 (1993): 83–94.

Alcoff, Linda Martín, "Is Latino/a Identity a Racial Category?" In *Hispanics and Latinos in the United States*, ed. Jorge J. E. Gracia and Pablo DeGreiff, pp. 23–44. London: Routledge, 2000.

——. "Philosophy and Racial Identity." *Radical Philosophy* 75 (1996): 5–14.

——. "Philosophy and Racial Identity." *Philosophy Today* 41 (1997): 67–76.

——. "Racism." In *A Companion to Feminist Philosophy*, ed. Alison M. Jaggar and Iris Young, pp. 475–84. Cambridge: Blackwell, 1998.

——. "Towards a Phenomenology of Racial Embodiment." *Radical Philosophy* 95 (1999): 15–26.

——. "What Should White People Do?" *Hypatia* 13 (1998): 6–26.

Allen, Wayne. "Eric Voegelin on the Genealogy of Race." *International Philosophical Quarterly* 39 (1999): 317–37.

Allport, Gordon W. *The Nature of Prejudice*. New York: Doubleday Anchor Books, 1958.

Almaguer, T. "Historical Notes on Chicano Oppression." *Aztlan* (1974).

Alston, William P. "Epistemic Circularity." *Philosophy and Phenomenological Research* 47 (1986): 1–30.

Alter, Torin. "Review of George Schedler's 'Racist Symbols and Reparations: Philosophical Reflections on Vestiges of the American Civil War.'" *Social Theory and Practice* 26 (2000): 153–71.

Altman, Andrew. "Expressive Meaning, Race, and the Law: The Racial Gerrymandering Cases." *Legal Theory* 5 (1999): 75–99.

——. "Legal Realism, Critical Legal Studies, and Dworkin." In *Philosophy of Law*, ed.

Joel Feinberg and Hyman Gross, 5th ed., pp. 176–91. Belmont, Calif.: Wadsworth, 1995.

———. "Policy, Principle, and Incrementalism: Dworkin's Jurisprudence of Race." *Journal of Ethics* 5 (2001): 241–62.

———. "Race and Democracy: The Controversy over Racial Vote Dilution." *Philosophy and Public Affairs* 27 (1998): 175–201.

Andelson, Robert V. "Black Reparations: A Study in Gray." *Personalist* 59 (1978): 173–83.

Anderson, John R. *Cognitive Psychology and Its Implications.* New York: W. H. Freeman, 1985.

Anderson, William L., ed. *Cherokee Removal.* Athens: University of Georgia Press, 1991.

Andreasen, Robin O. "A New Perspective on the Race Debate." *British Journal for the Philosophy of Science* 49 (1998): 199–225.

Anglas-Grande, Sandy Marie. "Beyond the Ecologically Noble Savage: Deconstructing the White Man's Indian." *Environmental Ethics* 21 (1999): 307–20.

Appiah, Anthony. "But Would That Still Be Me? Notes on Gender, Race, Ethnicity, as Sources of Ethnicity." *Journal of Philosophy* 77 (1990): 493–499.

———. "Race, Culture, and Identity: Misunderstood Connections." In *The Tanner Lectures on Human Values,* ed. Grethe B. Peterson. Salt Lake City: University of Utah Press, 1996.

———. "Racism and Moral Pollution." *Philosophical Forum* 18 (1987): 185–202.

———. "Racisms." In *Anatomy of Racism,* ed. David Goldberg, pp. 3–17. Minneapolis: University of Minnesota Press, 1990).

———. "The Uncompleted Argument: DuBois and the Illusion of Race." In *The Idea of Race,* ed. Robert Bernasconi and Tommy Lott, pp. 118–35. Indianapolis: Hackett, 2000.

Applebaum, Barbara. "Good Liberal Intentions Are not Enough! Racism, Intentions, and Moral Responsibility." *Journal of Moral Education* 26 (1997), pp. 409–21.

Appleton, Nicholas. "On Choosing an Ethnic Identity." *Philosophy of Education* 37 (1981): 211–18.

Arnold, N. Scott. "Affirmative Action and the Demands of Justice." *Social Philosophy and Policy* 15 (1998): 133–75.

Axelsen, Diana. "With All Deliberate Delay: On Justifying Preferential Policies in Education." *Philosophical Forum* 9 (1978): 264–88.

Baier, Kurt. "Merit and Race." *Philosophia* 8 (1978): 121–51.

Bailey, Garrick, and Roberta Glenn Bailey. *A History of the Navajos.* Santa Fe: School of American Research Press, 1986.

Baker, Judith, ed. *Group Rights.* Toronto: University of Toronto Press, 1994.

Baldwin, James. *Evidence of Things Not Seen.* New York: Holt, Rinehart and Winston, 1985.

———. *The Fire Next Time.* New York: Dial Press, 1963.

Balfour, Lawrie. "A Most Disagreeable Mirror: Race Consciousness as Double Consciousness." *Political Theory* 26 (1998): 346–69.

Banner, William. "Reverse Discrimination: Misconception and Confusion." *Journal of Social Philosophy* 10 (1979): 15–18.

Barnard, William A., and Mark S. Benn. "Belief Congruence and Prejudice Reduction in an Interracial Contact Setting." *Journal of Social Psychology* 128 (1988): 125–34.

Bar-On, Dorit. "Discrimination, Individual Justice, and Preferential Treatment." *Public Affairs Quarterly* 4 (1990): 111–137.

Bayles, Michael D. "Reparations to Wronged Groups." *Analysis* 33 (1973): 182–84.

Beauchamp, Tom L. "In Defense of Affirmative Action." *Journal of Ethics* 2 (1998): 143–58.

Beckwith, Francis J. "The 'No One Deserves His or Her Talents' Argument for Affirmative Action: A Critical Analysis." *Social Theory and Practice* 25 (1999): 52–60.

Beckwith, Martha. *Hawai'ian Mythology*. Honolulu: University of Hawai'i Press, 1976.

Bedau, Hugo Adam. "Compensatory Justice and the Black Manifesto." *Monist* 56 (1972): 20–42.

Bell, Derrick. *Faces at the Bottom of the Well*. New York: Basic Books, 1992.

———. *And We Are Not Saved*. New York: Basic Books, 1987.

Benatar, David. "Prejudice in Jest: When Racial and Gender Humor Harms." *Public Affairs Quarterly* 13 (1999): 191–203.

Benedict, Ruth. *Patterns of Culture*. Boston: Houghton and Mifflin, 1934.

Berkhofer, Robert Jr. *Salvation and the Savage*. New York: Atheneum, 1965.

Bernasconi, Robert, and Tommy Lott, eds. *The Idea of Race*. Indianapolis: Hackett, 2000.

Bigelow, John, Robert Pargetter, and Robert Young. "Land, Well-Being, and Compensation." *Australasian Journal of Philosophy* 68 (1990): 330–46.

Bishop, John D. "Locke's Theory of Original Appropriation and the Right of Settlement in Iroquois Territory." *Canadian Journal of Philosophy* 27 (1997): 311–38.

Bittker, Boris. *The Case for Black Reparations*. New York: Random House, 1973.

———. "Identifying the Beneficiaries." In *Reverse Discrimination*, ed. Barry Gross. Buffalo: Prometheus Books, 1977.

Blackburn, Daniel. "Why Race Is Not a Biological Concept." In *Race and Racism in Theory and Practice*, ed. Berel Lang, pp. 3–26. Lanham, Md.: Rowman and Littlefield, 2000.

Blackstone, William T. "Compensatory Justice and Affirmative Action." *Proceedings and Addresses of the American Philosophical Association* 49 (1975): 218–27.

———. "Is Preferential Treatment Just or Unjust?" In *Ethics, Free Enterprise, and Public Policy*, ed. Richard De George, pp. 99–115. New York: Oxford University Press, 1978.

———. "Reverse Discrimination and Compensatory Justice." *Social Theory and Practice* 3 (1975): 253–88.

Blackstone, William T., and Robert D. Heslep, eds. *Social Justice and Preferential Treatment*. Athens: University of Georgia Press, 1977.

Blanchard Jr., Kenneth C. "Ethnicity and the Problem of Equality." *Interpretation* 20 (1993): 309–24.

Blauner, Robert. *Racial Oppression in America*. New York: Harper & Row, 1972.

Blum, Lawrence. "Ethnicity, Identity, and Community." In *Justice and Caring*, ed. Michael S. Katz, Nel Noddings, and Kenneth A. Strike, pp. 127–45. New York: Teachers College Press, 1999.

———. *I'm Not a Racist, But . . .* Ithaca: Cornell University Press, 2002.

———. "Philosophy and the Values of a Multicultural Community." *Teaching Philosophy* 14 (1991): 127–34.

Boubia, Fawzi. "Hegel's Internationalism: World History and Exclusion." *Metaphilosophy* 28 (1997): 417–32.

Bowie, Norman E., ed. *Equal Opportunity*. Boulder, Colo.: Westview Press, 1988.

Boxill, Bernard R. *Blacks and Social Justice*. Totowa, N.J.: Rowman and Littlefield, 1984.

——. "Equality, Discrimination, and Preferential Treatment." In *A Companion to Ethics,* ed. Peter Singer, pp. 333–42. Cambridge: Blackwell, 1991.

——. "The Morality of Reparations." *Social Theory and Practice* 2 (1972): 113–22.

——. "Power and Persuasion." *Journal of Social Philosophy* 32 (2001): 382–85.

Bracken, Harry. "Essence, Accident, and Race." *Hermathena* 16 (1973): 81–96.

——. "Philosophy and Racism." *Philosophia* 8 (1978): 241–60.

Bricker, David C. "Autonomy and Culture: Will Kymlicka on Cultural Minority Rights." *Southern Journal of Philosophy* 36 (1998): 47–59.

Brooks, D. H. M. "Why Discrimination Is Especially Wrong." *Journal of Value Inquiry* 17 (1983): 305–12.

Browder, John O. "Redemptive Communities: Indigenous Knowledge, Colonist Farming Systems, and Conservation of Tropical Forests." *Agriculture and Human Values* 12 (1995): 17–30.

Brown, Dee. *Bury My Heart at Wounded Knee.* New York: Henry Holt, 1970.

Byrnes, Deborah A., and Gary Kiger. "Prejudice-Reduction Simulations: Ethics, Evaluations, and Theory into Practice." *Simulation & Gaming* 23 (1992): 457–71.

——. "Prejudice-Reduction Simulations: Notes on Their Use and Abuse—A Reply to Williams and Giles." *Simulation & Gaming* 23 (1992): 485–89.

Callicott, J. Baird. "Many Indigenous Worlds or 'the' Indigenous World? A Reply to My 'Indigenous' Critics." *Environmental Ethics* 22 (2000): 291–310.

Campbell, Joseph. *The Hero with a Thousand Faces.* Princeton: Princeton University Press, 1949.

——. *The Masks of God.* 4 vols. New York: Viking Press, 1968.

Campbell, Stanley W. *The Slave Catchers: Enforcement of the Fugitive Slave Laws, 1850–1860.* New York: Norton, 1970.

Canadian Journal of Law and Jurisprudence 4 (1991).

Cane, Peter. *Responsibility in Law and Morality.* Oxford: Hart, 2002.

Cerutti, Furio. "Can There Be a Supranational Identity?" *Philosophy and Social Criticism* 18 (1992): 147–62.

Cheney, Jim, and Anthony Weston. "Environmental Ethics as Environmental Etiquette: Toward an Ethics-Based Epistemology." *Environmental Ethics* 21 (1999): 115–34.

Churchill, Ward. *From a Native Son.* Boston: South End Press, 1996.

Cochran, David Carroll. *The Color of Freedom: Race and Contemporary American Liberalism.* Albany: State University of New York Press, 1999.

Cohen, Carl. "Preference by Race Is Neither Just Nor Wise." *Philosophic Exchange* 28 (1998): 29–42.

——. "Who Are Equals?" *National Forum* 58 (1978): 10–14.

Cohen, G. A. *History, Labour, and Freedom.* Oxford: Oxford University Press, 1988.

Cohen, Marshall, Thomas Nagel, and Thomas Scanlon, eds. *Equality and Preferential Treatment.* Princeton: Princeton University Press, 1977.

Cohen, Stephen. "Arguing About Prejudice and Discrimination." *Journal of Value Inquiry* 28 (1994): 391–400.

Coleman, Jules. "Corrective Justice and Property Rights." *Social Philosophy and Policy* 11 (1994): 124–38.

——. "Corrective Justice and Wrongful Gain." *Journal of Legal Studies* 11 (1982): 421–40.

Collins, Patricia Hill. "It's All in the Family: Intersections of Gender, Race, and Nation." *Hypatia* 13 (1998): 62–82.

Cone, James H. *Black Theology and Black Power*. New York: Seabury, 1969.
——. *A Black Theology of Liberation*. Philadelphia: Lippencott, 1970.
——. *For My People: Black Theology and the Black Church*. Maryknoll: Orbis, 1984.
——. *God of the Oppressed*. Maryknoll: Orbis, 1997.
——. *Risks of Faith*. Boston: Beacon, 1999.
Cooney, William, "Affirmative Action and the Doctrine of Double Effect." *Journal of Applied Philosophy* 6 (1989): 201–4.
Cordero, Ronald. "Unwitting Discrimination." *Journal of Social Philosophy* 27 (1996): 172–88.
Corlett, J. Angelo. "Analyzing Racism." *Public Affairs Quarterly* 12 (1998): 23–50.
——. *Analyzing Social Knowledge*. Lanham, Md.: Rowman and Littlefield, 1996.
——. "Dworkin's *Empire* Strikes Back!" *Statute Law Review* 21 (2000): 43–56.
——. "Epistemic Responsibility," forthcoming.
——. "Epistemologia sociale e filosofia sociale." *Fenomenologia e societa* 1 (1998): 2–10.
——. "Epistemology, Psychology, and Goldman." *Social Epistemology* 5 (1991): 91–100.
——. "Goldman and the Foundations of Social Epistemics." *Argumentation* 8 (1994): 145–56.
——. "Latino Identity." *Public Affairs Quarterly* 13 (1999): 273–95.
——. "Latino/a Identity." *American Philosophical Association Newsletter on Hispanic/Latino Issues in Philosophy* 1 (2001): 97–104.
——. "Latino Identity and Affirmative Action." In *Hispanics/Latinos in the United States: Ethnicity, Race and Rights*, ed. Jorge J. L. Gracia and Pablo DeGreiff, pp. 223–34. London: Routledge, 2000.
——. "Making *More* Sense of Retributivism: Desert as Responsibility and Proportionality," *Philosophy*, forthcoming.
——. "Moral Compatibilism: Rights, Responsibility, Punishment, and Compensation," Ph.D. dissertation, Department of Philosophy, University of Arizona, 1992.
——. "Parallels of Ethnicity and Gender." In *Race/Sex: Their Sameness, Difference, and Interplay*, ed. Naomi Zack, pp. 163–84. London: Routledge, 1996.
——. "The Problem of Collective Moral Rights." *Canadian Journal of Law and Jurisprudence* 6 (1993): 237–59.
——. "Racism and Affirmative Action." *Journal of Social Philosophy* 24 (1993): 163–75.
——. "Reparations to Native Americans?" In *War Crimes and Collective Wrongdoing*, ed. Alexander Jokic, pp. 236–69. London: Blackwell, 2000.
——. *Responsibility and Punishment*. Dordrecht: Kluwer Academic, 2001.
——. "Ruminations on Reparations," In *Reparations*, ed. Howard McGary. Lanham, Md.: Rowman and Littlefield, forthcoming.
——. "Social Epistemology and Social Cognition." *Social Epistemology* 5 (1991): 135–49.
——. "Surviving Evil: Jewish, African, and Native-Americans." *Journal of Social Philosophy* 31 (2000): 207–23.
——. *Terrorism: A Philosophical Analysis*. Dordrecht: Kluwer Academic, Philosophical Studies Series, 2003.
——, ed. *Equality and Liberty: Analyzing Rawls and Nozick*. London: Macmillan, 1990.
Corlett, J. Angelo, and Robert Francescotti. "Foundations of a Theory of Hate Speech." *Wayne Law Review*, forthcoming.

Cortese, Anthony J. *Ethnic Ethics: The Restructuring of Moral Theory.* Albany: State University of New York Press, 1990.

Cotingham, John. "Race and Individual Merit." *Philosophy* 55 (1980): 525–31.

Cover, Robert. *Justice Accused.* New Haven: Yale University Press, 1975.

Cowen, J. L. "Inverse Discrimination." *Analysis* 33 (1972): 10–12.

Cowan, Tyler. "Discounting and Restitution." *Philosophy and Public Affairs* 26 (1997): 168–85.

Curtin, Deane, ed. *Institutional Violence.* Amsterdam: Rodopi, 1999.

——. "Making Peace with the Earth: Indigenous Agriculture and the Green Revolution." *Environmental Ethics* 17 (1995): 59–74.

D'Amico, Robert. "Reply to the Introduction to *Telos* 108." *Telos* 110 (1998): 141–47.

Danley, John R. "Liberalism, Aboriginal Rights, and Cultural Minorities." *Philosophy and Public Affairs* 20 (1991): 168–85.

Darley, J. M., et al. "Dispelling Negative Expectancies: The Impact of Interaction Goals and Target Characteristics on the Expectancy Confirmation Process." *Journal of Experimental Social Psychology* 24 (1988): 19–36.

Davis, Angela. *Women, Race, and Class.* New York: Random House, 1981.

Davis, Michael. "Race as Merit." *Mind* 92 (1983): 347–67.

——. "Racial Quotas, Weights, and Real Possibilities: A Moral For Moral Theory." *Social Theory and Practice* 7 (1981): 49–84.

Debo, Angie. *A History of the Indians of the United States.* Norman: University of Oklahoma Press, 1970.

——. *And Still the Waters Run.* Norman: University of Oklahoma Press, 1989.

Delgado, Richard, and Vicky Palacios. "Mexican Americans as a Legally Cognizable Class." In *The Latino/a Condition: A Critical Reader,* ed. Richard Delgado and Jean Stefancic, pp. 284–90. New York: New York University Press, 1998.

De Marco, Joseph P. "The Concept of Race in the Social Thought of W. E. B. DuBois." *Philosophical Forum* 3 (1972): 227–41.

De Waal, Alex. "Group Identity, Rationality, and the State." *Critical Review* 11 (1997): 279–89.

Dodds, Susan. "Justice and Indigenous Land Rights." *Inquiry* 41 (1998): 187–205.

Dougherty, Michael. *To Steal a Kingdom: Probing Hawai'ian History.* Waimanalo: Island Style Press, 1992.

DuBois, W. E. B. *The Souls of Black Folk.* New York: Fawcett, 1961.

Duckitt, John. "Locus of Control and Racial Prejudice." *Psychological Reports* 54 (1984).

Du Toit, Louise. "Cultural Identity as Narrative and Performance." *South African Journal of Philosophy* 16 (1997): 85–93.

Dworkin, Ronald. *Law's Empire.* Cambridge: Harvard University Press, 1986.

——. "Review of Robert Cover, *Justice Accused.*" *Times Literary Supplement,* 5 December 1975.

——. *Taking Rights Seriously.* Cambridge: Harvard University Press, 1978.

Ehle, John. *Trail of Tears.* New York: Anchor Books, 1988.

Elenes, Alejandra C. "Reclaiming the Borderlands: Chicana/o Identity, Difference, and Critical Pedagogy." *Educational Theory* 47 (1997): 359–75.

Elkins, Stanley. *Slavery.* Chicago: University of Chicago Press, 1968.

Endicott, Timothy. "Are There Any Rules?" *Journal of Ethics* 5 (2001): 199–220.

English, Parker. "Education and Preferential Treatment." In *Values and Education,* ed. Thomas Magnell, pp. 125–37. Amsterdam: Rodopi, 1998.

———. "Preferential Hiring and Just War Theory." *Journal of Social Philosophy* 25 (1994): 119–38.

Ezorsky, Gertrude. *Racism and Justice: The Case for Affirmative Action.* Ithaca: Cornell University Press, 1991.

Feagan, Joe R. *Race and Ethnic Relations.* 2d ed. Englewood Cliffs: Prentice-Hall, 1984.

Feinberg, Joel. *Doing and Deserving.* Princeton: Princeton University Press, 1970.

———. *Freedom and Fulfillment.* Princeton: Princeton University Press, 1992.

———. *Harm to Others.* Oxford: Oxford University Press, 1984.

——— "Limits to the Free Expression of Opinion." In *Philosophy of Law,* ed. Joel Feinberg and Hyman Gross, 4th ed. pp. 295–310. Belmont, Calif.: Wadsworth, 1991.

———. "The Moral and Legal Responsibility of the Bad Samaritan." In Joel Feinberg, *Freedom and Fulfillment,* pp. 175–96. Princeton: Princeton University Press, 1992.

———. "The Nature and Value of Rights." In Joel Feinberg, *Rights, Justice, and the Bounds of Liberty.* Princeton: Princeton University Press, 1980.

———. *Offense to Others.* Oxford: Oxford University Press, 1985.

———. *Rights, Justice, and the Bounds of Liberty.* Princeton: Princeton University Press, 1980.

Felice, William F. "The Case for Collective Human Rights: The Reality of Group Suffering." *Ethics and International Affairs* 10 (1996): 47–61.

Ferguson, Ann. "Moral Responsibility and Social Change: A New Theory of Self." *Hypatia* 12 (1997): 116–41.

Fiske, Susan, and Shelley Taylor. *Social Cognition.* Menlo Park: Addison-Wesley, 1984.

Flew, Antony. *Atheistic Humanism.* Buffalo: Prometheus, 1993.

———. "Education against Racism: Three Comments." *Journal of Philosophy of Education* 21 (1987): 313–37.

———. "Education: Anti-racist, Multi-ethnic, and Multi-cultural." In *Logical Foundations,* ed. Indira Mahalingam, pp. 194–205. New York: St. Martin's Press, 1991.

Foreman, Grant. *Indian Removal.* Norman: University of Oklahoma Press, 1932.

Franklin, John Hope. *From Slavery to Freedom: A History of Negro Americans.* 3d ed. New York: Alfred A. Knopf, 1987.

French, Peter A. *Corporate and Collective Responsibility.* New York: Columbia University Press, 1984.

———. *Responsibility Matters.* Lawrence: University Press of Kansas, 1990.

Freyre, Gilberto. "Ethnic Groups and Culture." *Diogenes* 25 (1959): 41–59.

Fried, Marlene Gerber. "The Invisibility of Oppression." *Philosophical Forum* 11 (1979): 18–29.

Fuchs, Stephen, and Charles E. Case. "Prejudice as Lifeform." *Sociological Inquiry* 59 (1989): 301–17.

Fullinwider, Robert K. "The Case for Reparations." *Institute for Philosophy and Public Policy* 20 (2000): 1–11.

———. "The Life and Death of Racial Preferences." *Philosophical Studies* 85 (1997): 163–80.

———. *The Reverse Discrimination Controversy.* Totowa, N.J.: Rowman and Littlefield, 1980.

Gaita, Raimond. *A Common Humanity.* London: Routledge, 1998.

Gahringer, Robert E. "Race and Class: The Basic Issue of the Bakke Case." *Ethics* 90 (1979): 97–114.

García, Jorge L. A. "Current Conceptions of Racism: A Critical Examination of Some Recent Social Philosophy." *Journal of Social Philosophy* 28 (1997): 5–42.

——. "The Heart of Racism." *Journal of Social Philosophy* 27 (1996): 5–46.

——. "How Latina? More Latina? In Debate with Angelo Corlett." *American Philosophical Association Newsletter on Hispanic/Latino Issues in Philosophy* 1 (2001): 93–97.

Garcia, Melinda A. "Responsibility Versus Defensiveness: Inclusion of Ethnicity in the Conceptualization of Theory." *Ethics and Behavior* 5 (1995): 373–75.

Garrett, Aaron. "Hume's Revised Racism Revisited." *Hume Studies* 26 (2000): 171–77.

Geels, Donald E. "How to Be a Consistent Racist." *Personalist* 52 (1971): 662–79.

Gilbert, Margaret. "Collective Guilt and Collective Guilt Feelings." *Journal of Ethics* 6 (2002): 115–43.

——. "Collective Remorse." In *War Crimes and Collective Wrongdoing*, ed. Aleksandar Jokic, pp. 216–35. London: Blackwell, 2001.

——. "Group Wrongs and Guilt Feelings." *Journal of Ethics* 1 (1997): 65–84.

——. *On Social Facts*. Princeton: Princeton University Press, 1989.

——. *Sociality and Responsibility*. Lanham, Md.: Rowman and Littlefield, 2000.

Gilbert, Paul. "Just War: Theory and Application." *Journal of Applied Philosophy* 4 (1987): 217–22.

Gilroy, Paul. *Against Race*. Cambridge: Harvard University Press, 2000.

Ginsberg, Robert. "Institutional Violence as Systemic Evil." In *Institutional Violence*, ed. Dean Curtin, ed. Amsterdam: Rodopi, 1999.

Glass, Marvin. "Anti-Racism and Unlimited Freedom of Speech: An Untenable Dualism." *Canadian Journal of Philosophy* 8 (1978): 559–75.

——. "Jensen's Pseudo Anti-racism: A Reply to Puccetti's 'Glass on Racism.'" *Canadian Journal of Philosophy* 11 (1981): 73–76.

Glazer, Nathan. "Blacks and Ethnic Groups: The Difference and Political Difference It Makes." *Social Problems* 18 (1971).

Glazer, Nathan, and Daniel P. Moynihan, eds. *Ethnicity: Theory and Experience*. Cambridge: Harvard University Press, 1975.

Goldberg, David Theo. "A Grim Dilemma about Racist Referring Expressions." *Metaphilosophy* 17 (1986): 224–29.

——. *The Racial State*. London: Blackwell, 2002.

——. "Racism and Rationality: The Need for a New Critique." *Philosophy of the Social Sciences* 20 (1990): 317–50.

——. *Racist Culture*. London: Blackwell, 1993.

——. "Racist Exclusions." *Philosophical Forum* 26 (1994): 1–32.

Goldman, Alan H. "Affirmative Action." *Philosophy and Public Affairs* 5 (1976): 178–95.

——. *Justice and Reverse Discrimination*. Princeton: Princeton University Press, 1979.

——. "Reparations to Individuals or Groups?" *Analysis* 35 (1975): 168–70.

Goldman, Alvin I. *Epistemology and Cognition*. Cambridge: Harvard University Press, 1986.

——. "Ethics and Cognitive Science." *Ethics* 103 (1993): 337–60.

——. *Philosophical Applications of Cognitive Science*. Boulder, Colo.: Westview Press, 1993.

Gomberg, Paul. "Patriotism Is Like Racism." *Ethics* 101 (1990): 144–50.

Gonzalez, Moishe. "Affirmative Action and Its Discontents." *Telos* 106 (1996): 157–64.

Goodin, Robert E. "Negating Positive Desert Claims." *Political Theory* 13 (1985): 575–98.

——. "Waitangi Tales." *Australasian Journal of Philosophy* 78 (2000): 309–33.

Gooding-Williams, Robert. "Race, Multiculturalism, and Democracy." *Constellations* 5 (1998): 18–41.

Gossett, Thomas F. *Race.* New York: Schocken Books, 1965.

Gracia, Jorge J. E. "Affirmative Action for Hispanics? Yes and No." In *Hispanics/Latinos in the United States,* ed. Jorge J. E. Gracia and Pablo DeGreiff, pp. 201–21. London: Routledge, 2000.

——. "Ethnic Labels and Philosophy: The Case of Latin-American Philosophy." *Philosophy Today* 43 (1999): 42–49.

——. *Hispanic/Latino Identity.* London: Blackwell, 2000.

——. "Hispanic Philosophy: Its Beginning and Golden Age." *Review of Metaphysics* 46 (1993): 475–502.

——. "The Nature of Ethnicity with Special Reference to Hispanic/Latino Identity." *Public Affairs Quarterly* 13 (1999): 25–42.

Gracia, Jorge J. E., and Pablo DeGreiff, eds. *Hispanics/Latinos in the United States.* London: Routledge, 2000.

Graham, Kevin M. "The Political Significance of Social Identity: A Critique of Rawls's Theory of Agency." *Social Theory and Practice* 26 (2000): 201–22.

Green, Michael D. *The Politics of Indian Removal.* Lincoln: University of Nebraska Press, 1982.

Greenawalt, Kent. *Discrimination and Reverse Discrimination.* New York: Knopf, 1983.

Greenberg, Stanley B. *Race and State in Capitalist Development.* New Haven: Yale University Press, 1980.

Griffin, Nicholas. "Aboriginal Rights: Gauthier's Arguments for Despoilation." *Dialogue: Canadian Philosophical Review* 20 (1981): 690–96.

Groarke, Leo. "Affirmative Action as a Form of Restitution," *Journal of Business Ethics* 9 (1990): 207–13.

Gross, Barry R. "Is Turnabout Fair Play?" *Journal of Critical Analysis* 5 (1975): 126–35.

——, ed. *Reverse Discrimination.* Buffalo: Prometheus Books, 1977.

Gutmann, Amy. *Liberal Equality.* Cambridge: Cambridge University Press, 1980.

——. "Responding to Racial Injustice." In *The Tanner Lectures on Human Values,* ed. Grethe B. Peterson. Salt Lake City: University of Utah Press, 1996.

Hamilton, David L., et al. "Stereotype-Based Expectancies: Effects on Information-Processing and Social Behavior." *Journal of Social Issues* 46 (1990): 35–60.

Handlin, Oscar. *Race and Nationality in American Life.* New York: Doubleday, 1957.

Harding, Sandra G., ed. *The 'Racial' Economy of Science.* Bloomington: Indiana University Press, 1993.

Harris, Leonard, ed. *The Philosophy of Alain Locke.* Philadelphia: Temple University Press, 1989.

——. *Philosophy Born of Struggle.* Dubuque, Iowa: Kendall/Hunt, 1983.

——. *Racism: Key Concepts in Critical Theory.* Amherst: Humanity Books, 1999.

Harwood, Sterling. "Affirmative Action Is Justified: A Reply to Newton." *Contemporary Philosophy* (1990): 14–17.

Haslanger, Sally. "Gender and Race: (What) Are They? (What) Do We Want Them to Be?" *Nous* 34 (2000): 31–55.

Heilke, Thomas W. *Voegelin on the Idea of Race: An Analysis of Modern European Racism.* Baton Rouge: Louisiana State University Press, 1990.

Held, Virginia. "Can a Random Collection Be Morally Responsible?" *Journal of Philosophy* 67 (1970): 471–80.

——. "Corporations, Persons, and Responsibility." In *Shame, Responsibility, and the Corporation,* ed. Hugh Curtler. New York: Haven, 1986.

——. "Group Responsibility for Ethnic Conflict." *Journal of Ethics* 6 (2002): 157–78.

Hester, Lee, Dennis McPherson, and Annie L. Booth. "Indigenous Worlds and Callicott's Land Ethic." *Environmental Ethics* 22 (2000): 273–90.

Higins, Robert R. "Race, Pollution, and the Mastery of Nature." *Environmental Ethics* 16 (1994): 251–64.

Hill, Thomas E. Jr. "The Message of Affirmative Action." *Social Philosophy and Policy* 8 (1991): 108–29.

Hitlon, J. L., and J. M. Darley. "Constructing Other Persons: A Limit on the Effect." *Journal of Experimental Social Psychology* 21 (1985): 1–18.

Hochschild, Jennifer L. "Yes, But . . . : Principles and Caveats in American Racial Attitudes." *Nomos* 32 (1990): 308–35.

Hocking, Barbara Ann, and Barbara Joyce Hocking. "Australian Aboriginal Property Rights as Issues of Indigenous Sovereignty and Citizenship." *Ratio Juris* 12 (1999): 196–225.

Hoekema, David A. "Philosophers in the United States." *Proceeding and Addresses of the American Philosophical Association* 65 (1992): 39–54.

Holly, Marilyn. "Handsome Lake's Teachings: The Shift from Female to Male Agriculture in Iroquois Agriculture." *Agriculture and Human Values* 26 (1990): 80–94.

——. "The Persons of Nature Versus the Power Pyramid: Locke, Land, and American Indians." *International Studies in Philosophy* 26 (1994): 13–31.

Holt, Thomas C. *Black Over White.* Urbana: University of Illinois Press, 1977.

——. *The Problem of Race in the Twenty-first Century.* Cambridge: Harvard University Press, 2000.

hooks, bell. *Ain't I a Woman: Black Women in Feminism.* Boston: South End Press, 1981.

——. *Talking Back: Thinking Feminist, Thinking Black.* Boston: South End Press, 1989.

——. *Yearning: Race, Gender, and Cultural Politics.* Boston: South End Press, 1990.

Horowitz, Donald L. *Ethnic Groups in Conflict.* Berkeley: University of California Press, 1985.

Hudson, James L. "The Ethics of Immigration Restriction." *Social Theory and Practice* 10 (1984): 201–40.

The Langston Hughes Reader. New York: George Braziller, 1958.

Hull, Gordon. "The Jewish Question Revisited: Marx, Derrida, and Ethnic Nationalism." *Philosophy and Social Criticism* 23 (1997): 47–77.

Ingram, David. *Group Rights: Reconciling Equality and Difference.* Lawrence: Kansas University Press, 2000.

Irele, Dipo. "Appiah and the Trope of Race." *International Studies in Philosophy* 30 (1998): 39–46.

Isaacs, Harold. "Basic Group Identity." In Nathan Glazer and Daniel P. Moynihan, eds., *Ethnicity: Theory and Experience.* Cambridge: Harvard University Press, 1975.

Jaggar, Alison. "Punishment and Race." *Southern Journal of Philosophy* 34 (1996): 21–51.

Jayal, Niraja Gopal. "Ethnic Diversity and the Nation State." *Journal of Applied Philosophy* 10 (1993): 147–53.

Johnson, E. Pauline. *Flint and Feather: The Complete Poems of E. Pauline Johnson Tekahionwake.* Ontario: Paperjacks, 1972.

Jones, Gary E. "Preferential Treatment and Individual Rights." *Pacific Philosophical Quarterly* 63 (1982): 289–95.

Jordan, Jeff. "The Doctrine of Double-Effect and Affirmative Action." *Journal of Applied Philosophy* 7 (1990): 213–16.

Jordan, Winthrop D. *White Over Black.* Baltimore: Penguin, 1968.

The Journal of Ethics 1:3 (1997): Special Issue on African-American Political Philosophy.

The Journal of Ethics 6:2 (2002): Special Issue on Collective Responsibility.

The Journal of Ethics 7:1 (2003): Special Issue on Race, Racism, and Reparations.

Kant, Immanuel. *The Metaphysics of Morals.* Translated and edited by Mary Gregor. Cambridge: Cambridge University Press, 1996.

———. "Of the Different Human Races." In *The Idea of Race,* ed. Robert Bernasconi and Tommy Lott, pp. 8–22. Indianapolis: Hackett, 2000.

Kaplan, Laura D. "Devaluing Others to Enhance Our Self-Esteem: A Moral Phenomenology of Racism." In *Institutional Violence,* ed. Deane Curtin and Robert Litke, pp. 197–203. Ansterdam: Rodopi, 1999.

Karenga, Maulana. *Kwanza: Celebration of Family, Community, and Culture.* Los Angeles: San Kore Press, 1998.

Kershnar, Stephen. "Are the Descendants of Slaves Owed Compensation for Slavery?" *Journal of Applied Philosophy* 16 (1999): 95–101.

———. "Intrinsic Moral Value and Racial Differences." *Public Affairs Quarterly* 14 (2000): 205–24.

———. "Strong Affirmative Action Programs and Disproportionate Burdens." *Journal of Value Inquiry* 33 (1999): 201–9.

———. "Uncertain Damages to Racial Minorities and Strong Affirmative Action." *Public Affairs Quarterly* 13 (1999): pp. 83–93.

Ketchum, Sara Ann. "Evidence, Statistics and Rights: A Reply to Simon." *Analysis* 39 (1979): 148–53.

Ketchum, Sara Ann, and Christine Pierce. "Implicit Racism." *Analysis* 36 (1976): 91–95.

King, James C. *The Biology of Race.* New York: Harcourt Brace Jovanovich, 1971.

King, Martin Luther, Jr. "Letter from Birmingham Jail." In *A Testament of Hope: The Essential Writings and Speeches of Martin Luther King, Jr.,* ed. James M. Washington, pp. 289–302. San Francisco: Harper Collins, 1986.

Kleinig, John. "Good Samaritanism." In *Philosophy of Law,* ed. Joel Feinberg and Hyman Gross, 5th ed., pp. 529–32. Belmont, Calif.: Wadsworth, 1995.

Klosko, George. "Racism in Plato's *Republic.*" *History of Political Thought* (1991): 1–13.

Kolenda, Konstantin. "Humanism and Ethnicity." *Humanist* 41 (1981): 39–42.

Korsgaard, Christine. "Taking the Law into Our Own Hands: Kant on the Right to Revolution." In *Reclaiming the History of Ethics: Essays for John Rawls,* ed. Andrews Reath, Barbara Herman, and Christine Korsgaard, pp. 297–328. Cambridge: Cambridge University Press, 1997.

Kukathas, Chandran. "Are There Any Cultural Rights?" *Political Theory* 20 (1992): 105–39.

Kymlicka, Will. *Liberalism, Community, and Culture.* Oxford: Oxford University Press, 1989.

———. *Multicultural Citizenship.* Oxford: Oxford University Press, 1995.

———, ed. *The Rights of Minority Cultures.* Oxford: Oxford University Press, 1995.

Laitin, David D. "Liberal Theory and the Nation." *Political Theory* 26 (1998): 221–36.

Lang, Berel. *Race and Racism in Theory and Practice.* Lanham, Md.: Rowman and Littlefield, 2000.

Lauer, Henle. "Realities of Social Construction: A Comment on Appiah's 'Illusions of Race.'" *Quest* 7 (1993): 106–13.

———. "Treating Race as a Social Construction." *Journal of Value Inquiry* 30 (1996): 445–51.

Lauter, Paul. "The Race for Class." In *Race and Racism in Theory and Practice,* ed. Berel Lang. Lanham, Md.: Rowman and Littlefield, 2000.

Lawson, Bill E., ed. *The Underclass Question.* Philadelphia: Temple University Press, 1992.

Lawson, Gary. "Proving Ownership." *Social Philosophy and Policy* 11 (1994): 139–52.

Lea, David R. "Do Communication Values Justify Papua New Guinean and/or Fijian Systems of Land Tenure?" *Agriculture and Human Values* 14 (1997): 115–26.

Leicester, Mal. "Racism, Responsibility, and Education." *Journal of Philosophy of Education* 22 (1988): 201–6.

Lesser, Harry. "Can Racial Discrimination Be Proved?" *Journal of Applied Philosophy* 1 (1984): 253–62.

Levin, Michael. "Is Racial Discrimination Special?" *Journal of Value Inquiry* 15 (1981): 225–34.

———. "Race, Biology, and Justice." *Public Affairs Quarterly* 8 (1994): 267–85.

———. "Responses to Race Differences in Crime." *Journal of Social Philosophy* 23 (1992): 5–29.

Levinson, Sanford. "Responsibility for Crimes of War." *Philosophy and Public Affairs* 2 (1973): 244–73.

Lindgren, J. Ralph. "The Irrelevance of Philosophical Treatments of Affirmative Action." *Social Theory and Practice* 7 (1981): 1–19.

Lloyd, Genevive. "No One's Land: Australia and the Philosophical Imagination." *Hypatia* 15 (2000): 26–39.

Locke, John. *The Second Treatise of Government.* Indianapolis: Bobbs-Merrill, 1952.

Lomasky, Loren. *Persons, Rights, and the Moral Community.* Oxford: Oxford University Press, 1987.

Loury, Glenn C. "Why Should We Care about Group Inequality?" *Social Philosophy & Policy* 5 (1987): 249–71.

Lyons, David. "The New Indian Claims and Original Rights to Land." *Social Theory and Practice* 6 (1977): 249–72.

MacCormick, D. N. "The Obligation of Reparations." *Proceedings of the Aristotelian Society* 78 (1977–78): 175–93.

McGary, Howard. "Justice and Reparations." *Philosophical Forum* 9 (1978): 250–63.

———. "Morality and Collective Liability." *Journal of Value Inquiry* 20 (1986): 156–65.

———. "Philosophy and Diversity: The Inclusion of African and African American Materials." *American Philosophical Association Newsletter on Feminism and Philosophy* 92 (1993): 51–53.

———. *Race and Social Justice.* London: Blackwell, 1999.

———. "On Violence in the Struggle for Liberation." In *Existence in Black: An Anthology of Black Existential Philosophy,* ed. Lewis R. Gordon, pp. 263–72. New York: Routledge, 1997.

———, and Bill E. Lawson. *Between Slavery and Freedom.* Bloomington: Indiana University Press, 1992.

Mackie, J. L. "The Third Theory of Law." In *Philosophy of Law,* ed. Joel Feinberg and Hyman Gross, 5th ed., pp. 162–68. Belmont, Calif.: Wadsworth, 1995.

Margalit, A., and G. Motzkin. "The Uniqueness of the Holocaust." *Philosophy and Public Affairs* 25 (1996): 65–83.

Marti, Oscar R. "Is There a Latin American Philosophy?" *Metaphilosophy* 14 (1983): 46–52.

Martin, Thomas. "The Role of Emotion in Sartre's Portrait of Anti-Semitism." *Australasian Journal of Philosophy* 76 (1998): 141–51.

Marx, Karl, and F. Engels. *Collected Works.* New York: International Publishers, 1975–95.

Massey, Stephen J. "Rethinking Affirmative Action." *Social Theory and Practice* 7 (1981): 21–47.

Matsuda, Mari. "Looking to the Bottom: Critical Legal Studies and Reparations." In *Critical Race Theory,* ed. Kimberle Crenshaw, Neil Gotanda, Gary Peller, and Kendall Thomas, eds. New York: New Press, 1995.

May, Larry. *The Morality of Groups.* Notre Dame, Ind.: University of Notre Dame Press, 1987.

——. *Sharing Responsibility.* Chicago: University of Chicago Press, 1992.

May, Larry, and Stacey Hoffman, eds. *Collective Responsibility.* Savage, Md.: Rowman and Littlefield, 1991.

Medina, Vicente. "The Possibility of an Indigenous Philosophy: A Latin American Perspective." *American Philosophical Quarterly* 29 (1992): 373–80.

Meier, August, and Elliott Rudwick, eds. *The Making of Black America: Essays in Negro Life and History.* Vol. 1. *The Origins of Black Americans.* New York: Atheneum, 1969.

Michaels, Walter Benn. "Critical Response II: The No-Drop Rule." *Critical Inquiry* 20 (1994): 758–69.

Miles, Robert. *Racism.* London: Routledge, 1989.

Miller, David. "Deserving Jobs." *Philosophical Quarterly* 42 (1992): 161–81.

Miller, S. R. "Just War Theory: The Case of South Africa." *Philosophical Papers* (1990): 143–61.

Mills, Charles W. "Black Trash." In *Faces of Environmental Racism,* ed. Laura Westra and Bill Lawson, pp. 73–91. Lanham, Md.: Rowman and Littlefield, 2001.

——. *Blackness Visible.* Ithaca: Cornell University Press, 1998.

——. "Dark Ontologies: Blacks, Jews, and White Supremacy." In *Autonomy and Community,* ed. Jane E. Kneller, pp. 131–68. New York: State University of New York Press, 1998.

——. "Do Black Men Have a Moral Duty to Marry Black Women?" *Journal of Social Philosophy* 25 (1994): 131–53.

——. "Prophetic Pragmatism as Political Philosophy." In *Cornel West,* ed. George Yancy, ed., pp. 192–223. London: Blackwell, 2001.

——. "Race and the Social Contract Tradition." *Social Identities* 6 (2000): 441–62.

——. *The Racial Contract.* Ithaca: Cornell University Press, 1997.

——. "Under Class Under Standings." *Ethics* 104 (1994): 855–81.

——. "White Supremacy and Racial Justice, Here and Now." In *Social and Political Philosophy,* ed. James Sterba, pp. 321–37. London: Routledge, 2001.

Modood, Tariq. "Race in Britain and the Politics of Difference." In *Philosophy and Pluralism,* ed. David Archard. New York: Cambridge University Press, 1996.

Momaday, N. Scott. "Personal Reflections." In *The American Indian and the Problem of History,* ed. Calvin Martin. Oxford: Oxford University Press, 1987.

Montagu, Ashley. *Man's Most Dangerous Myth.* Cleveland: World, 1964.

——. *Race, Science, and Humanity.* New York: Van Nostrand Reinhold, 1963.

Moody-Adams, Michele M. "A Commentary on Color Conscious: The Political Morality of Race." *Ethics* 109 (1999): 408–23.

Morrison, Toni. "Unspeakable Things Unspoken: The Afro-American Presence in American Literature." In *The Tanner Lectures on Human Values,* ed. Grethe B. Peterson, pp. 121–63. Salt Lake City: University of Utah Press, 1990.

Mosley, Albert G. *Affirmative Action: Social Justice or Unfair Preference?.* Lanham, Md.: Rowman and Littlefield, 1996.

——. "Negritude, Nationalism, and Nativism: Racists or Racialists?" In Kwame Anthony Appiah, ed., *African Philosophy: Selected Readings.* Englewood Cliffs, N.J.: Prentice Hall, 1995.

——. "Preferential Treatment and Social Justice." In *Terrorism, Justice and Social Values,* ed. Creighton Peden. Lewiston: Mellen Press, 1990.

Murphy, Jeffrie G. *Character, Liberty, and the Law.* Dordrecht: Kluwer Academic, 1998.

Murray, Robert. "Liberalism, Culture, and Aboriginal Rights." *Canadian Journal of Philosophy* 29 (1999): 109–38.

Musschenga, Albert W. "Intrinsic Value as a Reason for the Preservation of Minority Cultures." *Ethical Theory and Moral Practice* 1 (1998): 201–25.

Musselman, John D. "Critical Race Theory on Hate Speech as a Bias Crime." *Contemporary Philosophy* 17 (1995): 2–8.

Nagel, Thomas. "Equal Treatment and Compensatory Discrimination." *Philosophy and Public Affairs* 2 (1973): 348–63.

——. *Mortal Questions.* Cambridge: Cambridge University Press, 1979.

Nelson, William. "Equal Opportunity." *Social Theory and Practice* 10 (1984): 157–84.

Neuberg, S. L. "The Goal of Forming Accurate Impressions During Social Interactions: Attenuating the Impact of Negative Expectations." *Journal of Personality and Social Psychology* 56 (1989): 374–86.

Neugebauer, Christian. "Hegel and Kant—A Refutation of Their Racism." *Quest* (1991): 50–73.

Neumann, Michael R. "Bad Beliefs." *Public Affairs Quarterly* 12 (1998): 333–46.

Newton, Lisa H. "Corruption of Thought, Word, and Deed: Reflections of Affirmative Action and its Current Defenders." *Contemporary Philosophy* (1991): 14–16.

Nickel, James. "Ethnocide and Indigenous Peoples." *Journal of Social Philosophy* 25 (1994): 84–98.

——. "Should Reparations Be to Individuals or to Groups?" *Analysis* 34 (1974): 154–60.

——. "What's Wrong with Ethnic Cleansing?" *Journal of Social Philosophy* 26 (1995): 5–15.

Novak, Michael. "Ethnicity for Individuals: What to Do and Why?" *Review Journal of Philosophy and Social Science* 1 (1980): 67–89.

Nozick, Robert. *Anarchy, State, and Utopia.* New York: Basic Books, 1974.

——. "Distributive Justice." *Philosophy and Public Affairs* 3 (1973): 45–126.

Oboler, Suzanne. *Ethnic Labels/Latino Lives.* Minneapolis: University of Minnesota Press, 1995.

Outlaw, Lucius. "On Race and Philosophy." *Graduate Faculty Philosophy Journal* 18 (1995): 175–99.

Owen, William B. "On the Alleged Uniqueness and Incomprehensibility of the Holocaust." *Philosophy in the Contemporary World* 2 (1995): 8–16.

Palter, Robert. "Hume and Prejudice." *Hume Studies* 21 (1995): 3–23.

Pappas, Gregory Fernando. "Dewey's Philosophical Approach to Racial Prejudice." *Social Theory and Practice* 22 (1996): 47–65.

Patterson, Orlando. *The Ordeal of Integration.* Washington, D.C.: Civitas/Counterpoint, 1997.

Paul, Diane. "In the Interests of Civilization: Marxist Views of Race and Culture in the Nineteenth Century." *Journal of the History of Ideas* 42 (1981): 115–38.

Paul, Ellen Frankel, ed. *Equal Opportunity.* New York: Blackwell, 1987.

——. "Set-Asides, Reparations, and Compensatory Justice." *Nomos* 33 (1991): 97–139.

Peffer, Rodney. "A Failed Reconciliation: Further Reflections on Sterba's Project." *Journal of Social Philosophy* 25 (1994): 206–21.

Penz, Peter G. "Development Refugees and Distributive Justice: Indigenous Peoples, Land, and the Developmentalist State." *Public Affairs Quarterly* 6 (1992): 105–31.

Perhac, Ralph M. "Environmental Justice: The Issue of Disproportionality." *Environmental Ethics* 21 (1999): 81–92.

Perrett, Roy W. "Indigenous Language Rights and Political Theory: The Case of TE REO MAŌRI." *Australasian Journal of Philosophy* 78 (2000): 405–17.

——. "Indigenous Rights and Environmental Justice." *Environmental Ethics* 20 (1998): 337–91.

Perry, Bruce, ed. *Malcolm X: The Last Speeches.* New York: Pathfinder, 1989.

Pettigrew, Thomas, and Joanne Martin. "The Fruits of Critical Discussion: A Reply to Commentators." *Journal of Social Issues* 43 (1987): 151f.

Philips, Michael. "Linguistic Choice and Moral Choice: A Reply to Richter's on Philips and Racism." *Canadian Journal of Philosophy* 16 (1986): 795–800.

——. "Racist Acts and Racist Humor." *Canadian Journal of Philosophy* 14 (1984): 75–96.

Pinkney, Alphonso. *Black Americans.* Englewood Cliffs, N.J.: Prentice-Hall, 1969.

Piper, Adrian. *Higher-Order Discrimination in Identity, Character, and Morality.* Cambridge: MIT Press, 1990.

Pittman, John P. "Punishment and Race." *Utilitas* 9 (1997): 115–30.

Pojman, Louis. "The Moral Status of Affirmative Action." *Public Affairs Quarterly* 6 (1992): 181–206.

Pojman, Louis, and Owen McLeod, eds. *What Do We Deserve?* Oxford: Oxford University Press, 1999.

Poole, Ross. "Justice or Appropriation?: Indigenous Claims and Liberal Theory." *Radical Philosophy* 101 (2000): 5–17.

——. *Nation and Identity.* London: Routledge, 1999.

Popkin, Richard H. "Hume's Racism." *Philosophical Forum* 9 (1978): 211–26.

Postow, B. C. "Thomas on Sexism." *Ethics* 90 (1980): 251–56.

Powell, Thomas. *The Persistence of Racism in America.* Lanham, Md.: Littlefield and Adams, 1993.

Priest, Graham. "What Is So Bad about Contradictions?" *Journal of Philosophy* 95 (1998): 410–26.

Puccetti, Roland. "Glass on Racism." *Canadian Journal of Philosophy* 11 (1981): 69–71.

Purdy, Laura. "Why Do We Need Affirmative Action?" *Journal of Social Philosophy* 25 (1994): 133–43.

Puzzo, Dante A. "Racism and the Western Tradition." *Journal of the History of Ideas* 25 (1964): 579–86.

Quarles, Benjamin. *The Negro in the Making of America.* New York: Collier, 1964.

Radin, Margaret Jane. "Affirmative Action Rhetoric." *Social Philosophy & Policy* (1990): 130–49.

Raikka, Juha. "On Disassociationg Oneself from Collective Responsibility." *Social Theory and Practice* 23 (1997): 93–108.

Rawls, John. *Collected Papers.* Cambridge: Harvard University Press, 1999.

——. *Justice as Fairness: A Restatement.* Cambridge: Harvard University Press, 2001.

——. *The Law of Peoples.* Cambridge: Harvard University Press, 1999.

——. *Lectures on the History of Moral Philosophy.* Cambridge: Harvard University Press, 2000.

——. *Political Liberalism.* New York: Columbia University Press, 1993.

——. *A Theory of Justice.* Cambridge: Harvard University Press, 1971.

Remini, Robert V. *The Legacy of Andrew Jackson.* Baton Rouge: Louisiana State University Press, 1988.

Richter, Reed. "On Philips and Racism: Comment on Racist Acts and Racist Humor." *Canadian Journal of Philosophy* 16 (1986): 785–94.

Ricourt, Milagros, and Ruby Danta. *Hispanas de Queens.* Ithaca: Cornell University Press, 2002.

Riser, John. "Marxism and Affirmative Action." *Social Praxis* 8 (1981): 89–98.

Roback, Jennifer. "Plural but Equal: Group Identity and Voluntary Integration." *Social Philosophy & Policy* (1991): 60–80.

Roberts, Rodney C. "The Morality of a Moral Statute of Limitations on Injustice." *Journal of Ethics* 7 (2003): 115–38.

——. Why Have the Injustices Perpetrated against Blacks in America not Been Rectified?" *Journal of Social Philosophy* 32 (2001): 357–73.

Robinson, Randall. *The Debt.* New York: Dutton, 1999.

Rodriguez, Alicia P. "Latino Education, Latino Movement." *Educational Theory* 49 (1999): 381–400.

Rohatyn, Dennis A. "Black Reparations: A Black and White Issue?" *Personalist* 60 (1979): 433–37.

Romero, Mary. *Maid in the U.S.A..* London: Routledge, 1992.

Root, Michael. "How We Divide the World." *Philosophy of Science* 67 (2000): 628–39.

——. "The Problem of Race in Medicine." *Philosophy of the Social Sciences* 31 (2001): 20–39.

Rose, Peter I. *The Subject Is Race.* New York: Oxford University Press, 1968.

Rosenfeld, Michel. *Affirmative Action and Justice: A Philosophical and Constitutional Inquiry.* New Haven: Yale University Press, 1991.

Santiago-Irizarry, Vilma. *Medicalizing Ethnicity.* Ithaca: Cornell University Press, 2001.

Sapadin, Eugene. "Race Isn't Merit." *Reason Papers* 15 (1990): 141–48.

Sasaki, Ken-ichi. "Should/Can Philosophy Be Ethnic? Varieties of Internationalism in Philosophy." *Metaphilosophy* 28 (1997): 351–58.

Schleifer, Michael. "The Flew-Jensen Uproar." *Philosophy* 48 (1973): 386–90.

Schmid, Thomas W. "The Definition of Racism." *Journal of Applied Philosophy* 13 (1996): 31–40.

Schmitt, Richard. "A New Hypothesis about the Relations of Class, Race, and Gender: Capitalism as a Dependent System." *Social Theory and Practice* 14 (1988): 345–65.

Schutte, Ofelia. *Cultural Identity and Social Liberation in Latin American Thought.* Albany: State University of New York Press, 1993.

——. "Negotiating Latina Identities." In *Hispanics/Latinos in the United States,* ed. Jorge J. E. Gracia and Pablo DeGreiff, pp. 61–76. London: Routledge, 2000.

Scully, Judith A. M. "Why Respectability Is Not Enough." *Criminal Justice Ethics* 19 (2000): 29–43.

Shapiro, Ian, and Will Kymlicka, eds. *Ethnicity and Group Rights.* New York: New York University Press, 1997.

Shaw, Bill. "Affirmative Action: An Ethical Evaluation." *Journal of Business Ethics* 7 (1988): 763–70.

Sher, George. *Approximate Justice.* Totowa, N.J.: Rowman and Littlefield, 1997.

——. "Diversity." *Philosophy and Public Affairs* 28 (1999): 85–104.

——. "Groups and Justice." *Ethics* 87 (1977): 174–81.

Shiner, Roger. "Individuals, Groups, and Inverse Discrimination." *Analysis* 33 (1973): 185–87.

Silvestri, Philip. "The Justification of Inverse Discrimination." *Analysis* 34 (1973): 31.

Simmons, A. John. *The Edge of Anarchy.* Princeton: Princeton University Press, 1993.

——. "Historical Rights and Fair Shares." *Law and Philosophy* 14 (1995): 149–84.

——. *The Lockean Theory of Rights.* Princeton: Princeton University Press, 1992.

——. "Makers' Rights." *Journal of Ethics* 2 (1998): 63–84.

Simon, Robert. "Individual Rights and 'Benign' Discrimination." *Ethics* 90 (1979): 88–97.

——. "Preferential Treatment: For Groups or for Individuals?" *National Forum* 58 (1978): 7–9.

——. "Rights, Groups and Discrimination: A Reply to Ketchum." *Analysis* 40 (1980): 109–12.

Simon, Thomas. "Group Harm." *Journal of Social Philosophy* 26 (1995): 123–37.

Simons, Jeanne Reidy. "Octavio Paz on Socialism in Latin America." *Philosophy Today* 26 (1982): 234–39.

Singer, Beth. "The Democratic Solution to Ethnic Pluralism." *Philosophy and Social Criticism* 19 (1993): 97–114.

Singer, M. S. "Justice in Preferential Hiring." *Journal of Business Ethics* 10 (1991): 797–803.

Singer, Marcus G. "Some Thoughts on 'Race' and 'Racism.' " *Philosophia* 8 (1978): 153–85.

Singer, Peter. "All Animals Are Equal." *Philosophic Exchange* 1 (1974): 103–16.

——. "Is Racial Discrimination Arbitrary?" *Philosophia* 8 (1978): 185–203.

Sistare, Christine, Larry May, and Leslie Francis, eds. *Groups and Group Rights.* Lawrence: University Press of Kansas, 2001.

Skillen, Anthony. "Racism: Flew's Three Concepts of Racism." *Journal of Applied Philosophy* 10 (1993): 73–89.

Skovira, Robert. "Cultural Pluralism, Categories of Identity, and Definitions of Ethnicity in Educational Discourse." *Philosophical Studies in Education* (1978): 64–71.

Sparrow, Robert. "History and Collective Responsibility." *Australasian Journal of Philosophy* 78 (2000): 346–59.

Stanage, Sherman Miller, ed. *Reason and Violence: Philosophical Investigations.* Totowa, N.J.: Rowman and Littlefield, 1974.

Stannard, David E. *American Holocaust: The Conquest of the New World.* Oxford: Oxford University Press, 1992.

Stanton, Elizabeth Cady, Susan B. Anthony, and Matilda Joslyn Gage. *History of Woman Suffrage.* Vol. 2. New York: Charles Mann, 1881.

Stavenhagen, Rodolfo. "Indian Ethnic Movements and State Policies in Latin America." *Praxis International* 2 (1982): 241–54.

Steele, Ian K. *Warpaths.* Oxford: Oxford University Press, 1994.

Stenson, Anthony, and Tim S. Gray. "An Autonomy Based Justification for Intellectual Property Rights of Indigenous Communities." *Environmental Ethics* 21 (1999): 177–90.

Sterba, James P. "Understanding Evil: American Slavery, the Holocaust, and the Conquest of the American Indians." *Ethics* 106 (1996): 424–48.

Stroud, Sarah. "The Aim of Affirmative Action." *Social Theory and Practice* 25 (1999): 385–408.

Stroup, Timothy. "Affirmative Action and the Police." *Applied Philosophy* 1 (1982): 1–19.

Sumner, L. W. *The Moral Foundations of Rights.* Oxford: Oxford University Press, 1987.

Sustein, Cass R. "The Limits of Compensatory Justice." *Nomos* 33 (1991): 281–310.

Swann, W. B., Jr., and R. J. Ely. "A Battle of Wills: Self-Verification Versus Behavioral Confirmation." *Journal of Personality and Social Psychology* 46 (1984): 1287–1302.

Tajfel, Henri. "Cognitive Aspects of Prejudice." *Journal of Social Issues* 25 (1969): 79–98.

Taylor, Gabrielle. *Pride, Shame, and Guilt.* Oxford: Oxford University Press, 1985.

Taylor, Paul C. "Appiah's Uncompleted Argument: W. E. B. DuBois and the Reality of Race." *Social Theory and Practice* 26 (2000): 103–28.

——. "Context and Color-Confrontation: Cress Theory and the Necessity of Racism." In *Institutional Violence,* ed. Deane Curtin, pp. 205–13. Amsterdam: Rodopi, 1999.

Taylor, Paul W. "Reverse Discrimination and Compensatory Justice." *Analysis* 33 (1973): 177–82.

Tessman, Lisa. "The Racial Politics of Mixed Race." *Journal of Social Philosophy* 30 (1999): 276–94.

Thalberg, Irving. "Justifications of Institutional Racism." *Philosophical Forum* 3 (1972): 243–63.

——. "Themes in the Reverse Discrimination Debate." *Ethics* 91 (1980): 138–50.

——. "Visceral Racism." *Monist* 56 (1972): 43–63.

Thomas, Laurence. "American Slavery and the Holocaust: Their Ideologies Compared." *Public Affairs Quarterly* 5 (1991): 191–210.

——. "Morality, Consistency, and the Self: A Lesson From Rectification." *Journal of Social Philosophy* 32 (2001): 374–81.

——. "Sexism and Racism: Some Conceptual Differences." *Ethics* 90 (1980): 239–50.

——. *Vessels of Evil.* Philadelphia: Temple University Press, 1993.

Thompson, Janna. "Historical Injustice and Reparation: Justifying Claims of Descendants." *Ethics* 112 (2001): 114–35.

——. "Historical Obligations." *Australasian Journal of Philosophy* 78 (2000): 334–45.

——. "Land Rights and Aboriginal Sovereignty." *Australasian Journal of Philosophy* 68 (1990): 313–29.

——. *Taking Responsibility for the Past.* Cambridge: Polity, 2002.

Thomson, Judith J. *The Realm of Rights.* Cambridge: Harvard University Press, 1990.

Tomasi, John. "Kymlicka, Liberalism, and Respect for Cultural Minorities." *Ethics* 105 (1995): 580–603.

Trafzer, Clifford E. *The Kit Carson Campaign.* Norman: University of Oklahoma Press, 1982.

Trotter, Griffin. "Royce, Community, and Ethnicity." *Transactions of the Charles S. Peirce Society* 30 (1994): 231–69.

Tully, James. "Aboriginal Property and Western Theory: Recovering a Middle Ground." *Social Philosophy & Policy* 11 (1994): 153–80.

Tushnet, Mark. "Change and Continuity in the Concept of Civil Rights: Thurgood Marshall and Affirmative Action." *Social Philosophy & Policy* 8 (1991): 150–71.

Udell, Larry. "Racism and Prejudice." In *Institutional Violence*, ed. Deane Curtin, pp. 225–31. Amsterdam: Rodopi, 1999.

Valls, Andrew. "The Libertarian Case for Affirmative Action." *Social Theory and Practice* 25 (1999): 299–323.

Vandeveer, Donald. "Coercive Restraint of Offensive Actions." *Philosophy and Public Affairs* 8 (1979): 175–93.

van Roojen, Mark. "Affirmative Action, Non-Consequentialism, and Responsibility for the Effects of Past Discrimination." *Public Affairs Quarterly* 11 (1997): 281–301.

van Patten, Jim. "Affirmative Action: Retrospect and Prospect." *Contemporary Philosophy* 17 (1995): 2–7.

Vanterpool, Rudolph V. "Affirmative Action Revisited: Justice and Public Policy Considerations." *Public Affairs Quarterly* 3 (1989): 47–59.

Varouxakis, Georgios. "John Stuart Mill on Race." *Utilitas* 10 (1998): 17–32.

Verkuyten, Maykel. "Personhood and Accounting for Racism in Conversation." *Journal for the Theory of Social Behavior* 28 (1998): 147–67.

Vigil, James Diego. *From Indians to Chicanos.* Prospect Heights, Ill.: Waveland, 1980.

Wade, Richard C. *Slavery in the Cities: The South, 1820–1960.* Oxford: Oxford University Press, 1964.

Waldron, Jeremy. *Nonsense upon Stilts.* London: Methuen, 1987.

——. *The Right to Private Property.* Oxford: Oxford University Press, 1988.

——. "Superceding Historical Injustice." *Ethics* 103 (1992): 4–28.

——. "Two Worries About Mixing One's Labor." *Philosophical Quarterly* 33 (1983): 37–44.

Walker, Jesse. "Every Man a Sultan: Indigenous Responses to the Somalia Crisis." *Telos* 103 (1995): 163–72.

Wallace, Anthony. *Jefferson and the Indians.* Cambridge: Harvard University Press, 1999.

Walzer, Michael. *Just and Unjust Wars.* 3d ed. New York: Basic Books, 2000.

——. *The Politics of Ethnicity.* Cambridge: Harvard University Press, 1982.

——. *Radical Principles.* New York: Basic Books, 1980.

——. *Spheres of Justice.* New York: Basic Books, 1983.

——. *On Toleration.* New Haven: Yale University Press, 1997.

Ware, Vron. "Moments of Danger: Race, Gender, and Memories of Empire." *History and Theory* 31 (1992): 116–37.

Warnke, Georgia. "Affirmative Action, Neutrality, and Integration." *Journal of Social Philosophy* 29 (1998): 87–103.

Washington, James, ed. *A Testament of Hope: The Essential Writings and Speeches of Martin Luther King, Jr.* San Francisco: Harper Collins, 1986.

Wassermann, Gerhard D. "Wittgenstein on Jews: Some Counter Examples." *Philosophy* (1990): 355–65.

Wasserstrom, Richard. "A Defense of Programs of Preferential Treatment." *National Forum* 58 (1978): 15–18.

———. *Philosophy and Social Issues: Five Studies.* Notre Dame, Ind.: University of Notre Dame Press, 1980.

———. "Preferential Treatment, Color-Blindness, and the Evils of Racism and Discrimination." *Proceedings and Addresses of the American Philosophical Association* 61 (1987): 27–42.

———. "Rights, Human Rights, and Racial Discrimination." *Journal of Philosophy* 61 (1964): 628–40.

Weaver, J., ed. *Defending Mother Earth: Native American Perspectives on Environmental Justice.* New York: Orbis, 1996.

Weigel, Russell H., and Paul W. Howes. "Conceptions of Racial Prejudice: Symbolic Racism Reconsidered." *Journal of Social Issues* 41 (1985): 117–38.

Wellman, Carl. *The Proliferation of Rights.* Boulder, Colo.: Westview, 1999.

———. *A Theory of Rights.* Totowa, N.J.: Rowman and Littlefield, 1988.

Wertheimer, Alan. "Jobs, Qualifications, and Preferences." *Ethics* 94 (1983): 99–112.

West, Cornel. *Keeping Faith: Philosophy and Race in America.* New York: Routledge, 1993.

———. "Marxist Theory and the Specificity of Afro-American Oppression." In *Marxism and the Interpretation of Culture,* ed. Cary Nelson. Chicago: University of Illinois Press, 1988.

———. *Race Matters.* Boston: Beacon, 1993.

Westra, Laura. "Environmental Racism and the First Nations of Canada: Terrorism at Oka." *Journal of Social Philosophy* 30 (1999): 103–24.

Wheeler III, Samuel C. "Reparations Reconstructed." *American Philosophical Quarterly* 34 (1997): 301–38.

Wicclair, Mark R. "Preferential Treatment and Desert." *Social Theory and Practice* 12 (1986): 287–308.

Wilkins, Burleigh. *Terrorism and Collective Responsibility.* London: Routledge: 1992.

———. "A Third Principle of Justice." *Journal of Ethics* 1 (1997): 355–74.

Willett, Cynthia. *The Soul of Justice.* Ithaca: Cornell University Press, 2001.

Williams, Angie, and Howard Giles. "Prejudice-Reduction Simulations: Social Cognition, Intergroup Theory, and Ethics." *Simulation & Gaming* 23 (1992): 472–84.

Williams, Johnny E. "Race and Class: Why All the Confusion?" In *Race and Racism in Theory and Practice,* ed. Berel Lang, pp. 215–27. Lanham, Md.: Rowman & Littlefield, 2000.

Williams, Rhonda M. "Consenting to Whiteness." In *Marxism in the Postmodern Age,* ed. Antonio Callari, pp. 301–8. New York: Guilford, 1995,

Williamson, C. "Prejudices and Generalisations." *International Journal of Moral and Social Studies* 2 (1987): 95–104.

Wilshire, Bruce. *The Primal Roots of American Philosophy: Pragmatism, Phenomenology, and Native American Thought.* University Park, Pa.: Pennsylvania State University Press, 2000.

Wittgenstein, L. *Philosophical Investigations.* New York: Macmillan, 1958.

Wood, Peter H., Gregory A. Waselkov, and M. Thomas Hatley, eds. *Powhatan's Mantle.* Lincoln: University of Nebraska Press, 1989.

Woodruff, Paul. "What's Wrong with Discrimination?" *Analysis* 36 (1976): 158–60.

Woodward, Grace Steele. *The Cherokees.* Norman: University of Oklahoma Press, 1963.

Zack, Naomi, ed. *American Mixed Race: The Culture of Microdiversity.* Lanham, Md.: Rowman and Littlefield, 1995.

———. *Bachelors of Science: Seventeenth-Century Identity, Then and Now.* Philadelphia: Temple University Press, 1996.

——. "The Family and Radical Family Theory." In *Feminism and Families*, ed. Hilde Lindemann, pp. 43–53. New York: Routledge, 1997.

——. *Philosophy of Science and Race*. London: Routledge, 2002.

——. "Lockean Money, Indigenism, and Globalism." *Canadian Journal of Philosophy* (Supplementary Volume) 25 (1999): 31–54.

——. "Mixed Black and White Race and Public Policy." *Hypatia* 10 (1995): 120–32.

——. "On Being and Not-Being Black and Jewish." In *The Multiracial Experience*, ed. Maria Root. Thousand Oaks: Sage, 1996.

——. "Philosophy and Racial Paradigms." *Journal of Value Inquiry* 33 (1999): 299–317.

——. *Race and Mixed Race*. Philadelphia: Temple University Press, 1993.

——, ed. *Race/Sex: Their Sameness, Difference, and Interplay*. New York: Routledge, 1997.

——. *Thinking About Race*. Belmont, Calif.: Wadsworth, 1998.

Zelinski, Wilbur. *The Enigma of Ethnicity*. Iowa City: University of Iowa Press 2001.

Index

acquired rights trumping original land
  rights objection, 154, 174–178, 195
affirmative action, 1–4, 16–17, 22–23, 25,
  28, 32, 44, 46, 49, 55–60, 71–72, 116–
  120, 122–4, 126, 132–141, 144, 164,
  196, 214, 217–18, 222–23
affirmative action objection, 154, 164–65,
  195
African American, 1, 3–5, 10–13, 15, 20,
  24, 37, 43, 49–50, 56, 64, 66–68, 70–
  74, 76, 78, 86–88, 90–92, 94–96, 115,
  117, 119–20, 133–40, 144, 146, 161–
  65, 169, 192–203, 205–10, 212–20,
  222–26
  narrative, 94–110, 112
Alcoff, Linda, 13, 27, 50, 52
anti-private-property-rights objection, 154,
  180–82, 195, 215–17
Appiah, Anthony, 2, 7–8, 12, 17, 63–65,
  92, 125, 127
apology, 151, 153, 158, 164, 209, 225–26

Blum, Lawrence, 17, 44, 65, 77, 92
Boxill, Bernard, 90–91, 116, 134, 165, 196,
  198–99, 202–03, 208, 210

Chicano. *See* Latinos
cognitive-behavioral theory of racism, 3, 64,
  66, 80, 87, 92, 115, 222
collective moral (liability) responsibility,
  155, 157–60, 177, 196–200, 203–6,
  210–13

color-blindness, 91, 93, 127, 136
compensatory justice, 1, 4, 49, 52, 55, 58,
  125–29, 134, 136–37, 139, 144, 146,
  150, 152–55, 159, 176–77, 180–81,
  183–85, 187, 190, 192, 198, 202, 212,
  218, 221, 223, 225
corrective justice, 24–25, 122, 126, 136,
  153, 169, 186, 192
counterfactual objection, 154, 182–85,
  195, 215–17

Davis, Angela Y., 73–74, 101, 121, 135
distributive justice, 24–25, 41, 118, 122,
  129, 134, 154, 165, 174, 223
DuBois, W. E. B., 64, 68, 86, 101

ethnic classification, 1, 7, 9–11, 16–21, 26–
  27, 29, 36, 44–46, 50, 52–55, 60, 115,
  120, 122–24, 126–28, 131, 139, 143–
  44, 146, 222–23
ethnic discrimination, 66, 69, 71, 74–76,
  79–80, 82, 84, 87, 89, 90–93, 116–19,
  144
ethnic identity, 10–11, 16, 17–18, 20–21,
  25–26, 29, 36–41, 44–6, 49–50, 52, 54,
  56–8, 60, 115, 128–31, 136, 139–46
ethnic in-group identification, 12–13, 22,
  27, 35–36, 41, 43, 45, 50–51, 119,
  129, 130–32, 146
ethnic out-group identification, 12–13, 19,
  22, 25, 27, 35–36, 41, 46, 50–51, 86,
  99, 129–32, 146

ethnic prejudice. *See* racist belief

ethnic self-identification, 10, 16, 22, 25, 27, 35, 40–41, 46, 51, 98, 129–31, 139, 145, 169

ethnicity, 2, 6–15, 17–18, 21, 23–27, 30–32, 35–37, 40–47, 50–58, 60, 61–62, 68, 71, 75, 79, 85–86, 91, 94, 115–16, 123, 126–28, 130–34, 136, 142, 169, 219

   concept of, 1–2, 8, 14–16, 18, 21, 26, 28, 40, 46–47, 50–51, 94, 115, 127, 129, 131, 133

   degrees of, 9–10, 12–14, 39, 45, 55, 126, 130, 132

   ethics of, 130, 133, 143–45

   metaphysics of, 25, 58, 130–31, 143–44

evil, 3–5, 13, 35, 49, 70, 75, 85, 92–94, 97, 101, 105, 107, 110–12, 115, 137, 145, 150, 154, 157, 162–65, 174, 182, 184, 189, 193, 196, 200–203, 206, 208, 210–12, 216, 218–20, 222–26

Feinberg, Joel, 66, 78, 113, 150–51, 157–58, 166, 175, 204–7, 211

García, Jorge, 17, 52, 54, 56–57, 60, 64, 69, 70, 80

genealogy (genealogical), 10, 12–16, 23–26, 28–40, 41–43, 45, 49–60, 126–27, 129–33, 139, 142–46

genealogical conception of ethnic identity, 2, 4, 51, 54, 59, 126, 128–31, 142–43, 146, 169, 219, 221

genealogical conception of Latino identity, 2, 4, 25, 29, 31, 34–35, 37–42, 44, 51, 54, 58–60, 115, 124, 129, 131, 221

genocide (of Native Americans), 3, 158, 173, 181–82, 185, 193, 199, 222–24

Goldberg, David Theo, 6, 16, 63–65, 68, 74, 79, 81, 92

Goldman, Alvin I., 79–80, 116

Gracia, Jorge, 18–20, 22–23, 27–28, 39, 41, 46–47, 50, 116–19, 121

harm(s), 4, 47, 49, 52, 56, 61, 66–67, 76, 89, 92, 98, 114, 117–18, 120, 122, 128, 134, 136–38, 140–41, 150, 152–55, 157–58, 161, 182, 185, 187, 193–6, 199–200, 202–3, 205, 209–12, 214–16, 218, 220, 222–23

Hispanic(s), 18–9, 22–23, 27, 29, 39, 46–48, 50, 52, 57, 117–18

historic injustice, 148, 154, 159–60, 166, 174, 176, 178–80, 182–83, 190–91, 195

Hobbes, Thomas, 27

holocaust, 3, 94, 105, 107, 110, 113, 133, 159, 181–82, 184, 222

Hume, David, 125, 144

intentional racism, 75, 79, 89, 142

intergenerational justice, 199–200, 209, 213

International Criminal Court (ICC), 196, 225

Jewish persons, 3, 71–72, 94–95, 97–101, 104–9, 112–13, 115, 133–34, 181, 199–200

Jim Crow, 3, 66–67, 74, 194, 196–98, 200, 202–10, 212–13, 215–16, 219, 222–23

justice, 4, 21, 41, 46, 53, 59–60, 113–14, 125, 127–28, 134, 136–37, 140–41, 145, 150, 156, 162, 172, 174, 176, 179, 184–85, 189, 198–200, 205, 207–08, 214, 217–18, 220, 222, 226

Kant, Immanuel, 6, 62, 125, 144, 156, 176

King, Martin Luther, Jr., 73, 75, 77, 101, 162

Kymlicka, Will, 17–18, 58, 153, 166

Laches Doctrine, 176, 180

Latino(s), 2–4, 12, 16, 18–39, 41–43, 46–52, 54–61, 71, 88, 115–24, 128, 130–31, 133–34, 137–39, 141–44, 214

   culture, 18, 23, 25–26, 28–35, 37, 39, 42–43, 51, 55–57, 131–32, 142–43

   identity(ies), 2, 16, 18–39, 41–44, 46–49, 50–61, 115–17, 126, 130–31

   language, 18, 23, 25–35, 37–38, 43, 51, 55, 71, 131–32, 142–43

   name(s), 23, 25–35, 42–43, 51, 57, 131–32

Latinohood (degrees of), 19, 23–25, 28–35, 37–39, 43, 51–52, 54, 56, 130

Lehrer, Keith, 45

liability, 175

   for racist harms, 128, 194, 198, 201

   for wrongdoings, 139, 151, 157, 174, 177, 189–90, 194, 198, 201

Locke, John, 165, 168, 171, 174–75, 177–79

Lyons, David, 148, 152, 174–75

Malcolm X, 73, 77, 101

manifest destiny, 110–11, 145, 161, 173, 183, 193

Marx, Karl, 97, 156, 181, 197

McGary, Howard, 86–87, 90, 93, 116, 134, 197–201, 217–18

Mills, Charles, 6, 29, 69, 125, 127

mixed ethnicity(ies), 10–17, 28, 41, 126, 130, 133

mixed race(s), 6, 8–10, 12, 27, 45, 51, 125, 130

Montagu, Ashley, 1, 63

moral responsibility (duty), 1, 68, 86, 114, 124–25, 152, 154, 180, 183–84, 192, 196, 198, 226

moral responsibility (liability), 69, 86, 89, 90, 145, 158, 174, 200–01, 207, 210
    for racist harms, 125, 128, 158, 174, 183–84, 198, 201, 210
    for wrongdoings, 158, 177, 189, 198, 210

Native American(s), 1, 3–5, 20, 49, 94–96, 109–15, 127, 133–34, 136–40, 143–49, 152–93, 195–96, 203–4, 206, 214–15, 217–20, 222–26

no Native American concept of moral rights objection, 154, 165–68, 195

Nozick, Robert, 10, 155–56, 174, 177

objection:
    to collective responsibility, 154, 157–60, 175, 177, 195, 211, 213
    from historical complexity, 154–55, 175, 195, 213
    from historical and normative progress, 154, 161–64, 195
    from the indeterminacy of Native American identity, 154, 168–70, 195
    from inter-nation conquests, 154, 160–61, 195
    from social utility, 154, 171–73, 195, 215–16, 219

offense, 66–67, 78, 84, 92, 175

oppression, 3–5, 16, 54, 65, 67, 73–74, 95–97, 100–103, 105, 107–9, 112–13, 115, 120–21, 125, 127–28, 133–40, 144–46, 159, 162–63, 181, 184, 193, 200, 207, 209–10, 213–14, 216, 218–20, 222–26

primitive race theories, 6–10, 13, 15, 18, 26, 45, 125, 127–28, 131, 143–44, 221

principle of morally just acquisitions and transfers, 5, 152, 155, 156, 159, 160–61, 170–72, 175–78, 181, 184–87, 189, 195, 202, 206, 212, 224

public policy (administration), 1–3, 16, 19–24, 32, 35, 38, 40–42, 46–47, 49, 51–53, 55–61, 94, 114, 116, 123–25, 127–34, 138–46, 219, 221, 223

race(s), 6, 8–10, 12–13, 15, 17, 21, 27, 38, 44, 55, 59, 61–63, 91, 116, 121, 124, 126, 134–35, 144, 150
    concept of, 1–2, 5–6, 8, 10, 16, 21, 26, 44–45, 61, 63, 94, 115, 125, 127, 144, 221
    ethics of, 125, 127, 144
    metaphysics of, 125, 127, 131, 133, 144, 221

racialism. *See* racial classification

racial classification, 1, 8–9, 13, 21, 26, 45, 50, 52, 112, 124–28

racial discrimination, 54, 64–65, 67, 70, 83, 93, 125, 135, 141, 164, 207

racial prejudice. *See* racist belief

racism, 1–6, 13, 17, 21, 33, 35, 42, 47, 54, 61–81, 83–93, 96, 104, 108–10, 115, 118–22, 124–28, 134–36, 139, 142–43, 145, 189, 202, 205, 208–9, 221–23
    degrees of, 3, 64, 66, 69–70, 72, 76–77, 81, 84, 88, 109, 113, 120, 134–35, 223
    moral status of, 85, 88–90
    nature of, 63–79, 92, 221
    origins of, 64, 80–84, 92

racist belief, 32, 65–66, 68–69, 71, 75, 79, 84, 87, 122, 222

racist harm, 1, 4–5, 21, 23–24, 49, 55, 58, 66–67, 84, 90, 94, 115, 122, 125, 128–29, 131, 134–36, 140, 145, 209, 221, 223

racist motive, 3, 20, 64, 69, 71, 74, 76, 84–85, 88, 102, 119, 146, 168

Rawls, John, 18, 58, 60, 129, 140, 145, 153, 176, 211

rectification, 21, 24, 59, 115, 153, 155, 159, 184, 194–96, 202, 205, 211, 223, 225–26

religious freedom objection, 154, 173–74, 195

reparations, 1, 3–5, 25, 47, 49, 57–58,
114–19, 133, 136–37, 139–40, 150–
54, 185, 187, 189, 191–93, 195–212,
214–21, 223–26
reparations argument, 5, 146, 153, 158,
160–61, 191, 193–95, 202, 204, 215–
17, 219–20, 223
reparations policies, 5, 16, 46–47, 137,
155, 164, 172, 184, 185–90, 192
reparative justice, 3, 118–19, 136–37, 139,
146, 150, 152, 157, 162, 192, 199, 213
retributive justice, 41, 126, 152, 159, 161,
171, 186

Schutte, Ofelia, 46–49, 52–55
sexism, 4, 13, 67, 121–22, 134–36, 138–
39, 145
Simmons, A. John, 149, 151, 155, 174, 177
Singer, Marcus, 64–65
slavery, 3–4, 85, 90, 94–96, 99–100, 102,
105–06, 108–11, 163, 194, 196–98,
200–203, 205–8, 210, 212–13, 215–
16, 219, 222
of Africans in the U.S., 3, 64, 79, 90, 95,
101–2, 104, 107, 114, 163, 191,
193, 196–98, 200–208, 210, 212–
13, 215–19, 222, 224
of Native Americans in the U.S., 163,
193
social class, 24, 47, 53, 73, 97, 121, 135,
163–64, 214
stereotyping, 48, 51, 53, 55, 64, 71, 77, 80–
83, 85, 109, 124, 132
supersession of historic injustice objection,
154, 178–80, 195, 213

Tully, James, 148, 165, 168, 171

unintentional racism, 75–76, 79, 85, 142

Waldron, Jeremy, 18, 151, 166, 174–76,
178–80, 182–83, 213, 216
Wasserstrom, Richard, 13, 93, 116, 145
Wittgenstein, Ludwig, 27, 39, 40
wrongdoing(s), 137, 139, 149, 152, 157–
58, 175, 177, 186, 189, 190, 193–95,
198–99, 205, 210, 212, 214–23

Zack, Naomi, 8–10, 12–13, 16, 27, 45,
125–27, 178

ABOUT THE AUTHOR

J. Angelo Corlett earned his Ph.D. in philosophy from the University of Arizona (1992) and is the author of more than seventy philosophy articles in many leading philosophy journals. He is the author of *Analyzing Social Knowledge* (Rowman and Littlefield, 1996), *Responsibility and Punishment* (Kluwer, 2001), *Terrorism: A Philosophical Analysis* (Kluwer, Philosophical Studies Series, 2003). He is the editor-in-chief of *The Journal of Ethics: An International Philosophical Review;* editor of *Equality and Liberty: Analyzing Rawls and Nozick* (Macmillan, 1990), and currently serves as professor of philosophy and ethics at San Diego State University. His areas of specialization are ethics; moral, social, legal and political philosophy; and theory of knowledge.